THE ILLUST

Peter Badcock

THE ILLUSTRATED BOSMAN

Jonathan Ball Publishers
Johannesburg

Human & Rousseau
Cape Town and Pretoria

Central News Agency (Pty) Ltd
CNA Building, Laub Street,
New Centre, Johannesburg 2001

This book has been designed and produced for CNA
by Jonathan Ball Publishers, Johannesburg
and
Human & Rousseau, Cape Town

Published in this form in 1985 by
Jonathan Ball Publishers, P O Box 548, Bergvlei 2012, Johannesburg
and
Human & Rousseau, 3–9 Rose Street, Cape Town

ISBN 0 86850 112 3

Design and phototypesetting by Book Productions, Johannesburg
Reproduction by Hirt & Carter, Natal
Printed by National Book Printers, Goodwood, Cape

CONTENTS

BOSMAN'S GENIUS

"Genius", with all its glorious, eccentric and tainted associations, is a thoroughly appropriate word for the standing of Herman Charles Bosman. It prepares us for originality, it prepares us for range – above all it prepares us for indefinable and surprising splendours in the achievement, a deep human resonance – and all this without precluding the possibility of flaws, lapses and mistakes.

It was in the nature of Bosman's creativity (as, indeed, of his personality) that he trusted to chance and ran great risks. That the work of such a writer impresses us with qualities such as beauty and subtlety of accomplishment, truth, wisdom and compassion is evidence that the concept of "inspiration" is no myth and is a tribute to the mystery of art.

Beyond Bosman the literary artist, we must take account of a Bosman who in unpredictable sequence or simultaneity took on the roles of entertainer and clown, philosopher of art, mocking prankster, imperious priest of a demonic aestheticism, salary hack, romantic rebel, patriot, perilous creature of unguarded passion and aberration, whose revulsions could make him contemptuous and cruel, who could invite such labels as extortionist, blasphemer and abortionist, idiosyncratic admirer of Jesus and of the simplest people, convict for murder, man of immeasurable geniality and tenderness, lover, friend, husband and teacher.

Bosman's own defiant romanticism and strange assertions about lies of various sorts ought not, I believe, to sanction a laxity in reconstructing the facts of a highly significant life. At the same time the force and originality of his imagination, his preternatural nervous sensitivity, his highly individual way of responding to whatever occurred, must be borne in mind as modifying the meaning of the facts.

The outline of his life was conventional enough during the first twenty years. He was born of Afrikaner parents on 3rd February 1905 at Kuils River near Cape Town. A brother, Pierre, was born 18 months later. His mother, evidently, was a woman of strong personality and some culture. His father, a miner, took the family to the Witwatersrand, where he died in 1921. Herman went to Jeppe Boys' High School, the University of the Witwatersrand and Normal College where he qualified as a teacher. This outline, however, was filled in with uneasy singularity of character, conspicuous selective brilliance, originality and humour. Very little is known about the inwardness of his childhood. Legend has it that his mother required her sons to be successful rather than good, and that, in Herman's words, "she imposed on me the gloomy grandeur of genius" (a telling phrase with its implication that he could see genius as a role rather than as a matter of capacity). Bernard Sachs, who was a schoolmate of his, Aegidius Jean Blignaut and others who encountered him during his adolescence, testify to his intensity and wildness; to his pursuit of excitement and laughter that more than once got him into trouble. He is reported to have tried his hand, while a schoolboy, at conducting a questionable money-making scheme exploiting public gullibility, until warned off by the police; to have contributed a series of storyettes to *The Sunday Times* whose editors were disconcerted when they discovered they had been paying good money to a youth of 16; to have remarked of his father's death, "I was moved almost to tears"; to have joined the Young Communists League as a sort of non-political provocateur for the sake of the opportunities it afforded for pranks; to have written a letter proclaiming his mastery of English in lieu of the answers to a mathematics examination; to have secured a minor prize in a poetry competition at Wits and then revealed that his entry was borrowed from Shelley; and so forth.

Literature was a religious passion to him, and he seems to have encountered some of his enduring favourites early on – the Elizabethans, the Romantics and the American humorists. He records as a crucial moment his discovery of Edgar Allan Poe in the school library. The work and personality of Poe were to exercise a singular hold on his imagination throughout the rest of his life.

In Bosman's twenty-first year his life style began to yield to the pressures of his intense individual way of seeing and feeling. He contracted a marriage which seems to have had for him a purely symbolic value, for it was never to be domesticated. Neither his family nor that of his young bride, Vera Sawyer, knew of the marriage and when shortly afterwards he went off to take up his first teaching appointment in the Groot Marico district, she stayed behind in Johannesburg. Could the gesture of this wedding have been meant as a comment on his mother's re-marriage which had happened only months before?

A measure of the intensity with which he experienced his spell in the bushveld is that these six months provided him with the setting for scores of short stories which he was to start writing some six years later, and that the same setting was to recur in work he was doing in the last year of his life. It appears that he did not greatly enjoy his platteland sojourn, but it must have been made desirably memorable by the catastrophe that redirected his life in the immediately following period. Home for the school holidays, at the house of his mother and her new husband in Bellevue East, Herman shot his stepbrother, David Russell, with a rifle he had bought in the bushveld. He had fired into a darkened room in which David and Pierre were embroiled in a tussle, and he attempted suicide immediately afterwards. The motive was never perfectly illuminated. He stood trial for murder and was convicted and sentenced to death. His words to the judge after sentence had been passed included the statement: "In that tragic moment, the happenings of which are still not quite clear to me, I was impelled by a wild and chaotic impulse, in which there was no suggestion of malice or premeditation." The death sentence was commuted and he served some four years in prison.

The bushveld experience was to feed into at least four volumes of Bosman's writings. The far longer prison term would produce very little more than one volume, the "unimpassioned chronicle" *Cold Stone Jug*, to be published nearly twenty years after his release. It was also written a long time after the events, so I shall only say at this point that it brings oblique testimony of all the horror such an experience must have contained for a young man of Bosman's temperament.

On his release in 1930 he assumed the *nom de plume* or alias Herman Malan, from his mother's maiden name. Why he did so is nowhere explained. In any case, it signalled the advent of a persona in whom certain elements of Bosman's make-up were at times intensified even to the point of distortion, so as to throw up some of the enigmas of his character with perplexing force.

After a few months in retreat with some solicitous cousins, Malan (as I shall call him for the time being) again encountered Aegidius Jean Blignaut, a writer and journalist five or six years his senior who, with the support of a businessman, John Webb, was about to launch a literary magazine. Malan and Blignaut found each other uncommonly congenial and commenced a particularly close and productive association that was to endure until 1934 and, incidentally, to set Johannesburg by the ears.

In the course of time Blignaut launched and edited not only the magazine, *The Touleier*, but also a series of publications that addressed themselves more to a mass readership, including *The New L.S.D.* and *The New Sjambok*. They carried some literary material, but their essential fare was satire, protests and exposés of Johannesburg society and they drew no genteel line at scandal and sensation. Malan was Blignaut's full collaborator on these provocative papers which landed the pair repeatedly in lawyers' offices and in court on various suits and charges, including libel, indecency and blasphemy, as well as at least one spell behind bars, and incurred them a banning or two. Sharing quarters as well as offices and ideas, the two were pursuing a sort of cultural Robin Hood existence – hecklers in print as well as on the City Hall steps or wherever likely targets of their derision might show themselves – for the sake of livelihood, imaginative freedom, fun and sheer mischief.

Early in 1931 they invited one of their literary contributors, a young woman named Ellie Beemer, to join them on the staff of *The Touleier*. A strong attraction arose between her and Malan but it wasn't long before she yielded to pressure from her family to sever this relationship and contract an acceptable marriage.

Whatever the explanation, from (and perhaps very especially during) 1931, Malan sporadically displayed a frame of mind which I think it is fair to describe as of a certain ugliness or perversity and which was expressed in some of his writings. There is a discernible need to revenge himself for his disappointment in love. And there is a set of attitudes presumably arising from other needs: he makes excessive proclamations of his own artistic and spiritual superiority to the point of claiming a special relationship to deity; he claims supranormal sexual and moral rights for "poets" and especially for himself; he scorns and ridicules even the most innocent sexuality of ordinary people, as though it were comparable with artistic pretensions in the untalented; he sometimes revels in thoughts of cruelty; he defies the values of the world, particularly in relation to madness, lies and "divine unreason" and happily obfuscates the lines of his own arguments as whim dictates; he defends or attacks chosen figures in diatribes in which the noise of his own praises or denunciations displaces any attempt at persuasive logic or proof.

To illustrate the quality of this perverse mood, I quote two brief passages from items published in 1931. The first is from a story called "The Man-Eater": "He's a pot-bellied Philistine ... He's a slave with a dirty soul. I wouldn't even be surprised if he's a devoted husband." The second is from the preface to *The Blue Princess*, Malan's first slender volume of poems, on love and its loss: "I have found a finality that has not been found before, although Baudelaire came near finding it ... The mob will not understand these verses. It would be an insult to me if they pretended that they did. A little sane logical man understanding the mad glories of a poet with his head in the stars and his feet on the white sand. But here and there will be those whom God has purposely made different from their fellows. They will understand ..."

The dark side of the Bosman-Malan persona continued to show itself during the entire thirteen- or fourteen-year period that Bosman used this name, and indeed beyond. Partly I have made this emphasis in order to point up a wonderful if bewildering paradox that emerges when we consider what Malan was writing from the start of his association with Blignaut. The latter had been an admirer of his younger friend's literary gifts since their first acquaintance in 1923, and when they met again in 1930 he had a significant body of his own work which he gave Malan to read in manuscript. It included a series of stories in English narrated by an old Hottentot, Ruiter, who is understood to be speaking Afrikaans.

These tales, fortuitously encountered at the moment when Malan was at last free to plunge into literary creation, appear to have provided precisely the model he needed for the shaping of the imaginative matter he had perforce been storing in his memory since his bushveld sojourn. Blignaut's Hottentot fathered Malan's Boer narrator, Oom Schalk Lourens of the Groot Marico – foreshadowed his ironic humour, his folk character, his particular way of moving in and out of the action he recounts, his Afrikaans-in-English – and revealed how the bushveld memories could be transmuted into a setting and a language for the story-stuff that was generating in a very extraordinary creative mind.

A setting and a language, I say, because the Schalk Lourens stories are clearly something other than any sort of record or fictional exploitation of a twenty-one-year-old teacher's half-year in a corner of the Western Transvaal. The stories are full of lovingly named details of that actual world, but on the one hand the author himself is rarely if ever identifiable as a character in the fictions, and on the other the story-substance of which they are constituted, in terms of history and life-histories, geography, psychology and romance, goes immensely beyond the possible actual experience of that young transient, however intensely he may have observed, however hungrily he may have absorbed the tales of the locals he encountered. It is fair to say that however convincingly Schalk Lourens' Groot Marico and the rest of his world looks and sounds and smells like the actual platteland, it is in fact substantially a geographical phantom, an aesthetic invention. The regionalism, the realism of these stories is only apparent, a cloak, a sort of ectoplasm to render visible a population of creatures whose native home is the author's imagination, whose real raw material is his entire experience and perception both of the specific truths of South Africa and of what he liked to call "the eternal verities".

What has enabled these stories to be widely loved as well as widely admired, on very different critical levels, is that the profundity of their feeling for human reality has been conveyed with a stylistic lightness that makes their meaning and their delights very generally accessible. This extraordinary achievement, in which humour plays a major role, makes of Bosman (alias Herman Malan, the arch-élitist!) one of the most democratic of great writers. The greatness consists partly in the originality of the vision, the way the narrator's playfulness traces a roundabout line and catches the reader's awareness in the flank (connecting ideas as they have never been connected before), and partly in the humane affirmativeness that underlies all the satire, mockery and curiosity, all the mischievous and tragic sense of human fallibility: there is almost an assumption that characters will be in some way weak, self-seeking, foolish or mendacious, that any who approach any sort of excellence are more than likely to be ill-fated – these are the conditions of human flesh – and yet the regard is full of warmth and tenderness, full of the bemused (how on earth does it come about?) implicit affirmation that mankind, such as it is, is the salt and the treasure and the inexhaustible wonder of God's universe.

Besides the shortlived *Touleier*, the scandal sheets and the pamphlets, the "underground press" – early abandoned by John Webb and thenceforward under the independent direction of Blignaut and Malan – also issued several slim volumes of their own writings in tiny editions. The Ruiter stories were collected under the title *The Hottentot's God* with a laudatory preface by Herman Malan, and from his pen *The Blue Princess* was followed by verse volumes called *Jesus*, *Rust* and *Mara*, the last of which contained a sort of dramatized essay on incest as well as ten poems. One of these was a long love ode called "Ellaleen" which was addressed to Ella Manson whom Malan married after divorcing the unobtrusive Vera Sawyer (who remained a remote sympathetic presence in his life to the end). He was to write of Ella as a descendant of the Vikings, and it is to some blizzardy half-lit fantasy world that she seems to have belonged. Less ambivalently than he, she soared in the high altitudes of romanticism. She believed herself possessed of magical powers and peopled the air with spirits and demons. She lived out the faith that her husband was a unique genius and spiritual aristocrat, all of which made a heady draught for the devotee of Poe, Baudelaire and Wilde.

In 1934 the Blignaut-Malan partnership came to an end when Herman and Ella departed for Europe. Until 1940 they lived mainly in London, with brief spells in Paris and Brussels, and Malan's life continued to be attended by contradiction. He wrote for *The Sunday Citizen*, a newspaper edited by John Webb who now lived in London, taunted the Mosleyites, flirted with Hitlerism and slated T.S. Eliot's *Murder in the Cathedral*. Herman and Ella became publishers under the imprint Arden Godbold, which was one more of the *noms de plume* he used. The legend goes that Ella's organizational drive helped the press achieve some kind of spectacular success. Nevertheless their vicissitudes were such that at one stage they were destitute.

The outbreak of war caused the couple to return to South Africa at the same time as it brought the soldierly Blignaut to Britain, so they missed each other. The two former brothers-in-arms were never to meet again. For a while Herman and Ella lived in Natal and then in Johannesburg. The details of this period are hardly less vague than of the European years, but it is recalled that their style of life was wildly bohemian and that one of the ways in which Herman earned his livelihood was as a building labourer (an experience he would draw upon in his novel *Jacaranda in the Night)*. Early in 1943 he accepted an appointment as editor of *The Zoutpansberg Review* in the Northern Transvaal town of Pietersburg, a newspaper supporting the United Party and the war. This spell lasted less than a year but was as turbulent a time as any. Politics, passion and the police all erupted into Malan's life, and by the time the chapter was closed his marriage with Ella was in dissolution. He had become deeply involved with Helena Stegmann, a schoolteacher, who became his third wife in Johannesburg in 1944.

A familiar photograph shows an ebullient Bosman walking between Ella and Helena in a city street, all three smiling. But in fact Ella did not outlive her divorce by many months, dying under circumstances that suggest the possibility of suicide in the building in which she and her new husband were neighbours to the Bosmans. Notwithstanding this shadow, there is a sense in which the years with Helena, the last eight years of Bosman's life, represent reintegration, restoration and peace, symbolized by the fact that he now dropped the *nom de plume* Herman Malan. His publications in this period were relatively voluminous. As literary editor of Bernard Sachs's revived *S. A. Opinion*, which after a while was incorporated with *Trek*, he contributed humorous essays, regularly, as well as criticism on literature, painting, theatre and other arts, and many Schalk Lourens stories (though not all of these last may have been newly written). After his connection with *Trek* was severed, during his last eighteen months, he contributed a story a week to *The Forum* under the rubric "In die Voorkamer". These years also saw his work being issued for the first time in book form by independent publishers. First, in 1947, came *Jacaranda in the Night* from APB, followed by *Mafeking Road* from CNA, and in 1949, *Cold Stone Jug* from APB.

The comparatively settled character of this period (though he and Helena lived in no fewer than eight places in their time) may be related to Helena's character. Of his own Cape Afrikaner origins, she must have embodied the idea of home and the earth for his imagination.

The chronicle of Bosman's imprisonment, *Cold Stone Jug* (included in part in this selection) was written about 1948. Perhaps the most startling characteristic of this document is that it is pre-eminently humorous, largely a raconteur's holiday. Why did Bosman not rush to embrace this tragically romantic material and claim, like Poe, these extremities of guilt and suffering to "bejewel his genius"? Instead he waited some seventeen years and then wrote as though the only significance of his homicidal act was that it had landed him in prison, and as though a sojourn in the death cell and the miseries of imprisonment were essentially comic adventures, and perhaps as though he had never heard of Edgar Allan Poe or the word "genius". The answer to this mystery has to be a complicated one. Part of it lies in Bosman's own precept that the obvious is untrustworthy. To have romanticized the romantic material, or even to have treated his own calamity with sombre seriousness would have been to falsify or cheapen it. It is a tribute to Bosman's creative genuineness and psychological insight that the chronicle of his gaol years is not a document of self-glorification, self-pity or indignation. *Cold Stone Jug* is totally original and, under its vast funniness, fully charged with intimations of horror and pity and misery so that it ends by being overwhelmingly poignant. The daringly light hand reveals all the awfulness of what men do to each other; the suffering of the narrator and his fellow prisoners, though rarely stressed, is after all thoroughly illustrated and evoked; and even the guilt, to which only one flippant phrase near the beginning has overtly referred, the unconfessable after-shock of having killed, I believe haunts the book to its end, being one of the emotions that energize the unique aching laughter. The obvious in many guises has been spurned, including the obvious mask of a tragically fated romantic genius. But in the throwaway roughness of this jokey fictionalized memoir Bosman expressed truth and beauty in rich and difficult ways, and has manifested something we can only call genius.

The Voorkamer sketches survive the pressures of the haste in which they were written in Bosman's urgent last eighteen months, with a remarkable freight of exuberant and incisive excellence. These sketches, or stories in the form of conversations go back to the Groot Marico of, by now, happy association for their setting. All in all the output of this period includes much of Bosman at his humane, wise, humorous and totally original best.

Despite this outpouring and the degree of recognition that was coming his way (*Mafeking Road* had been widely acclaimed from the first and declared the collection "the best short stories that have ever come out of South Africa" and so on), Bosman had, during this period as always, to scratch for a living. He tried to teach at Damelin College where Helena was the Afrikaans mistress, but his nerves were not equal to the confrontation with raucous adolescents; he sold advertising space for *S.A. Opinion*, *Trek* and *S.A. Jewish Times* and worked as a sub-editor on the last. From 1949 he was a proof-reader on *The Sunday Express*. Eventually he was able to place a deposit on a house in Milton Road, Lombardy East, on the outskirts of Johannesburg.

Attending his shifts, turning out his weekly Voorkamer story, pressing on with his new novel, he was apparently too preoccupied with work at first to celebrate his move to Lombardy East. Some months passed before friends were invited to a house-warming party, on Friday 12th October. It would have been a memorable party in any case because a storm in the night churned the unmade roads of the suburb to mud and many of the guests were forced to sleep over. But it goes down as a singular occasion because on Sunday the 14th Bosman died of a heart attack. It was 1951 and he was 46 years old.

Lionel Abrahams
Johannesburg, 1985.

BOSMAN'S BOSVELD

Text and pictures by David Goldblatt

In 1964 I visited the Marico bushveld in search of Bosman's milieu. I took with me a map which showed only two places Bosman mentions in his stories: Nietverdiend and Derdepoort. A policeman at Derdepoort border post told me that the person in the area who knew the bushveld best was Oom Ben Welgemoed.

So to Oom Ben I went. Yes, he knew the bushveld. But no, he had never heard of Abjaterskop or of the farm Drogedal, or of a schoolmaster called Herman Bosman. I headed south toward the Dwarsberg and Nietverdiend, looking vaguely for the links with Bosman that I felt had to be there. At evening I came to a line of tall gum trees and a sign: *Transvaal Provincial Library Depot*.

Hoping to find water and the corner of a garden for my sleeping-bag, I turned in. Koos Niehaus was the name of the young man who welcomed me; not a librarian, but a farmer. Within minutes he had arranged that I should sleep in the rondavel adjoining his house. And then we drove to his lands where he was to give instructions for the night's ploughing. As we went I explained my mission. He knew of neither Bosman nor his works.

'But do you know Abjaterskop?' I asked.

'Yes, there it is', he pointed.

'And the farm, Drogedal?'

'Yes, that is where we are ploughing.'

As the last light touched the Dwarsberg, I watched Koos Niehaus plough an arrow-straight furrow in the black turf soil near Abjaterskop. It was here, in the story 'Funeral Earth', that the Mtosas surrendered to the conquering Boers.

This was Bosman's country, and I think Koos and his young wife Anne were as excited as I was. We chatted late into the night. And as they mentioned the names of people living in the district it dawned on me that not only had Bosman used real place names but, it seemed, in blissful disregard of the conventions, the real names of people too.

There were not many of Bosman's characters left in the district. But when Koos and Anne had read the stories they helped me to track down a number of them, and these remembered Bosman, not, I must record, with any great fondness. He came there in 1925 as assistant to young Charles Terblanche, at the Heimweeberg Farm School. The two seem to have spent a pranksome year raising hell in the Dwarsberg, Bosman being regarded as wild and rowdy. Then after he had shot his step-brother he disappeared to prison. Yet the people of Marico thought well of his stories. In answer to my question, Did he write truthfully of life in the bushveld? they would say invariably, 'Ja, dit was ons'. They seemed neither flattered nor incensed at having their own families' names and characters thus enlarged upon. If Bosman were to return to the Marico Bushveld today, I think he would find that while the people have retained the qualities he knew, bushveld life has lost much of its *élan*. Years of drought and overgrazing have in great areas completely destroyed the grass and its roots. Over these bald patches the bush, thorny and hostile, encroaches. As a result the area is being depopulated and those farmers who have survived now run vast consolidated estates. They are for the most part the middle-aged and old, with their children. The nubile girls and uncouth lads of *Mafeking Road* and *Unto Dust* are hardly seen. They go to the towns and seldom return. Bosman's bushveld is passing away.

An abandoned farmhouse in the Marico and the encroaching haak-en-steek. Years of drought and overgrazing destroyed the grass where 'once it grew so high that sitting on a mule cart one could hardly see the back of an ox as it went by,' Tant Nellie Haasbroek said.

Oom Koos Nienaber appears in Bosman. He and his wife, although still together, had not spoken to one another for thirty years before she died.

'There were no roads in the old days,' he said. 'Ons het sommer gery. When the tyres were punctured we stopped.'

When he lost a motor car part (he had the first car in the Marico) he suspected his dog of having swallowed it. He shot the dog but did not find the car part.

He lived alone on his farm near Abjaterskop, but said he would marry again.

Oom Koos's grandson, Koos Niehaus, building a dam on the farm Drogedal or Droëdal near Nietverdiend. This farm and its people, like others in the district, appears in several of Bosman's stories.

Years ago there was a more primitive dam here and from it Bosman's characters, the 'conservative' Bekkers and de Bruyns, drew water.

Through the thorn trees of Drogedal you can see Abjaterskop, which, when you're lying in the grass, 'looks like the toe of your boot'.

At the verge of the farm Drogedal, not far from Krisjan Geel's shop at Zwingli, on the 'Government' road to Bechuanaland (Botswana), the remains of Jurie Bekker's post-office – the voorhuis and stoep – may still be seen.

Here, in real life and in Bosman's stories, the farmers used to discuss the news of the day.

Frik Loubser, shopkeeper and postmaster in the Marico, sat before the bakoond in which his wife baked bread. He spoke of his son, the fastest runner at Nietverdiend school, of the regrettable tendency to serve instant coffee on Marico stoeps, and of the bushveld he loves.

In a place densely covered with thorn trees, he nurtured a swarthaak in his backyard through the drought.

Tant Nellie Haasbroek was Bosman's landlady and Heimweeberg School was on her land. She told how she and her husband were wakened one night by shots. They found Bosman and his colleague Terblanche firing live rounds. She told her husband, 'He will end on the gallows', and described Bosman as a friendless man.

Oom At Geel, who arrived in the Marico bushveld in 1925, was still farming, at seventy-nine, near Nietverdiend, with his new wife – his second. The names of several of the Geel family are to be found in Bosman's stories.

Oom At was chairman of the school committee when Bosman taught in the Marico, and he recalled that Bosman gave them a lot of trouble.

At the shooting range one day Oom At held up a rifle and called:

'Who'll give me £3 for this?'

'I will', cried Bosman.

When Oom At asked Bosman what he would do with the weapon, he replied:

'Ek wil daarmee in Johannesburg gaan pronk.'

A few weeks later Bosman shot and killed his stepbrother, probably with this rifle.

Oom At's son (overleaf), Krisjan Geel, who was taught by Bosman, behind the counter serving his friends in his store near Zwingli.

Simms

THE ILLUSTRATED BOSMAN

Peter Badcock

IN THE WITHAAK'S SHADE

Leopards? - Oom Schalk Lourens said - Oh, yes, there are two varieties on this side of the Limpopo. The chief difference between them is that the one kind of leopard has got a few more spots on it than the other kind. But when you meet a leopard in the veld, unexpectedly, you seldom trouble to count his spots to find out what kind he belongs to. That is unnecessary. Because, whatever kind of leopard it is that you come across in this way, you only do one kind of running. And that is the fastest kind.

I remember the occasion that I came across a leopard unexpectedly, and to this day I couldn't tell you how many spots he had, even though I had all the time I needed for studying him. It happened about midday, when I was out on the far end of my farm, behind a koppie, looking for some strayed cattle. I thought the cattle might be there because it is shady under those withaak trees, and there is soft grass that is very pleasant to sit on. After I had looked for the cattle for about an hour in this manner, sitting up against a tree-trunk, it occurred to me that I could look for them just as well, or perhaps even better, if I lay down flat. For even a child knows that cattle aren't so small that you have got to get onto stilts and things to see them properly.

So I lay on my back, with my hat tilted over my face, and my legs crossed, and when I closed my eyes slightly the tip of my boot, sticking up into the air, looked just like the peak of Abjaterskop.

Overhead a lonely *aasvoël* wheeled, circling slowly round and round without flapping his wings, and I knew that not even a calf could pass in any part of the sky between the tip of my toe and that *aasvoël* without my observing it immediately. What was more, I could go on lying there under the withaak and looking for the cattle like that all day, if necessary. As you know, I am not the sort of farmer to loaf about the house when there is a man's work to be done.

The more I screwed up my eyes and gazed at the toe of my boot, the more it looked like Abjaterskop. By and by it seemed that it actually was Abjaterskop, and I could see the stones on top of it, and the bush trying to grow up its sides, and in my ears there was a far-off humming sound, like bees in an orchard on a still day. As I have said, it was very pleasant.

Then a strange thing happened. It was as though a huge cloud, shaped like an animal's head and with spots on it, had settled on top of Abjaterskop. It seemed so funny that I wanted to laugh. But I didn't. Instead, I opened my eyes a little more and felt glad to think that I was only dreaming. Because otherwise I would have to believe that the spotted cloud on Abjaterskop was actually a leopard, and that he was gazing at my boot. Again I wanted to laugh. But then, suddenly, I knew.

And I didn't feel so glad. For it was a leopard, all right - a large-sized, hungry-looking leopard, and he was sniffing suspiciously at my feet. I was uncomfortable. I knew that nothing I could do would ever convince that leopard that my toe was Abjaterskop. He was not that sort of leopard: I knew that without even counting the number of his spots. Instead, having finished with my feet, he started sniffling higher up. It was the most terrifying moment of my life. I wanted to get up and run for it. But I couldn't. My legs wouldn't work.

Every big-game hunter I have come across has told me the same story about how, at one time or another, he has owed his escape from lions and other wild animals to his cunning in lying down and pretending to be dead, so that the beast of prey loses interest in him and walks off. Now as I lay there on the grass, with the leopard trying to make up his mind about me, I understood why, in such a situation, the hunter doesn't move. It's simply that he can't move. That's all. It's not his cunning that keeps him down. It's his legs.

In the meantime the leopard had got up as far as my knees. He was studying my trousers very carefully, and I started getting embarrassed. My trousers were old and rather unfashionable. Also, at the knee, there was a torn place, from where I had climbed through a barbed-wire fence, into the thick bush, the time I saw the Government tax-collector coming over the bult before he saw me. The leopard stared at that rent in my trousers for quite a while, and my embarrassment grew. I felt I wanted to explain about the Government tax-collector and the barbed-wire. I didn't want the leopard to get the impression that Schalk Lourens was the sort of man who didn't care about his personal appearance.

When the leopard got as far as my shirt, however, I felt better. It was a good blue flannel shirt that I had bought only a few weeks ago from the Indian store at Ramoutsa, and I didn't care how many strange leopards saw it. Nevertheless, I made up my mind that next time I went to lie on the grass under the withaak, looking for strayed cattle, I would first polish up my veldskoens with sheep's fat, and I would put on my black hat that I only wear to Nagmaal. I could not permit the wild animals of the neighbourhood to sneer at me.

But when the leopard reached my face I got frightened again. I knew he couldn't take exception to my shirt. But I wasn't so sure about my face. Those were terrible moments. I lay very still, afraid to open my eyes and afraid to breathe. Sniff-sniff, the huge creature went, and his breath swept over my face in hot gasps. You hear of many frightening experiences that a man has in a lifetime. I have also been in quite a few perilous situations. But if you want something to make you suddenly old and to turn your hair white in a few moments, there is nothing to beat a leopard - especially when he is standing over you, with his jaws at your throat, trying to find a good place to bite.

The leopard gave a deep growl, stepped right over my body, knocked off my hat, and growled again. I opened my eyes and saw the animal moving away clumsily. But my relief didn't last long. The leopard didn't move far. Instead, he turned over and lay down next to me.

Yes, there on the grass, in the shade of the withaak, the leopard and I lay down together. The leopard lay half curled up, on his side, with his forelegs crossed, like a dog, and whenever I tried to move away he grunted. I am sure that in the whole history of the Groot Marico there have never been two stranger companions engaged in the thankless task of looking for strayed cattle.

Next day, in Fanie Snyman's voorkamer, which was used as a post office, I told my story to the farmers of the neighbourhood, while they were drinking coffee and waiting for the motor-lorry from Zeerust.

"And how did you get away from that leopard in the end?" Koos van Tonder asked, trying to be funny. "I suppose you crawled through the grass and frightened the leopard off by pretending to be a python."

"No, I just got up and walked home," I said. "I remembered that the cattle I was looking for might have gone the other way and strayed into your kraal. I thought they would be safer with the leopard."

"Did the leopard tell you what he thought of General Pienaar's last speech in the Volksraad?" Frans Welman asked, and they all laughed.

I told my story over several times before the lorry came with our letters, and although the dozen odd men present didn't say much while I was talking, I could see that they listened to me in the same way that they listened when Krisjan Lemmer talked. And everybody knew that Krisjan Lemmer was the biggest liar in the Bushveld.

To make matters worse, Krisjan Lemmer was there, too, and when I got to the part of my story where the leopard lay down beside me, Krisjan Lemmer winked at me. You know that kind of wink. It was to let me know that there was now a new understanding between us, and that we could speak in future as one Marico liar to another.

I didn't like that.

"Kêrels," I said in the end, "I know just what you are thinking. You don't believe me, and you don't want to say so."

"But we do believe you," Krisjan Lemmer interrupted me, "very wonderful things happen in the Bushveld. I once had a twenty-foot mamba that I named Hans. This snake was so attached to me that I couldn't go anywhere without him. He would even follow me to church on Sunday, and because he didn't care much for some of the sermons, he would wait for me outside under a tree. Not that Hans was irreligious. But he had a sensitive nature, and the strong line that the predikant took against the serpent in the Garden of Eden always made Hans feel awkward. Yet he didn't go and look for a withaak to lie under, like your leopard. He wasn't stand-offish in that way. An ordinary thorn-tree's shade was good enough for Hans. He knew he was only a mamba, and didn't try to give himself airs."

I didn't take notice of Krisjan Lemmer's stupid lies, but the upshot of this whole affair was that I also began to have doubts about the existence of that leopard. I recalled queer stories I had heard of human beings that could turn themselves into animals, and although I am not a superstitious man I could not shake off the feeling that it was a spook thing that had happened. But when, a few days later, a huge leopard had been seen from the roadside near the poort, and then again by Mtosas on the way to Nietverdiend, and again in the turf-lands near the Malopo, matters took a different turn.

At first people jested about this leopard. They said it wasn't a real leopard, but a spotted animal that had walked away out of Schalk Lourens' dream. They also said that the leopard had come to the Dwarsberge to have a look at Krisjan Lemmer's twenty-foot mamba. But afterwards, when they had found his spoor at several water-holes, they had no more doubt about the leopard.

It was dangerous to walk about in the veld, they said. Exciting times followed. There was a great deal of shooting at the leopard and a great deal of running away from him. The amount of Martini and Mauser fire I heard in the krantzes reminded me of nothing so much as the First Boer War. And the amount of running away reminded me of nothing so much as the Second Boer War.

But always the leopard escaped unharmed. Somehow, I felt sorry for him. The way he had first sniffed at me and then lain down beside me that day under the withaak was a strange thing that I couldn't understand. I thought of the Bible, where it is written that the lion shall lie down with the lamb.

But I also wondered if I hadn't dreamt it all. The manner in which those things had befallen me was also unearthly. The leopard began to take up a lot of my thoughts. And there was no man to whom I could talk about it who would be able to help me in any way. Even now, as I am telling you this story, I am expecting you to wink at me, like Krisjan Lemmer did.

Still, I can only tell you the things that happened as I saw them, and what the rest was about only Africa knows.

It was some time before I again walked along the path that leads through the bush to where the withaaks are. But I didn't lie down on the grass again. Because when I reached the place, I found that the leopard had got there before me. He was lying on the same spot, half curled up in the withaak's shade, and his forepaws were folded as a dog's are sometimes. But he lay very still. And even from the distance where I stood I could see the red splash on his breast where a Mauser bullet had gone.

THE MUSIC-MAKER

Of course, I know about history - Oom Schalk Lourens said - it's the stuff children learn in school. Only the other day, at Thys Lemmer's post office, Thys's little son Stoffel started reading out of his history book about a man called Vasco da Gama, who visited the Cape. At once Dirk Snyman started telling young Stoffel about the time when he himself visited the Cape, but young Stoffel didn't take much notice of him. So Dirk Snyman said that that showed you.

Anyway, Dirk Snyman said that what he wanted to tell young Stoffel was that the last time he went down to the Cape a kafir came and sat down right next to him in a tram. What was more, Dirk Snyman said, was that people seemed to think nothing of it.

Yes, it's a queer thing about wanting to get into history.

Take the case of Manie Kruger, for instance.

Manie Kruger was one of the best farmers in the Marico. He knew just how much peach brandy to pour out for the tax-collector to make sure that he would nod dreamily at everything Manie said. And at a time of drought Manie Kruger could run to the Government for help much quicker than any man I ever knew.

Then one day Manie Kruger read an article in the *Kerkbode* about a musician who said that he knew more about music than Napoleon did. After that - having first read another article to find out who Napoleon was - Manie Kruger was a changed man. He could talk of nothing but his place in history and of his musical career.

Of course, everybody knew that no man in the Marico could be counted in the same class with Manie Kruger when it came to playing the concertina.

No Bushveld dance was complete without Manie Kruger's concertina. When he played a vastrap you couldn't keep your feet still. But af-

Peter Badcock

ter he had decided to become the sort of musician that gets into history books, it was strange the way that Manie Kruger altered. For one thing, he said he would never again play at a dance. We all felt sad about that. It was not easy to think of the Bushveld dances of the future. There would be the peach brandy in the kitchen; in the voorkamer the feet of the dancers would go through the steps of the schottische and the polka and the waltz and the mazurka, but on the riempies bench in the corner where the musicians sat, there would be no Manie Kruger. And they would play "Die Vaal Hare en die Blou Oge" and "Vat Jou Goed en Trek, Ferreira", but it would be another's fingers that swept over the concertina keys. And when, with the dancing and the peach brandy, the young men called out "Dagbreek toe" it would not be Manie Kruger's head that bowed down to the applause.

It was sad to think about all this.

For so long, at the Bushveld dances, Manie Kruger had been the chief musician.

And of all those who mourned this change that had come over Manie, we could see that there was no one more grieved than Letta Steyn.

And Manie said such queer things at times. Once he said that what he had to do to get into history was to die of consumption in the arms of a princess, like another musician he had read about. Only it was hard to get consumption in the Marico, because the climate was so healthy.

Although Manie stopped playing his concertina at dances, he played a great deal in another way. He started giving what he called recitals. I went to several of them. They were very impressive.

At the first recital I went to, I found that the front part of Manie's voorkamer was taken up by rows of benches and chairs that he had borrowed from those of his neighbours who didn't mind having to eat their meals on candle-boxes and upturned buckets. At the far end of the voorkamer a wide green curtain was hung on a piece of string. When I came in, the place was full. I managed to squeeze in on a bench between Jan Terblanche and a young woman in a blue kappie. Jan Terblanche had been trying to hold this young woman's hand.

Manie Kruger was sitting behind the green curtain. He was already there when I came in. I knew it was Manie by his veldskoens, which were sticking out from underneath the curtain. Letta Steyn sat in front of me. Now and again, when she turned round, I saw that there was a flush on her face and a look of dark excitement in her eyes.

At last everything was ready, and Joel, the farm kafir to whom Manie had given this job, slowly drew the green curtain aside. A few of the younger men called out "Middag, ou Manie," and Jan Terblanche asked if it wasn't very close and suffocating, sitting there like that behind that piece of green curtain.

Then he started to play.

And we all knew that it was the most wonderful concertina music we had ever listened to. It was Manie Kruger at his best. He had practised a long time for that recital; his fingers flew over the keys; the notes of the concertina swept into our hearts; the music of Manie Kruger lifted us right out of that voorkamer into a strange and rich and dazzling world.

It was fine.

The applause right through was terrific. At the end of each piece the kafir closed the curtains in front of Manie, and we sat waiting for a few minutes until the curtains were drawn aside again. But after that first time there was no more laughter about this procedure. The recital lasted for about an hour and a half, and the applause at the end was even greater than at the start. And during those ninety minutes Manie left his seat only once. That was when there was some trouble with the curtain and he got up to kick the kafir.

At the end of the recital Manie did not come forward and shake hands with us, as we had expected. Instead, he slipped through behind the green curtain into the kitchen, and sent word that we could come and see him round the back. At first we thought this a bit queer, but Letta Steyn said it was all right. She explained that in other countries the great musicians and stage performers all received their admirers at the back. Jan Terblanche said that if these actors used their kitchens for entertaining their visitors in, he wondered where they did their cooking.

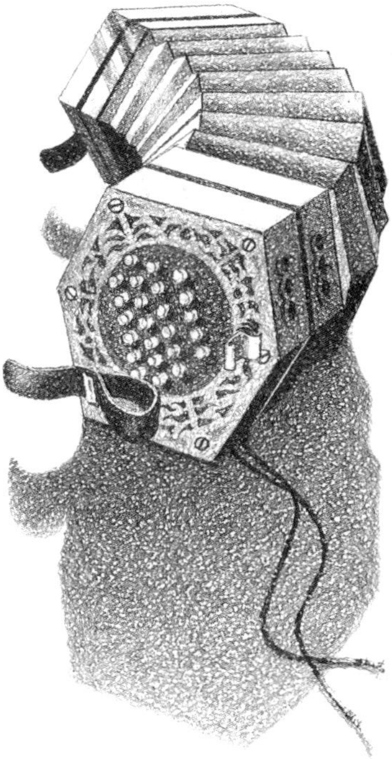

Nevertheless, most of us went round to the kitchen, and we had a good time congratulating Manie Kruger and shaking hands with him; and Manie spoke much of his musical future, and of the triumphs that would come to him in the great cities of the world, when he would stand before the curtain and bow to the applause.

Manie gave a number of other recitals after that. They were all equally fine. Only, as he had to practise all day, he couldn't pay much attention to his farming. The result was that his farm went to pieces and he got into debt. The court messengers came and attached half his cattle while he was busy practising for his fourth recital. And he was practising for his seventh recital when they took away his ox-wagon and mule-cart.

Eventually, when Manie Kruger's musical career reached that stage when they took away his plough and the last of his oxen, he sold up what remained of his possessions and left the Bushveld, on his way to those great cities that he had so often talked about. It was very grand, the send-off that the Marico gave him. The predikant and the Volksraad member both made speeches about how proud the Transvaal was of her great son. Then Manie replied. Instead of thanking his audience, however, he started abusing us left and right, calling us a mob of hooligans and soulless Philistines, and saying how much he despised us.

Naturally, we were very much surprised at this outburst, as we had always been kind to Manie Kruger and had encouraged him all we could. But Letta Steyn explained that Manie didn't really mean the things he said. She said it was just that every great artist was expected to talk in that way about the place he came from.

So we knew it was all right, and the more offensive the things were that Manie said about us, the louder we shouted, *"Hoor, hoor vir* Manie." There was a particularly enthusiastic round of applause when he said that we knew as much about art as a boomslang. His language was hotter than anything I had ever heard - except once. And that was when De Wet said what he thought of Cronje's surrender to the English at Paardeberg. We could feel that Manie's speech was the real thing. We cheered ourselves hoarse that day.

And so Manie Kruger went. We received one letter to say that he had reached Pretoria. But after that we heard no more of him.

Yet always, when Letta Steyn spoke of Manie, it was as a child speaks of a dream, half-wistfully, and always, with the voice of a wistful child, she would tell me how one day, one day he would return. And often, when it was dusk, I would see her sitting on the stoep, gazing out across the veld into the evening, down the dusty road that led between the thorn-trees and beyond the Dwarsberg, waiting for the lover who would come to her no more.

It was a long time before I again saw Manie Kruger. And then it was in Pretoria. I had gone there to interview the Volksraad member about an election promise. It was quite by accident that I saw Manie. And he was playing the concertina - playing as well as ever, I thought. I went away quickly. But what affected me very strangely was just that one glimpse I had of the green curtain of the bar in front of which Manie Kruger played.

FUNERAL EARTH

We had a difficult task, that time (Oom Schalk Lourens said), teaching Sijefu's tribe of Mtosas to become civilized. But they did not show any appreciation. Even after we had set fire to their huts in a long row round the slopes of Abjaterskop, so that you could see the smoke almost as far as Nietverdiend, the Mtosas remained just about as unenlightened as ever. They would retreat into the mountains, where it was almost impossible for our commando to follow them on horseback. They remained hidden in the thick bush.

"I can sense these kafirs all around us," Veldkornet Andries Joubert said to our "seksie" of about a dozen burghers when we had come to a halt in a clearing amid the tall withaaks. "I have been in so many kafir wars that I can almost smell when there are kafirs lying in wait for us with assegais. And yet all day long you never see a single Mtosa that you can put a lead bullet through."

He also said that if this war went on much longer we would forget altogether how to handle a gun. And what would we do then, when we again had to fight England?

Young Fanie Louw, who liked saying funny things, threw back his head and pretended to be sniffing the air with discrimination. "I can smell a whole row of assegais with broad blades and short handles," Fanie Louw said. "The stabbing assegai has got more of a selons-rose sort of smell about it than a throwing spear. The selons-rose that you come across in graveyards."

The veldkornet did not think Fanie Louw's remark very funny, however. And he said we all knew that this was the first time Fanie Louw had ever been on commando. He also said that if a crowd of Mtosas were to leap out of the bush on to us suddenly, then you wouldn't be able to smell Fanie Louw for dust. The veldkornet also said another thing that was even better.

Our group of burghers laughed heartily. Maybe Veldkornet Joubert could not think out a lot of nonsense to say just on the spur of the moment, in the way that Fanie Louw could, but give our veldkornet a chance to reflect, first, and he would come out with the kind of remark that you just had to admire.

Indeed, from the very next thing Veldkornet Joubert said, you could see how deep was his insight. And he did not have to think much, either, then.

"Let us get out of here as quick as hell, men," he said, speaking very distinctly. "Perhaps the kafirs are hiding out in the open turf-lands, where there are no trees. And none of this long tamboekie grass, either."

When we emerged from that stretch of bush we were glad to discover that our veldkornet had been right, like always.

For another group of Transvaal burghers had hit on the same strategy.

"We were in the middle of the bush," their leader, Combrinck, said to us, after we had exchanged greetings. "A very thick part of the bush, with withaaks standing up like skeletons. And we suddenly thought the Mtosas might have gone into hiding out here in the open."

You could see that Veldkornet Joubert was pleased to think that he had, on his own, worked out the same tactics as Combrinck, who was known as a skilful kafir-fighter. All the same, it seemed as though this was going to be a long war.

It was then that, again speaking out of his turn, Fanie Louw said that all we needed now was for the commandant himself to arrive there in the middle of the turf-lands with the main body of burghers. "Maybe we should even go back to Pretoria to see if the Mtosas aren't perhaps hiding in the Volksraad," he said. "Passing laws and things. You know how cheeky a Mtosa is."

"It can't be worse than some of the laws that the Volksraad is already passing now," Combrinck said, gruffly. From that we could see that why he had not himself been appointed commandant was because he had voted against the President in the last elections.

By that time the sun was sitting not more than about two Cape feet above a tall koppie on the horizon. Accordingly, we started looking about for a place to camp. It was muddy in the turf-lands, and there was no firewood there, but we all said that we did not mind. We would not pamper ourselves by going to sleep in the thick bush, we told one another. It was wartime, and we were on commando, and the mud of the turf-lands was good enough for us, we said.

It was then that an unusual thing happened.

For we suddenly did see Mtosas. We saw them from a long way off. They came out of the bush and marched right out into the open. They made no attempt to hide. We saw in amazement that they were coming straight in our direction, advancing in single file. And we observed, even from that distance, that they were unarmed. Instead of assegais and shields they carried burdens on their heads. And almost in that same moment we realized, from the heavy look of those burdens, that the carriers must be women.

For that reason we took our guns in our hands and stood waiting. Since it was women, we were naturally prepared for the lowest form of treachery.

As the column drew nearer we saw that at the head of it was Ndambe, an old native whom we knew well. For years he had been Sijefu's chief counsellor. Ndambe held up his hand. The line of women halted. Ndambe spoke. He declared that we white men were kings among kings and elephants among elephants. He also said that we were ringhals snakes more poisonous and generally disgusting than any ringhals snake in the country.

We knew, of course, that Ndambe was only paying us compliments in his ignorant Mtosa fashion. And so we naturally felt highly gratified. I can still remember the way Jurie Bekker nudged me in the ribs and said, "Did you hear that?"

When Ndambe went on, however, to say that we were filthier than the spittle of a green tree-toad, several burghers grew restive. They felt that there was perhaps such a thing as carrying these tribal courtesies a bit too far.

It was then that Veldkornet Joubert, slipping his finger inside the trigger guard of his gun, requested Ndambe to come to the point. By the expression on our veldkornet's face, you could see that he had had enough of compliments for one day.

They had come to offer peace, Ndambe told us then.

What the women carried on their heads were presents.

At a sign from Ndambe the column knelt in the mud of the turf-lands. They brought lion and zebra skins and elephant tusks, and beads and brass bangles and, on a long mat, the whole haunch of a red Afrikaner ox, hide and hoof and all. And several pigs cut in half. And clay pots filled to the brim with white beer. And also – and this we prized most – witch-doctor medicines that protected you against *goël* spirits at night and the evil eye.

Ndambe gave another signal. A woman with a clay pot on her head rose up from the kneeling column and advanced towards us. We saw then that what she had in the pot was black earth. It was wet and almost like turf-soil. We couldn't understand what they wanted to bring us that for. As though we didn't have enough of it, right there where we were standing and sticking to our veldskoens, and all. And yet Ndambe acted as though that was the most precious part of the peace offerings that his chief, Sijefu, had sent us.

It was when Ndambe spoke again that we saw how ignorant he and his chief and the whole Mtosa tribe were, really.

He took a handful of soil out of the pot and pressed it together between his fingers. Then he told us how honoured the Mtosa tribe was because we were waging war against them. In the past they had only had flat-faced Mshangaans with spiked knobkerries to fight against, he said, but now it was different. Our veldkornet took half a step forward, then, in case Ndambe was going to start flattering us again. So Ndambe said, simply, that the Mtosas would be glad if we came and made war against them later on, when the harvest had been gathered in. But in the meantime the tribe did not wish to continue fighting.

It was the time for sowing.

Ndambe let the soil run through his fingers, to show us how good it was. He also invited us to taste it. We declined.

We accepted his presents and peace was made. And I can still remember how Veldkornet Joubert shook his head and said, "Can you beat the Mtosas for ignorance?"

And I can still remember what Jurie Bekker said, also. That was when something made him examine the haunch of beef more closely, and he found his own brand mark on it.

It was not long afterwards that the war came against England.

By the end of the second year of the war the Boer forces were in a very bad way. But we would not make peace. Veldkornet Joubert was now promoted to commandant. Combrinck fell in the battle before Dalmanutha. Jurie Bekker was still with us, and so was Fanie Louw. And it was strange how attached we had grown to Fanie Louw during the years of hardship that we went through together in the field. But up to the end we had to admit that, while we had got used to his jokes, and we knew there was no harm in them, we would have preferred it that he should stop making them.

He did stop, and forever, in a skirmish near a blockhouse. We buried him in the shade of a thorn-tree. We got ready to fill in his grave, after which the commandant would say a few words and we would bare our heads and sing a psalm. As you know, it was customary at a funeral for each mourner to take up a handful of earth and fling it in the grave.

When Commandant Joubert stooped down and picked up his handful of earth, a strange thing happened. And I remembered that other war, against the Mtosas. And we knew – although we would not say it – what was now that longing in the heart of each of us. For Commandant Joubert did not straight away drop the soil into Fanie Louw's grave. Instead he kneaded the damp ground between his fingers. It was as though he had forgotten that it was funeral earth. He seemed to be thinking not of death then, but of life.

We patterned after him, picking up handfuls of soil and pressing it together. We felt the deep loam in it, and saw how springy it was, and we let it trickle through our fingers. And we could remember only that it was the time for sowing.

I understood then how, in an earlier war, the Mtosas had felt, they who were also farmers.

UNTO DUST

I have noticed that when a young man or woman dies, people get the feeling that there is something beautiful and touching in the event, and that it is different from the death of an old person. In the thought, say, of a girl of twenty sinking into an untimely grave, there is a sweet wistfulness that makes people talk all kinds of romantic words. She died, they say, young, she that was so full of life and so fair. She was a flower that withered before it bloomed, they say, and it all seems so fitting and beautiful that there is a good deal of resentment, at the funeral, over the crude questions that a couple of men in plain clothes from the landdrost's office are asking about cattle-dip.

But when you have grown old, nobody is very much interested in the manner of your dying. Nobody except you yourself, that is. And I think that your past life has got a lot to do with the way you feel when you get near the end of your days. I remember how, when he was lying on his deathbed, Andries Wessels kept on telling us that it was because of the blameless path he had trodden from his earliest years that he could compose himself in peace to lay down his burdens. And I certainly never saw a man breathe his last more tranquilly, seeing that right up to the end he kept on murmuring to us how happy he was, with heavenly hosts and invisible choirs of angels all around him.

Just before he died, he told us that the angels had even become visible. They were medium-sized angels, he said, and they had cloven hoofs and carried forks. It was obvious that Andries Wessels' ideas were getting a bit confused by then, but all the same I never saw a man die in a more hallowed sort of calm.

Once, during the malaria season in the Eastern Transvaal, it seemed to me, when I was in a high fever and like to die, that the whole world was a big burial-ground. I thought it was the earth itself that was a

Peter Badcock

graveyard, and not just those little fenced-in bits of land dotted with tombstones, in the shade of a Western Province oak-tree or by the side of a Transvaal koppie. This was a nightmare that worried me a great deal, and so I was very glad, when I recovered from the fever, to think that we Boers had properly marked out places on our farms for white people to be laid to rest in, in a civilized Christian way, instead of having to be buried just anyhow, along with a dead wild cat, maybe, or a Bushman with a clay-pot, and things.

When I mentioned this to my friend, Stoffel Oosthuizen, who was in the Low Country with me at the time, he agreed with me wholeheartedly. There were people who talked in a high-flown way of death as the great leveller, he said, and those high-flown people also declared that everyone was made kin by death. He would still like to see those things proved, Stoffel Oosthuizen said. After all, that was one of the reasons why the Boers trekked away into the Transvaal and the Free State, he said, because the British Government wanted to give the vote to any Cape Coloured person walking about with a *kroes* head and big cracks in his feet.

The first time he heard that sort of talk about death coming to all of us alike, and making us all equal, Stoffel Oosthuizen's suspicions were aroused. It sounded like out of a speech made by one of those liberal Cape politicians, he explained.

I found something very comforting in Stoffel Oosthuizen's words.

Then, to illustrate his contention, Stoffel Oosthuizen told me a story of an incident that took place in a bygone Transvaal kafir war. I don't know whether he told the story incorrectly, or whether it was just that kind of story, but, by the time he had finished, all my uncertainties had, I discovered, come back to me.

"You can go and look at Hans Welman's tombstone any time you are at Nietverdiend," Stoffel Oosthuizen said. "The slab of red sandstone is weathered by now, of course, seeing how long ago it all happened. But the inscription is still legible. I was with Hans Welman on that morning when he fell. Our commando had been ambushed by the kafirs and was retreating. I could do nothing for Hans Welman. Once, when I looked round, I saw a tall kafir bending over him and plunging an assegai into him. Shortly afterwards I saw the kafir stripping the clothes off Hans Welman. A yellow kafir dog was yelping excitedly around his black master. Although I was in grave danger myself, with several dozen kafirs making straight for me on foot through the bush, the fury I felt at the sight of what that tall kafir was doing made me hazard a last shot. Reining in my horse, and taking what aim I could under the circumstances, I pressed the trigger. My luck was in. I saw the kafir fall forward beside the naked body of Hans Welman. Then I set spurs to my horse and galloped off at full speed, with the foremost of my pursuers already almost upon me. The last I saw was that yellow dog bounding up to his master – whom I had wounded mortally, as we were to discover later.

"As you know, that kafir war dragged on for a long time. There were few pitched battles. Mainly, what took place were bush skirmishes, like the one in which Hans Welman lost his life.

"After about six months, quiet of a sort was restored to the Marico and Zoutpansberg districts. Then the day came when I went out, in company of a handful of other burghers, to fetch in the remains of Hans Welman, at his widow's request, for burial in the little cemetery plot on the farm. We took a coffin with us on a Cape-cart.

"We located the scene of the skirmish without difficulty. Indeed, Hans Welman had been killed not very far from his own farm, which had been temporarily abandoned, together with the other farms in that part, during the time that the trouble with the kafirs had lasted. We drove up to the spot where I remembered having seen Hans Welman lying dead on the ground, with the tall kafir next to him. From a distance I again saw that yellow dog. He slipped away into the bush at our approach. I could not help feeling that there was something rather stirring about that beast's fidelity, even though it was bestowed on a dead kafir.

"We were now confronted with a queer situation. We found that what was left of Hans Welman and the kafir consisted of little more than pieces of sun-dried flesh and the dismembered fragments of bleached skeletons. The sun and wild animals and birds of prey had done their work. There was a heap of human bones, with here and there leathery strips of blackened flesh. But we could not tell which was the white man and which the kafir. To make it still more confusing, a lot of bones were missing altogether, having no doubt been dragged away by wild animals into their lairs in the bush. Another thing was that Hans Welman and that kafir had been just about the same size."

Stoffel Oosthuizen paused in his narrative, and I let my imagination dwell for a moment on that situation. And I realized just how those Boers must have felt about it: about the thought of bringing the remains of a Transvaal burgher home to his widow for Christian burial, and perhaps having a lot of kafir bones mixed up with the burgher –

lying with him in the same tomb on which the mauve petals from the oleander overhead would fall.

"I remember one of our party saying that that was the worst of these kafir wars," Stoffel Oosthuizen continued. "If it had been a war against the English, and part of a dead Englishman had got lifted into that coffin by mistake, it wouldn't have mattered so much," he said.

There seemed to me in this story to be something as strange as the African veld. Stoffel Oosthuizen said that the little party of Boers spent almost a whole afternoon with the remains in order to try to get the white man sorted out from the kafir. By the evening they had laid all they could find of what seemed like Hans Welman's bones in the coffin in the Cape-cart. The rest of the bones and flesh they buried on the spot.

Stoffel Oosthuizen added that, no matter what the difference in the colour of their skin had been, it was impossible to say that the kafir's bones were less white than Hans Welman's. Nor was it possible to say that the kafir's sun-dried flesh was any blacker than the white man's. Alive, you couldn't go wrong in distinguishing between a white man and a kafir. Dead, you had great difficulty in telling them apart.

"Naturally, we burghers felt very bitter about this whole affair," Stoffel Oosthuizen said, "and our resentment was something that we couldn't explain, quite. Afterwards, several other men who were there that day told me that they had the same feelings of suppressed anger that I did. They wanted somebody – just once – to make a remark such as 'in death they were not divided'. Then you would have seen an outburst all right. Nobody did say anything like that, however. We all knew better. Two days later a funeral service was conducted in the little cemetery on the Welman farm, and shortly afterwards the sandstone memorial was erected that you can still see there."

That was the story Stoffel Oosthuizen told me after I had recovered from the fever. It was a story that, as I have said, had in it features as strange as the African veld. But it brought me no peace in my broodings after that attack of malaria. Especially when Stoffel Oosthuizen spoke of how he had occasion, one clear night when the stars shone, to pass that quiet graveyard on the Welman farm. Something leapt up from the mound beside the sandstone slab. It gave him quite a turn, Stoffel Oosthuizen said, for the third time – and in that way – to come across that yellow kafir dog.

MAFEKING ROAD

When people ask me - as they often do, how it is that I can tell the best stories of anybody in the Transvaal (Oom Schalk Lourens said, modestly), then I explain to them that I just learn through observing the way that the world has with men and women. When I say this they nod their heads wisely, and say that they understand, and I nod my head wisely also, and that seems to satisfy them. But the thing I say to them is a lie, of course.

For it is not the story that counts. What matters is the way you tell it. The important thing is to know just at what moment you must knock out your pipe on your veldskoen, and at what stage of the story you must start talking about the School Committee at Drogevlei. Another necessary thing is to know what part of the story to leave out.

And you can never learn these things.

Look at Floris, the last of the Van Barnevelts. There is no doubt that he had a good story, and he should have been able to get people to listen to it. And yet nobody took any notice of him or of the things he had to say. Just because he couldn't tell the story properly.

Accordingly, it made me sad whenever I listened to him talk. For I could tell just where he went wrong. He never knew the moment at which to knock the ash out of his pipe. He always mentioned his opinion of the Drogevlei School Committee in the wrong place. And, what was still worse, he didn't know what part of the story to leave out.

And it was no use my trying to teach him, because as I have said, this is the thing that you can never learn. And so, each time he had told his story, I would see him turn away from me, with a look of doom on his face, and walk slowly down the road, stoop-shouldered, the last of the Van Barnevelts.

On the wall of Floris's voorkamer is a long family tree of the Van Barnevelts. You can see it there for yourself. It goes back for over two hundred years, to the Van Barnevelts of Amsterdam. At one time it went even further back, but that was before the white ants started on the top part of it and ate away quite a lot of Van Barnevelts. Nevertheless, if you look at this list, you will notice that at the bottom under Floris's own name, there is the last entry, "Stephanus". And behind the name "Stephanus", between two bent strokes, you will read the words: "*Obiit* Mafeking".

At the outbreak of the Second Boer War, Floris van Barnevelt was a widower, with one son, Stephanus, who was aged seventeen. The commando from our part of the Transvaal set off very cheerfully. We made a fine show with our horses and our wide hats, and our bandoliers, and with the sun shining on the barrels of our Mausers.

Young Stephanus van Barnevelt was the gayest of us all. But he said there was one thing he didn't like about the war, and that was that, in the end, we would have to go over the sea. He said that, after we had invaded the whole of the Cape, our commando would have to go on a ship and invade England also.

But we didn't go overseas, just then. Instead, our veldkornet told us that the burghers from our part had been ordered to join the big commando that was lying at Mafeking. We had to go and shoot a man there called Baden-Powell.

We rode steadily on into the west. After a while we noticed that our veldkornet frequently got off his horse and engaged in conversation with passing kafirs, leading them some distance from the roadside and speaking earnestly to them. Of course, it was right that our veldkornet should explain to the kafirs that it was wartime now, and that the Republic expected every kafir to stop smoking so much dagga and to think seriously about what was going on. But we noticed that each time at the end of the conversation the kafir would point towards something, and that our veldkornet would take much pains to follow the direction of the kafir's finger.

Of course, we understood then, what it was all about. Our veldkornet was a young fellow, and he was shy to let us see that he didn't know the way to Mafeking.

Somehow, after that, we did not have so much confidence in our veldkornet.

After a few days we got to Mafeking. We stayed there a long while, until the English troops came up and relieved the place. We left then. We left quickly. The English troops had brought a lot of artillery with them. And if we had difficulty in finding the road to Mafeking, we had no difficulty in finding the road away from Mafeking. And this time our veldkornet did not need kafirs, either, to point with their fingers where we had to go. Even though we did a lot of travelling in the night.

Long afterwards I spoke to an Englishman about this. He said it gave him a queer feeling to hear about the other side of the story of Mafeking. He said there had been very great rejoicings in England when Mafeking was relieved, and it was strange to think of the other aspect of it - of a defeated country and of broken columns blundering through the dark.

I remember many things that happened on the way back from Mafeking. There was no moon. And the stars shone down fitfully on the road that was full of guns and frightened horses and desperate men. The veld throbbed with the hoofbeats of baffled commandos. The stars looked down on scenes that told sombrely of a nation's ruin; they looked on the muzzles of the Mausers that had failed the Transvaal for the first time.

Of course, as a burgher of the Republic, I knew what my duty was. And that was to get as far away as I could from the place where, in the sunset, I had last seen English artillery. The other burghers knew their duty also. Our commandants and veldkornets had to give very few orders. Nevertheless, although I rode very fast, there was one young man who rode still faster. He kept ahead of me all the time. He rode, as a burgher should ride when there may be stray bullets flying, with his head well down and with his arms almost round the horse's neck.

He was Stephanus, the young son of Floris van Barnevelt.

There was much grumbling and dissatisfaction some time afterwards, when our leaders started making an effort to get the commandos in order again. In the end they managed to get us to halt. But most of us felt that this was a foolish thing to do. Especially as there was still a lot of firing going on all over the place, in haphazard fashion, and we couldn't tell how far the English had followed us in the dark. Furthermore, the commandos had scattered in so many different directions that it seemed hopeless to try and get them together again until after the war. Stephanus and I dismounted and stood by our horses. Soon there was a large body of men around us. Their figures looked strange and shadowy in the starlight. Some of them stood by their horses. Others sat on the grass by the roadside. "*Vas staan*, Burghers, *vas staan*," came the commands of our officers. And all the time we could still hear what sounded a lot like lyddite. It seemed foolish to be waiting there.

"The next they'll want," Stephanus van Barnevelt said, "is for us to go back to Mafeking. Perhaps our commandant has left his tobacco pouch behind, there."

Some of us laughed at this remark, but Floris, who had not dismounted, said that Stephanus ought to be ashamed of himself for talking like that. From what we could see of Floris in the gloom, he looked quite impressive, sitting very straight in the saddle, with the stars shining on his beard and rifle.

"If the veldkornet told me to go back to Mafeking," Floris said, "I would go back."

"That's how a burgher should talk," the veldkornet said, feeling flattered. For he had had little authority since the time we found out what he was talking to the kafirs for.

"I wouldn't go back to Mafeking for anybody," Stephanus replied, "unless, maybe, it's to hand myself over to the English."

"We can shoot you for doing that," the veldkornet said. "It's contrary to military law."

"I wish I knew something about military law," Stephanus answered. "Then I would draw up a peace treaty between Stephanus van Barnevelt and England."

Some of the men laughed again. But Floris shook his head sadly. He said the Van Barnevelts had fought bravely against Spain in a war that lasted 80 years.

Suddenly, out of the darkness there came a sharp rattle of musketry, and our men started getting uneasy again. But the sound of the firing decided Stephanus. He jumped on his horse quickly.

"I am turning back," he said, "I am going to hands-up to the English."

"No, don't go," the veldkornet called to him lamely, "or at least, wait until the morning. They may shoot you in the dark by mistake." As I have said, the veldkornet had very little authority.

Two days passed before we again saw Floris van Barnevelt. He was in a very worn and troubled state, and he said that it had been very hard for him to find his way back to us.

"You should have asked the kafirs," one of our number said with a laugh. "All the kafirs know our veldkornet."

But Floris did not speak about what happened that night, when we saw him riding out under the starlight, following after his son and shouting to him to be a man and to fight for his country. Also, Floris did not mention Stephanus again, his son was not worthy to be a Van Barnevelt.

After that we got separated. Our veldkornet was the first to be taken prisoner. And I often felt that he must feel very lonely on St. Helena. Because there were no kafirs from whom he could ask the way out of the barbed-wire camp.

Then, at last, our leaders came together at Vereeniging, and peace was made. And we returned to our farms, relieved that the war was over, but with heavy hearts at the thought that it had all been for nothing and that over the Transvaal the Vierkleur would not wave again.

And Floris van Barnevelt put back in its place, on the wall of the voorkamer, the copy of his family tree that had been carried with him in his knapsack throughout the war. Then a new schoolmaster came to this part of the Marico, and after a long talk with Floris, the schoolmaster wrote behind Stephanus's name, between two curved lines, the two words that you can still read there: "*Obiit* Mafeking".

Consequently, if you ask any person hereabouts what "*obiit*" means, he is able to tell you right away, that it is a foreign word, and that it means to ride up to the English, holding your Mauser in the air, with a white flag tied to it, near the muzzle.

But it was long afterwards that Floris van Barnevelt started telling his story.

And then they took no notice of him. And they wouldn't allow him to be nominated for the Drogevlei School Committee on the grounds that a man must be wrong in the head to talk in such an irresponsible fashion.

But I knew that Floris had a good story, and that its only fault was that he told it badly. He mentioned the Drogevlei School Committee too soon. And he knocked the ash out of his pipe in the wrong place. And he always insisted on telling that part of the story that he should have left out.

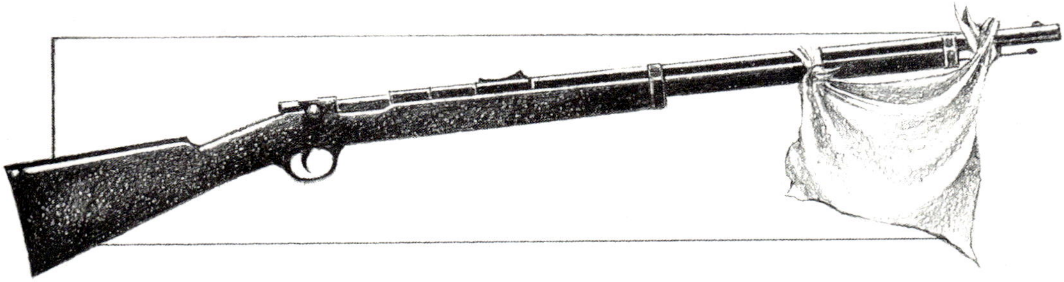

DRIEKA AND THE MOON

There is a queer witchery about the moon when it is full - Oom Schalk Lourens remarked - especially the moon that hangs over the valley of the Dwarsberge in the summertime. It does strange things to your mind, the Marico moon, and in your heart are wild and fragrant fancies, and your thoughts go very far away. Then, if you have been sitting on your front stoep, thinking these thoughts, you sigh and murmur something about the way of the world, and carry your chair inside.

I have seen the moon in other places besides the Marico. But it is not the same there.

Braam Venter, the man who fell off the Government lorry once, near Nietverdiend, says that the Marico moon is like a woman laying green flowers on a grave. Braam Venter often says things like that. Particularly since the time he fell off the lorry. He fell on his head, they say.

Always when the moon shines full like that it does something to our hearts that we wonder very much about and that we never understand. Always it awakens memories. And it is singular how different these memories are with each one of us.

Johannes Oberholzer says that the full moon always reminds him of one occasion when he was smuggling cattle over the Bechuanaland border. He says he never sees a full moon without thinking of the way it shone on the steel wire-cutters that he was holding in his hand when two mounted policemen rode up to him. And the next night Johannes Oberholzer again had a good view of the full moon; he saw it through the window of the place he was in. He says the moon was very large and very yellow, except for the black stripes in front of it.

And it was in the light of the full moon that hung over the thorn-trees that I saw Drieka Breytenbach.

Drieka was tall and slender. She had fair hair and blue eyes, and lots of people considered that she was the prettiest woman in the Marico. I thought so, too, that night I met her under the full moon by the thorn-trees. She had not been in the Bushveld very long. Her husband, Petrus Breytenbach, had met her and married her in the Schweizer-Reneke district, where he had trekked with his cattle for a while during the big drought.

Afterwards, when Petrus Breytenbach was shot dead with his own Mauser by a kafir working on his farm, Drieka went back to Schweizer-Reneke, leaving the Marico as strangely and as silently as she had come to it.

And it seemed to me that the Marico was a different place because Drieka Breytenbach had gone. And I thought of the moon, and the tricks it plays with your senses, and the stormy witchery that it flings at your soul. And I remembered what Braam Venter said, that the full moon is like a woman laying green flowers on a grave. And it seemed to me that Braam Venter's words were not so much nonsense, after all, and that worse things could happen to a man than that he should fall off a lorry on his head. And I thought of other matters.

But all this happened only afterwards.

When I saw Drieka that night she was leaning against a thorn-tree beside the road where it goes down to the drift. But I didn't recognize her at first. All I saw was a figure dressed in white with long hair hanging down loose over its shoulders. It seemed very unusual that a figure should be there like that at such a time of night. I remembered certain stories I had heard about white ghosts. I also remembered that a few miles back I had seen a boulder lying in the middle of the road. It was a fair-sized boulder and it might be dangerous for passing mule-carts. So I decided to turn back at once and move it out of the way.

I decided very quickly about the boulder. And I made up my mind so firmly that the saddle-girth broke from the sudden way in which I jerked my horse back on his haunches. Then the figure came forward and spoke and I saw it was Drieka Breytenbach.

"Good evening," I said in answer to her greeting, "I was just going back because I had remembered about something."

"About ghosts?" she asked.

"No," I replied truthfully, "about a stone in the road."

Drieka laughed at that. So I laughed too. And then Drieka laughed again. And then I laughed. In fact, we did quite a lot of laughing between us. I got off my horse and stood beside Drieka in the moonlight. And if somebody had come along at that moment and said that the predikant's mule-cart had been capsized by the boulder in the road I would have laughed still more.

That is the sort of thing the moon in the Marico does to you when it is full.

I didn't think of asking Drieka how she came to be there, or why her hair was hanging down loose, or who it was that she had been waiting for under the thorn-tree. It was enough that the moon was there, big and yellow over the veld, and that the wind blew softly through the trees and across the grass and against Drieka's white dress and against the mad singing of the stars.

Before I knew what was happening we were seated on the grass under the thorn-tree whose branches leant over the road. And I remember that for quite a while we remained there without talking, sitting side by side on the grass with our feet in the soft sand. And Drieka smiled at me with a misty sort of look in her eyes, and I saw that she was lovely.

I felt that it was not enough that we should go on sitting there in silence. I knew that a woman - even a moon-woman like Drieka - expected a man to be more than just good-humoured and honest. I knew that a woman wanted a man also to be an entertaining companion for her. So I beguiled the passing moments for Drieka with interesting conversation.

I explained to her how a few days before a pebble had worked itself into my veldskoen and had rubbed some skin off the top of one of my toes. I took off my veldskoen and showed her the place. I also told her about the rinderpest and about the way two of my cows had died of the miltsiek. I also knew a lot about blue-tongue in sheep, and about gallansiekte and the haarwurm, and I talked to her airily about these things, just as easily as I am talking to you.

But, of course, it was the moonlight that did it. I never knew before that I was so good in this idle, butterfly kind of talk. And the whole thing was so innocent, too. I felt that if Drieka Breytenbach's husband, Petrus, were to come along and find us sitting there side by side, he would not be able to say much about it. At least, not very much.

After a while I stopped talking.

Drieka put her hand in mine.

"Oh, Schalk," she whispered, and the moon and that misty look were in her blue eyes. "Do tell me some more."

I shook my head.

"I am sorry, Drieka," I answered, "I don't know any more."

"But you must, Schalk," she said very softly. "Talk to me about - about other things."

I thought steadily for some moments.

"Yes, Drieka," I said at length, "I have remembered something. There is one more thing I haven't told you about the blue-tongue in sheep ..."

"No, no, not that," she interrupted, "talk to me about other things. About the moon, say."

So I told her two things that Braam Venter had said about the moon. I told her the green flower one and the other one.

"Braam Venter knows lots more things like that about the moon," I explained, "you'll see him next time you go to Zeerust for the Nagmaal. He is a short fellow with a bump on his head from where he fell ..."

"Oh, no, Schalk," Drieka said again, shaking her head, so that a wisp of her fair head brushed against my face, "I don't want to know about Braam Venter. Only about you. You think out something on your own about the moon and tell it to me."

I understood what she meant.

"Well, Drieka," I said thoughtfully. "The moon - the moon is all right."

"Oh, Schalk!" Drieka cried. "That's much finer than anything Braam Venter could ever say - even with that bump on his head."

Of course, I told her that it was nothing and that I could perhaps say something even better if I tried. But I was very proud, all the same. And somehow it seemed that my words brought us close together. I felt that a handful of words, spoken under the full moon, had made a new and witch thing come into the life of Drieka and me.

We were holding hands then, sitting on the grass with our feet in the road, and Drieka leant her head on my shoulder, and her long hair stirred softly against my face, but I looked only at her feet. And I thought for a moment that I loved her. And I did not love her because her body was beautiful, or because she had red lips, or because her eyes were blue. In that moment I did not understand about her body or her lips or her eyes. I loved her for her feet; and because her feet were in the road next to mine.

And yet all the time I felt, far away at the back of my mind, that it was the moon that was doing these things to me.

"You have got good feet for walking on," I said to Drieka.

"Braam Venter would have said that I have got good feet for dancing on," Drieka answered, laughing. And I began to grow jealous of Braam Venter.

The next thing I knew was that Drieka had thrown herself into my arms.

"Do you think I am very beautiful, Schalk?" Drieka asked.

"You are very beautiful, Drieka," I answered slowly, "very beautiful."

"Will you do something for me, Schalk?" Drieka asked again, and her red lips were very close to my cheek. "Will you do something for me if I love you very much?"

"What do you want me to do, Drieka?"

She drew my head down to her lips and whispered hot words in my ear.

And so it came that I thrust her from me, suddenly. I jumped unsteadily to my feet; I found my horse and rode away. I left Drieka Breytenbach where I had found her, under the thorn-tree by the roadside, with her hot whisperings still ringing in my ears, and before I reached home the moon had set behind the Dwarsberge.

Well, there is not much left for me to tell you. In the days that followed, Drieka Breytenbach was always in my thoughts. Her long, loose hair and her red lips and her feet that had been in the roadside sand with mine. But if she really was the ghost that I had at first taken her to be, I could not have been more afraid of her.

And it seemed singular that, while it had been my words, spoken in the moonlight, that helped to bring Drieka and me closer together, it was Drieka's hot breath, whispering wild words in my ear, that sent me so suddenly from her side.

Once or twice I even felt sorry for having left in that fashion.

And later on when I heard that Drieka Breytenbach had gone back to Schweizer-Reneke, and that her husband had been shot dead with his own Mauser by one of the farm kafirs, I was not surprised. In fact, I had expected it. Only it did not seem right somehow, that Drieka should have got a kafir to do the thing that I refused to do.

WHITE ANT

Jurie Steyn was rubbing vigorously along the side of his counter with a rag soaked in paraffin. He was also saying things which, afterwards, in calmer moments, he would no doubt regret. When his wife came into the voorkamer with a tin of Cooper's dip, Jurie Steyn stopped using that sort of language and contented himself with observations of a general nature about the hardships of life in the Marico.

"All the same, they are very wonderful creatures, those little white ants," the schoolmaster remarked. "Among the books I brought here into the Marico, to read in my spare time, is a book called *The Soul of the White Ant*. Actually, of course, the white ant is not a true ant at all. The right name for the white ant is *isoptera* –"

Jurie Steyn had another, and shorter, name for the white ant right on the tip of his tongue. And he started saying it, too. Only, he remembered his wife's presence in time, and so he changed the word to something else.

"This isn't the first time the white ants have got in behind your counter," At Naudé announced. "The last lot of stamps you sold me had little holes eaten all round the edges."

"That's just perforations," Jurie Steyn announced. "All postage stamps are that way. Next time you have got a postage stamp in your hand, just look at it carefully, and you'll see. There's a law about it, or something. In the Department we talk of those little holes as perforations. It is what makes it possible for us, in the Department, to tear stamps off easily, without having to use a scissors. Of course, it's not everybody that knows that."

At Naudé looked as much hurt as surprised.

"You mustn't think I am so ignorant, Jurie," he announced severely. "Mind you, I'm not saying that, perhaps, when this post office was first opened, and you were still new to affairs, and you couldn't be expected to *know* about perforations and things, coming to this job raw, from behind the plough – I'm not saying that you mightn't have cut the stamps loose with a scissors, or a no. 3 pruning shears, even. At the start, mind you. And nobody would have blamed you for it, either. I mean, nobody ever has blamed you. We've all, in fact, admired the way you took to this work. I spoke to Gysbert van Tonder about it, too, more than once. Indeed, we both admired you. We spoke about how you stood behind that counter, with kraal manure in your hair, and all, just like you were Postmaster General. Bold as brass, we said, too."

The subtle flattery in At Naudé's speech served to mollify Jurie Steyn.

"You said all that about me?" he asked. "You did?"

"Yes," At Naudé proceeded smoothly. "And we also admired the neat way you learnt to handle the post office rubber stamp, Gysbert and I. We said you held onto it like it was a branding-iron. And we noticed how you would whistle, too, just before bringing the rubber stamp down on a parcel, and how you would step aside afterwards, quickly, just as though you half expected the parcel to jump up and poke you in the short ribs. To tell you the truth, Jurie, we were *proud* of you."

Jurie Steyn was visibly touched. And so he said that he admitted he had perhaps been a bit arrogant in the way he had spoken to At Naudé about the perforations. The white ants *had* got amongst his postage stamps, Jurie Steyn acknowledged – once. But what they ate you could hardly notice, he said. They just chewed a little around the edges.

But Gysbert van Tonder said that, all the same, that was enough. His youngest daughter was a member of the Sunshine Children's Club of the church magazine in Cape Town, Gysbert said. And his youngest daughter wrote to Aunt Susann, who was the woman editor, to say that it was her birthday. And when Aunt Susann mentioned his youngest daughter's birthday in the Sunshine Club corner of the church magazine, Aunt Susann wrote that she was a little girl staying in the lonely African wilds. *Gramadoelas* was the word that Aunt Susann used, Gysbert van Tonder said. And all just because Aunt Susann had noticed the way that part of the springbok on the stamp on his youngest daughter's letter had been eaten off by white ants, Gysbert van Tonder said.

He added that his daughter had lost all interest in the Sunshine

Children's Club, since then. It sounded so uncivilized, the way Aunt Susann wrote about her.

"As though we're living in a grass hut with a string of crocodiles around it, with their teeth showing," Gysbert van Tonder said. "As though it's all still konsessie farms and we haven't made improvements. And it's no use trying to explain to her, either, that she must just feel sorry for Aunt Susann for not knowing any better. You can't explain things like that to a child."

Nevertheless, while we all sympathized with Gysbert van Tonder, we had to concede that it was not in any way Jurie Steyn's fault. We had all had experience of white ants, and we knew that mostly, when you came along with the paraffin and Cooper's dip, it was too late. By the time you saw those little tunnels, which the white ants made by sticking grains of sand together with spit, all the damage had already been done.

The schoolmaster started talking some more about his book dealing with the life of the white ant, then, and he said that it was well known that the termite was the greatest plague of tropic lands. Several of us were able to help the schoolmaster right. As Chris Welman made it clear to him, the Marico was not in the tropics at all. The tropics were quite a long way up. The tropics started beyond Mochudi, even. A land surveyor had established that much for us, a few years ago, on a coloured map. It was loose talk about wilds and gramadoelas and tropics that gave the Marico a bad name, we said. Maybe we did have white ants here – lots of them, too – but we certainly weren't in the tropics, like some countries we knew, and that we could mention, also, if we wanted to. Maybe what had happened was that the white ants had come down here *from* the tropics, we said. From away down beyond Mochudi and other side Frik Bonthuys's farm, even. *There* was tropics for you, now, we said to the schoolmaster. Why, he should just see Frik Bonthuys's shirt. Frik Bonthuys wore his shirt outside of his trousers, and the back part of it hung down almost onto the ground.

The schoolmaster said that he thought we were perhaps just a little too sensitive about this sort of thing. He himself was interested in the white ant, he explained, mainly from the scientific point of view. The white ant belonged to the insect world, which was really very highly civilized, he said. All the insect world didn't have was haemoglobin. The insect had the same blood in his veins as a White man, the schoolmaster said, except for haemoglobin.

Gysbert van Tonder said that whatever that thing was, it was enough. Gysbert said it quite hastily, too. He said that when once you started making allowances for the white ant, that way, the next thing the white ant would want would be to vote. And *he* wouldn't go into a polling booth alongside of an ant, to vote, Gysbert van Tonder said, even if that ant *was* white.

This conversation was getting out of our depths. The talk had taken a wrong turning, but we couldn't make out where, exactly. Consequently, we were all pleased when Oupa Bekker spoke, and made things seem sensible again.

"The worst place I ever knew for white ants, in the old days," Oupa Bekker said, "was along the Malopo, just below where it joins the Crocodile River. *There* was white ants for you. I was a transport rider in those days, when all the transport was still by ox-wagon. My partner was Jan Theron. We called him Jan Mankie because of his wooden leg – a back wheel of the ox-wagon having gone over his kneecap one day when he had been drinking mampoer. Anyway, we had camped out beside the Malopo. And the next morning, when we inspanned, Jan Mankie was saying how gay and *light* he felt. He couldn't understand it. He even started thinking that it must be the drink again, that was this time affecting him in quite a new way. We didn't know, of course, that it was because the white ants had hollowed out all of his wooden leg while he had lain asleep.

"And what was still more queer was that the wagon, when he inspanned it, also seemed surprisingly light. It didn't strike us what the reason for that was, either, just then. Maybe we were not in a guessing frame of mind, that morning. But when our trek got through the Paradys Poort, into a stiff wind that was blowing across the vlakte, it all became very clear to us. For the sudden cloud of dust that went up was not just dust from the road. Our wagon and its load of planed Oregon pine were carried away in the finest kind of powder you can imagine, and all that our oxen were left pulling was the trek-chain. And Jan Mankie Theron was standing on one leg. His other trouser-leg, that was of a greyish-coloured moleskin, was flapping empty in the wind."

Thus, Oupa Bekker's factual account of a straightforward Marico incident of long ago, presenting the ways and characteristics of the termite in a positive light, restored us to a sense of current realities.

"But what are you supposed to do about white ants, anyway?" Johnny Coen asked after a while. "Cooper's dip helps, of course. But there should be a more permanent way of getting rid of them, I'd imagine."

It was then that we all turned to the schoolmaster, again. What did it say in that book of his about the white ant, we asked him.

Well, there was a chapter in his book on the destruction of termites, the schoolmaster said. At least, there had been a chapter. It was the last chapter in the book. But he had unfortunately left the book lying on his desk in the schoolroom over one week-end. And when he had got back on Monday morning there was a little tunnel running up his desk. And the pages dealing with how to exterminate the white ant had been eaten away.

WILLEM PRINSLOO'S PEACH BRANDY

No (Oom Schalk Lourens said) you don't get flowers in the Groot Marico. It is not a bad district for mealies, and I once grew quite good onions in a small garden I made next to the dam. But what you can really call flowers are rare things here. Perhaps it's the heat. Or the drought.

Yet whenever I talk about flowers, I think of Willem Prinsloo's farm on Abjaterskop, where the dance was, and I think of Fritz Pretorius, sitting pale and sick by the roadside, and I think of the white rose that I wore in my hat, jauntily. But most of all I think of Grieta.

If you walk over my farm to the hoogte, and look towards the north-west, you can see Abjaterskop behind the ridge of the Dwarsberge. People will tell you that there are ghosts on Abjaterskop, and that it was once the home of witches. I can believe that. I was at Abjaterskop only once. That was many years ago. And I never went there again. Still, it wasn't ghosts that kept me away; nor was it the witches.

Grieta Prinsloo was due to come back from the finishing school at Zeerust, where she had gone to learn English manners and dictation and other high-class subjects. Therefore Willem Prinsloo, her father, arranged a big dance on his farm at Abjaterskop to celebrate Grieta's return.

I was invited to the party. So was Fritz Pretorius. So was every white person in the district, from Derdepoort to Ramoutsa. What was more, practically everybody went. Of course, we were all somewhat nervous about meeting Grieta. With all the superior things she had learnt at the finishing school, we wouldn't be able to talk to her in a chatty sort of way, just as though she were an ordinary Boer girl. But what fetched us all to Abjaterskop in the end was our knowledge that Willem Prinsloo made the best peach brandy in the district.

Fritz Pretorius spoke to me of the difficulty brought about by Grieta's learning.

"Yes, jong," he said, "I am feeling pretty shaky about talking to her, I can tell you. I have been rubbing up my education a bit, though. Yesterday I took out my old slate that I last used when I left school seventeen years ago and I did a few sums. I did some addition and subtraction. I tried a little multiplication, too. But I have forgotten how it is done."

I told Fritz that I would have liked to have helped him, but I had never learnt as far as multiplication.

The day of the dance arrived. The post-cart bearing Grieta to her father's house passed through Drogedal in the morning. In the afternoon I got dressed. I wore a black jacket, fawn trousers, and a pink shirt. I also put on the brown boots that I had bought about a year before, and that I had never had occasion to wear. For I would have looked silly walking about the farm in a pair of shop boots, when everybody else wore home-made veldskoens.

I believed, as I got on my horse, and set off down the Government road, with my hat rakishly on one side, that I would be easily the best-dressed young man at that dance.

It was getting on towards sunset when I arrived at the foot of Abjaterskop, which I had to skirt in order to reach Willem Prinsloo's farm nestling in a hollow behind the hills. I felt, as I rode, that it was stupid for a man to live in a part that was reputed to be haunted. The trees grew taller and denser, as they always do on rising ground. And they also got a lot darker.

All over the place were queer, heavy shadows. I didn't like the look of them. I remembered stories I had heard of the witches of Abjaterskop, and what they did to travellers who lost their way in the dark. It seemed an easy thing to lose your way among those tall trees. Accordingly I spurred my horse on to a gallop, to get out of this gloomy region as quickly as possible. After all, a horse is sensitive about things like ghosts and witches, and it was my duty to see my horse was not frightened unnecessarily. Especially as a cold wind suddenly sprang up through the poort, and once or twice it sounded as though an evil voice were calling my name. I started riding fast then. But a few moments later I looked round and realized the position. It was Fritz Pretorius galloping along behind me.

"What was your hurry?" Fritz asked when I had slowed down to allow his overtaking me.

"I wished to get through those trees before it was too dark," I answered, "I didn't want my horse to get frightened."

"I suppose that's why you were riding with your arms round his neck," Fritz observed, "to soothe him."

I did not reply. But what I did notice was that Fritz was also very stylishly-dressed. True, I beat him as far as shirt and boots went, but he was dressed in a new grey suit, with his socks pulled up over the bottoms of his trousers. He also had a handkerchief which he ostentatiously took out of his pocket several times.

Of course, I couldn't be jealous of a person like Fritz Pretorius. I was only annoyed at the thought that he was making himself ridiculous by going to a party with an outlandish thing like a handkerchief.

We arrived at Willem Prinsloo's house. There were so many oxwagons drawn up on the veld that the place looked like a laager. Prinsloo met us at the door.

"Go right through, kêrels," he said, "the dancing is in the voorhuis. The peach brandy is in the kitchen."

Although the voorhuis was big it was so crowded as to make it almost impossible to dance. But it was not as crowded as the kitchen. Nor was the music in the voorhuis - which was provided by a number of men with guitars and concertinas - as loud as the music in the kitchen, where there was no band, but each man sang for himself.

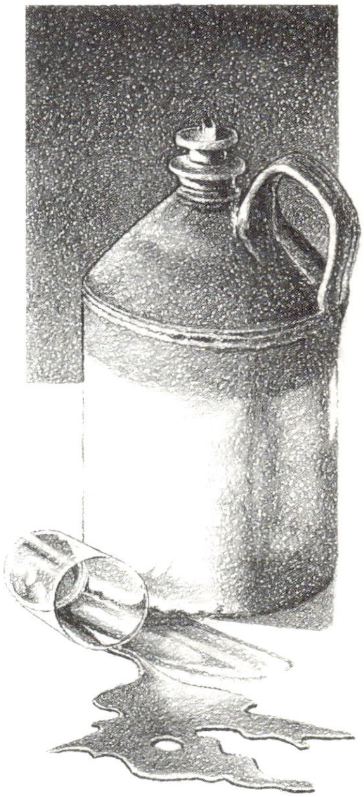

We knew from these signs that the party was a success.

When I had been in the kitchen for about half an hour I decided to go into the voorhuis. It seemed a long way, now, from the kitchen to the voorhuis, and I had to lean against the wall several times to think. I passed a number of other men who were also leaning against the wall like that, thinking. One man even found that he could think best by sitting on the floor with his head in his arms.

You could see that Willem Prinsloo made good peach brandy.

Then I saw Fritz Pretorius, and the sight of him brought me to my senses right away. Airily flapping his white handkerchief in time with the music, he was talking to a girl who smiled up at him with bright eyes and red lips and small white teeth.

I knew at once that it was Grieta.

She was tall and slender and very pretty, and her dark hair was braided with a wreath of white roses that you could see had been picked that same morning in Zeerust. And she didn't look the sort of girl, either, in whose presence you had to appear clever and educated. In fact, I felt I wouldn't really need the twelve times table which I had torn off the back of a school writing book, and had thrust into my jacket pocket before leaving home.

You can imagine that it was not too easy for me to get a word in with Grieta while Fritz was hanging around. But I managed it eventually, and while I was talking to her I had the satisfaction of seeing, out of the corner of my eye, the direction Fritz took. He went into the kitchen, flapping his handkerchief behind him - into the kitchen, where the laughter was, and the singing, and Willem Prinsloo's peach brandy.

I told Grieta that I was Schalk Lourens.

"Oh yes, I have heard of you," she answered, "from Fritz Pretorius."

I knew what that meant. So I told her that Fritz was known all over the Marico for his lies. I told her other things about Fritz. Ten minutes later, when I was still talking about him, Grieta smiled and said that I could tell her the rest some other night.

"But I must tell you one more thing now," I insisted. "When he knew that he would be meeting you here at the dance, Fritz started doing homework."

I told her about the slate and the sums, and Grieta laughed softly. It struck me again how pretty she was. And her eyes were radiant in the candlelight. And the roses looked very white against her dark hair. And all this time the dancers whirled around us, and the band in the voorhuis played lively dance tunes, and from the kitchen there issued weird sounds of jubilation.

The rest happened very quickly.

I can't even remember how it all came about. But what I do know is that when we were outside, under the tall trees, with the stars over us, I could easily believe that Grieta was not a girl at all, but one of the witches of Abjaterskop who wove strange spells.

Yet to listen to my talking nobody would have guessed the wild, thrilling things that were in my heart.

I told Grieta about last year's drought, and about the difficulty of keeping the white ants from eating through the door and window frames, and about the way my new brown boots tended to take the skin off my toes if I walked quickly.

Then I moved close up to her.

"Grieta," I said, taking her hand, "Grieta, there is something I want to tell you."

She pulled away her hand. She did it gently, though. Sorrowfully, almost.

"I know what you want to say," she answered.

I was surprised at that.

"How do you know, Grieta?" I asked.

"Oh, I know lots of things," she replied, laughing again, "I haven't been to finishing school for nothing."

"I don't mean that," I answered at once, "I wasn't going to talk about spelling or arithmetic. I was going to tell you that ..."

"Please don't say it, Schalk," Grieta interrupted me. "I - I don't know whether I am worthy of hearing it. I don't know, even ..."

"But you are so lovely," I exclaimed. "I have got to tell you how lovely you are."

But at the very moment I stepped forward she retreated swiftly, eluding me. I couldn't understand how she had timed it so well. For, try as I might, I couldn't catch her. She sped lightly and gracefully amongst the trees, and I followed as best I could.

Yet it was not only my want of learning that handicapped me. There were also my new boots. And Willem Prinsloo's peach brandy. And the shaft of a mule-cart - the lower end of the shaft, where it rests in the grass.

I didn't fall very hard, though. The grass was long and thick there. But even as I fell a great happiness came into my heart. And I didn't care about anything else in the world.

Grieta had stopped running. She turned round. For an instant her body, slender and misty in the shadows, swayed towards me. Then her hand flew to her hair. Her fingers pulled at the wreath. And the next thing I knew was that there lay, within reach of my hand, a small white rose.

I shall always remember the thrill with which I picked up that rose, and how I trembled when I stuck it in my hat. I shall always remember the stir I caused when I walked into the kitchen. Everybody stopped drinking to look at the rose in my hat. The young men made jokes about it. The older men winked slyly and patted me on the back.

Although Fritz Pretorius was not in the kitchen to witness my triumph, I knew he would get to hear of it somehow. That would make him realize that it was impudence for a fellow like him to set up as Schalk Lourens' rival.

During the rest of the night I was a hero.

The men in the kitchen made me sit on the table. They plied me with brandy and drank to my health. And afterwards, when a dozen of them carried me outside, onto an ox-wagon, for fresh air, they fell with me only once.

At daybreak I was still on that wagon.

I woke up feeling very sick - until I remembered about Grieta's rose. There was that white rose still stuck in my hat, for the whole world to know that Grieta Prinsloo had chosen me before all other men.

But what I didn't want people to know was that I had remained asleep on that ox-wagon hours after the other guests had gone. So I rode away very quietly, glad that nobody was astir to see me go.

My head was dizzy as I rode back, but in my heart it felt like green wings beating; and although it was day now, there was the same soft wind in the grass that had been there when Grieta flung the rose at me, standing under the stars.

I rode slowly through the trees on the slope of Abjaterskop, and had reached the place where the path turns south again, when I saw something that made me wonder if, at these fashionable schools, they did not perhaps teach the girls too much.

First I saw Fritz Pretorius's horse by the roadside.

Then I saw Fritz. He was sitting up against a thorn-tree, with his chin resting on his knees. He looked very pale and sick. But what made me wonder much about those finishing schools was that in Fritz's hat, which had fallen on the ground some distance away from him, there was a small white rose.

THE STILE

It created no small stir in the Marico (Oom Schalk Lourens said) when Piet Human came back after an absence of twenty years. His return was as unexpected as his departure had been sudden. It was quite a story, the manner of his leaving his farm his father had bought for him at Gemsbokvlei – and also the reasons for his leaving. Since it was a story of young love, the women took pleasure in discussing it in much detail. The result was that with the years the events surrounding Piet Human's sudden decision to move out of the Marico remained fresh in people's memories. More, the affair grew into something like a folk-tale, almost, with the passage of time.

Indeed, I had heard one version of the story of Piet Human and the girl Wanda Rossouw as far away as Schweizer-Reneke, where I had trekked with my cattle during a season of drought. It was told me by one of the daughters in the house of a farmer with whom I had made arrangements for grazing my cattle. The main feature in the story was the wooden stile between the two farms – Piet Human's farm and the farm of Wanda Rossouw's parents. If you brought that stile into it, you couldn't go wrong in the telling of the story, whatever else you added to it or left out.

And so the farmer's daughter in Schweizer-Reneke, because she mentioned the stile right at the beginning, related the story very pleasantly. Piet Human had been courting Wanda Rossouw for some time. And they had met often by the white-painted wooden fence that stood at the boundary of the two farms. And Wanda Rossouw had dark eyes and a wild heart. Now, it had been well known that, before Piet Human came to live at Gemsbokvlei, there had been another young man who had called very regularly at the Rossouw homestead. This young man was Gerhard Oelofse. He was somewhat of a braggart. But he had dashing ways. In his stride there was a kind of free-

dom that you couldn't help noticing. It was said that there were few girls in the Groot Marico that Gerhard Oelofse could not have for the asking.

One day Gerhard Oelofse rode off to join Van Pittius's free-booters in Stellaland. Later on he left for the Caprivi Strip. From then onwards we would receive, at long intervals, vague accounts of his activities in those distant parts. And in those fragmentary items of news about Gerhard Oelofse that reached us, there was little that did him credit.

Anyway, to return to Wanda Rossouw and Piet Human. There was an afternoon near to the twilight when they again met at the stile on the boundary between the two farms. It was a low stile, with only two cross-pieces. And the moment came inevitably when Piet Human, standing on his side of the fence, stooped forward to take Wanda Rossouw in his arms and to lift her over to him. And that was the moment in which Wanda Rossouw confessed to him of the thing that had happened, two years before, between Gerhard Oelofse and herself.

In that moment Piet Human left Wanda Rossouw.

He had her in his arms. And he put her down again, awkwardly. On her own side of the fence. Without a word Piet Human turned on his heel and walked away from her, into the deepening twilight. Shortly afterwards he sold his farm and left the Marico.

Because of the prominence she gave to that wooden stile, the daughter of the farmer in Schweizer-Reneke told the story of Piet Human and Wanda Rossouw remarkably well. She introduced into her narrative a few variations that were unfamiliar to us in the Groot Marico, but that made no difference to the quality of the story itself. When she came to the end of the tale, I mentioned to her that I actually knew that wooden fence, low, with two cross-rails, and painted white. I had seen that stile very often, I said. The farmer's daughter looked at me with a new sort of interest – she looked at me in such a way that for a little while I felt almost as though I was handsome.

On the spur of the moment, I went so far as to make up a lie, then. I told her that I had even carved my initials on that stile – on one of the lower cross-rails, I said. I felt it would have been too presumptuous if I had said one of the upper rails.

But even as I spoke I realized, by the far-off look in her eyes, that the farmer's daughter had already lost interest in me. Ah well, the story of Piet Human and Wanda Rossouw was a good love story. And I had no right to try to chop a piece of it out for myself, cutting – in imagination – "Schalk Lourens" into a strip of painted wood with a pocket-knife.

"If Piet Human had really loved Wanda Rossouw, he would have forgiven her for what had happened with Gerhard Oelofse," the daughter of the Schweizer-Reneke farmer said, dreamily. "At least, I think so. But I suppose you can never tell –"

Consequently, when Piet Human came back to the Groot Marico, the story of his sudden departure, twenty years earlier, was still fresh in people's memories – and with sundry additions.

I had heard of Piet Human's return several weeks before I met him. Needless to say, everybody north of the Dwarsberge knew he had come back. We talked of nothing else.

Where I again encountered Piet Human, after twenty years, was in Jurie Bekker's post office. Piet Human was staying with Jurie Bekker. I must admit that, as far as I was concerned, there were certain unhappy features about that meeting. And I have reason to believe that there were those of the older farmers in Jurie Bekker's post office that day – who had also known Piet Human long ago – who shared my feeling. Briefly, when Piet Human left us, he had been a youth of five-and-twenty summers. We saw him again now as a man of mature years, sun-tanned. But there were those wrinkles under his eyes. There were those grey hairs at his temples. In our sudden awareness of the fact that Piet Human had indeed grown twenty years older since we had seen him last, there was also the deeper knowledge that we, too, each one of us, had likewise aged.

How I knew that others felt the same way that I did was when I happened to glance across at Jurie Bekker. Jurie was sitting back in his chair, with his eyes cast down to his stomach. He gazed at his fat stomach with a certain measure of intentness, for some moments, and then he shook his head.

Nevertheless, it did not last long, this sense of melancholy that we had at having been brought face to face with the reality of the passage of time. Those intervening years that the locusts had eaten were no more than a quick sigh. We drank our coffee and listened to what Piet Human had to relate, and in a little while it was as though he had never gone away.

Piet Human told us that he had entered the Marico from the Bechuanaland side, and had journeyed through Ramoutsa. He had decided to stay with Jurie Bekker for a time, and had not yet, in the course of his visits to familiar scenes of twenty years before, proceeded any further to the west along the Government road.

I thought that this statement of Piet Human's was significant. Farther to the west lay the farm that had once been his, Gemsbokvlei – and adjoining it was the Rossouw farm, where Wanda Rossouw still lived with her widowed mother. During all those years, Wanda Rossouw, although attractive and sought-after, had remained unmarried.

Piet Human said that in some ways the Marico had changed a great deal, since he had been there last. In other respects there had been no changes at all. Some of the people he had known had died in that long interval. Others had trekked away. And children in arms had grown into young men and women. But there were just as many aspects of life in the Marico that had undergone no change.

"I came here through Rooigrond," Piet Human said. "That big white house that used to be the headquarters of the Van Pittius freebooter gang is still there. But it is today a coach-station."

But Piet Human said that when he learnt how much he had to pay for his coach-ticket to Ottoshoop, he realized that things had not really changed, after all. That big white house was still the headquarters of robbers.

He also mentioned those Mtosa huts on the way to Ramoutsa.

"I remembered that ring of huts very well," Piet Human said. "I had called there several times in the old days. And the chief used to lie on the ground in front of his hut, smoking his long dagga-pipe and moving round with the sun. The women were at work in the fields. When I went there this time, it was to find that the old chief was long dead. But his eldest son had taken his place as chief. The new chief was lying in front of his hut in the sun, smoking dagga. I noticed that it was still the same pipe, though."

Thus Piet Human entertained us with anecdotes. But I noticed that all his stories had a bearing on the places that lay only on the one side of the Goot Marico. He made no reference to that other side, where his old farm was, and where the Rossouws dwelt, and where his heart no doubt was also. Still I reflected, since he had not visited that part yet, it was perhaps still too early for him to talk to us about it, airily, as he talked of other things.

Others beside myself sensed Piet Human's reluctance to discuss what had, after all, been the most important thing in his life when he had lived in the Marico twenty years before. We were naturally very curious to know what his plans were. But there was nobody in the post office that afternoon shameless enough to broach the matter to Piet Human, even by way of indirect hint. We all felt that the story of Piet Human and Wanda Rossouw stood for something in our community.

There was a fineness about it that we had to respect.

Even Fritz van Tonder, who was known as a pretty rough character, waited until Piet Human had gone out of the voorkamer before he made a remark. And then all he said was, "Well, if Piet Human has decided to forgive Wanda Rossouw for that Gerhard Oelofse business – he'll find that she's still pretty. And she's waited long enough."

We passed over his comments in silence.

But the day did come when Piet Human paid a visit to that other part of the Marico where his old farm was. The white-painted wooden stile stood there still. The uprights, before being put into the ground, had been dipped in a Stockholm tar of a kind that you don't get today.

And it was when the twilight was beginning to fall that Piet Human again came across Wanda Rossouw by the stile. She wore a pale frock. And although her face had perhaps grown thinner with the years, the look in her dark eyes had not changed. The grass was heavy with the scents of a dying summer's day. Piet Human spoke urgent, burning words in a low voice. Then he stooped forward over the fence and took Wanda Rossouw in his arms.

It was when she struggled in his arms, thrusting him from her fiercely when he tried to lift her over the stile, that Piet Human understood. He realized then that it was that other worthless lover, who had forgotten her long ago, for whom, down the years, vainly, Wanda Rossouw had waited.

For the second time, thus, Piet Human walked back into the gathering dusk, alone.

THE NIGHT-DRESS

Johanna Snyman stood in front of the kitchen table, on which lay a pile of washing. It was ordinary farm clothing: her father's and brothers' blue denim shirts and trousers, her mother's and her own dresses and underwear.

Johanna took an iron off the stove, tilted it sideways and spat on it to see if it was hot. Then she went back to the table and commenced ironing.

It was a hot day in the Marico Bushveld. The heat from the sun and from the stove made the kitchen unbearable for Johanna's mother, who had gone to sit in front of the house with some sewing and a back number of the *Kerkbode*. Johanna's mother was known all over the district as Tant Lettie. She was thin and sallow-looking and complained regularly about her health. There was something the matter with her which rooi laventel, wit dulsies and other Boer remedies could not cure.

On the other hand, Johanna was strong and robustly made. Now, with the heat of the kitchen, there was a pink glow on her features. It was a flush that extended from her forehead right down to her neck and that part of her bosom which the blue print frock did not conceal. Her face was full and had just that tendency towards roundness that is much admired by the men of the Bushveld. But her nose was too small and too snub to remain attractive long after girlhood. And Johanna was twenty-three.

Tant Lettie, having put aside the *Kerbode*, began embroidering a piece of cheap material that she had bought from the Indian store at Ramotswa. She was making herself a night-dress. She held the partly finished garment to the light and examined it. She laughed softly. But it was not a meaningless laugh. There was too much bitterness for that. She wondered why she was taking all that trouble with her night-dress, sewing bits of pink tape on it and working French knots round the neck, for all the world as though she was making it for her honeymoon.

She remembered the time she got married. Twenty-four years ago. A long while beforehand she had made herself clothes. That was on the highveld, in the Potchefstroom district. Her father had sold some oxen to the Jewish trader and had given her the money to buy things for her marriage. That was a good time. She remembered that one night-dress she made. It was very fine stuff that cost a riksdaalder a yard. She sewed on a lot of lace, and put in all kinds of tucks and frills. When it was finished it was pretty. She ironed it out and put it right at the bottom of the kist in her bedroom. She didn't want any of her brothers or sisters to see that night-dress, because they would make improper jokes about it and she would feel uncomfortable. As it was, they already had too much to say.

They went by Cape-cart to Potchefstroom for the wedding. Frans Snyman looked very happy. He was excited and she was afraid he would drop the ring, and that would bring them bad luck. But he did not drop it. Yet they seemed to have got bad luck all the same. When the ceremony was over, Frans kissed her and said: "Now you will always be my wife." She felt afraid when he said that.

That night they stayed at her father's house. Then she and Frans left for the Government farm that Frans had bought in the Marico Bushveld. She remembered the way she had taken the night-dress out of the kist that evening after the wedding, and how she had laughed at the frills in it, and the ribbons and the lace, and had suddenly folded up the garment and pressed it against her breasts. But that was long ago.

She had kept the night-dress for many years. Often she looked at it and thought of the time when she had first worn it. But, somehow, it didn't seem the same. Each time she took it out it meant less to her than before. Afterwards she made a petticoat out of it for Johanna.

First Johanna was born. Then came, in turn, Willem and Adrian and Lourens. In the first year of their marriage there was a big drought, and it was only after half the stock had died that Frans decided to trek with the remainder of the stock to the Limpopo River. It was in the ox-wagon that Johanna was born. Tant Lettie remembered that she was alone nearly all that day, with only a black woman to attend to her. And Frans was in a bad temper because the blacks had been negligent and had allowed some oxen to get lost. Frans was also angry because she had not given birth to a man-child. He swore about it, as though it was her fault.

Later on, when Willem was born, Frans seemed a little more satisfied. But it was only for a while. There were other things that he had to concern himself with. It had rained and he had to sow mealies all day long while the ground remained wet. As for the two youngest children, Adrian and Lourens, Frans hardly noticed their coming.

Still, that was the way Frans was, and all men were like that. She knew he was sorry he had got married, and she didn't blame him for it. Only she thought that he need not always show it in such an open sort of way. For that matter, she was sorry also that she had got married. It would have been better if she had remained in her father's house. She knew she would have been unhappy there, and when her parents died she would have to go out and stay with somebody else. Or she might have been able to get work somewhere. But still, all that would have been better than to get married. Now she had brought four children into the world who would lead the same kind of life that she had led.

Tant Lettie put down her sewing. Her face turned slightly pale. Her hands dropped to her sides. She felt, coming on once more, that pain which rooi laventel and wit dulsies could not cure.

In the kitchen Johanna had at last finished with the ironing. Then she slipped quietly into her bedroom and came back with a garment which she unfolded in a way that had tenderness in it. She ran her fingers over the new linen, with the lace and ribbons and frills. Then, having ironed it, she took the night-dress to her bedroom and packed it away carefully at the bottom of her kist.

THE GRAMOPHONE

That was a terrible thing that happened with Krisjan Lemmer, Oom Schalk Lourens said. It was pretty bad for me, of course, but it was much worse for Krisjan.

I remember well when it happened, for that was the time when the first gramophone came into the Marico Bushveld. Krisjan bought the machine off a Jew trader from Pretoria. It's funny when you come to think of it. When there is anything that we Boers don't want you can be quite sure that the Jew traders will bring it to us, and that we'll buy it, too.

I remember how I laughed when a Jew came to my house once with a hollow piece of glass that had a lot of silver stuff in it. The Jew told me that the silver in the glass moved up and down to show you if it was hot or cold. Of course, I said that was all nonsense. I know when it is cold enough for me to put on my woollen shirt and jacket, without having first to go and look at the piece of glass. And I also know when it is too hot to work - which it is almost all the year round in this part of the Marico Bushveld. In the end I bought the thing. But it has never been the same since little Annie stirred her coffee with it.

Anyway, if the Jew traders could bring us the miltsiek, we would buy that off them as well, and pay them so much down, and the rest when all our cattle were dead.

Therefore, when a trader brought Krisjan Lemmer a second-hand gramophone, Krisjan sold some sheep and bought the thing. For many miles round the people came to hear the machine talk. Krisjan was very proud of his gramophone, and when he turned the handle and put in the little sharp pins, it was just like a child that has found something new to play with. The people who came to hear the gramophone said that it was very wonderful what things a man would think of making when once the devil had taken a hold on him properly.

Peter Badcock

They said that, if nothing else, the devil has got good brains. I also thought it was wonderful, not that the gramophone could talk, but that people wanted to listen to its doing something that a child of seven could do as well. Most of the songs the gramophone played were in English. But there was one song in Afrikaans. It was "O Brandewyn laat my staan". Krisjan played that often; the man on the round plate sang it rather well. Only the way he pronounced the words made it seem as though he was a German trying to make "O Brandewyn laat my staan" sound English. It was just like the rooineks, I thought. First they took our country and governed it for us in a better way than we could do ourselves; now they wanted to make improvements in our language for us.

But if people spoke much about Krisjan Lemmer's gramophone, they spoke a great deal more about the unhappy way in which he and his wife lived together. Krisjan Lemmer was then about thirty-five. He was a big, strongly-built man, and when he moved about you could see the muscles of his shoulders stand out under his shirt. He was also a surprisingly good-natured man who seldom became annoyed about anything. Even with the big drought, when he had to pump water for his cattle all day and the pump broke, so that he could get no water for his cattle, he just walked into the house, and lit his pipe and said that it was the Lord's will. He said that perhaps it was as well that the pump broke, because, if the Lord wanted the cattle to get water, He wouldn't have sent the drought. That was the kind of man Krisjan Lemmer was. And he would never have set hand to the pump again, either, was it not that the next day rain fell, whereby Krisjan knew that the Lord meant him to understand that the drought was over. Yet, when anything angered him he was bad.

But the unfortunate part of Krisjan Lemmer was that he could not get on with his wife Susannah. Always they quarrelled. Susannah, as we knew, was a good deal younger than her husband, but often she didn't look so very much younger. She was small and fair. Her skin had not been much darkened by the Bushveld sun, for she always wore a very wide kappie, the folds of which she pinned down over the upper part of her face whenever she went out of the house. Her hair was the colour of the beard you see on the yellow mealies just after they have ripened. She had very quiet ways. In company she hardly ever talked, unless it was to say that the Indian shopkeeper in Ramoutsa put roasted kremetart roots with the coffee he sold us, or that the spokes of the mule-cart came loose if you didn't pour water over them.

You see, what she said were things that everybody knew and that no one argued about. Even the Indian storekeeper didn't argue about the kremetart roots. He knew that was the best part of his coffee. And yet, although she was so quiet and unassuming, Susannah was always quarrelling with her husband. This, of course, was foolish of her, especially as Krisjan was a man with gentle ways until somebody purposely annoyed him. Then he was not quite so gentle. For instance, there was the time when the chief of the Mtosa kafirs passed him in the veld and said "Good morning" without taking the leopard skin off his head and calling Krisjan "baas". Krisjan was fined ten pounds by the magistrate and had to pay for the doctor during the three months that the Mtosa chief walked with a stick.

One day I went to Krisjan Lemmer's farm to borrow a roll of baling-wire for the teff. Krisjan had just left for the krantz to see if he could shoot a ribbok. Susannah was at home alone. I could see that she had been crying. So I went and sat next to her on the riempies-bank and took her hand.

"Don't cry, Susannah," I said, "everything will be all right. You must learn to understand Krisjan a little better. He is not a bad fellow in his way."

At first she was angry with me for saying anything against Krisjan, and she told me to go home. But afterwards she became more reasonable about it, allowing me to move up a bit closer to her and to hold her hand a little tighter. In that way I comforted her. I would have comforted her even more, perhaps, only I couldn't be sure how long Krisjan would remain in the krantz; and I didn't like what happened to the Mtosa kafir chief.

I asked her to play the gramophone for me, not because I wanted to hear it, but because you always pretend to take an interest in the things that your friends like, especially when you borrow a roll of baling-wire off them. When anybody visits me and gets my youngest son Willie to recite texts from the Bible, I know that before he leaves he is going to ask me if I will be using my mealie-planter this week.

So Susannah put the round plate on the thing, and turned the handle, and the gramophone played "O Brandewyn laat my staan". You couldn't hear too well what the man was singing, but I have said all that before.

Susannah laughed as she listened, and in that moment somehow she seemed very much younger than her husband. She looked very pretty, too. But I noticed also that when the music ended it was as though she was crying.

Then Krisjan came in. I left shortly afterwards. But I had heard his footsteps coming up the path, so there was no need for me to leave in a hurry.

But just before I went Susannah brought in coffee. It was weak coffee; but I didn't say anything about it. I am very much like an Englishman that way. It's what they call manners. When I am visiting strangers and they give me bad coffee I don't throw it out and say that the stuff isn't fit for a kafir. I just drink it and then don't go back to that house again. But Krisjan spoke about it.

"Vrou," he said, "the coffee is weak."

"Yes," Susannah answered.

"It's very weak," he went on.

"Yes," she replied.

"Why do you always ..." Krisjan began again.

"Oh, go to hell," Susannah said.

Then they went at it, swearing at one another, and they didn't even hear me when, on leaving in the manner of the Bushveld, I said, "Goodbye and may the good Lord bless us all."

It was a dark night that time, about three months later, when I again went to Krisjan Lemmer's house by mule-cart. I was leaving early in the morning for Zeerust with a load of mealies and I wanted to borrow Krisjan's wagon-sail. Before I was halfway to his house it started raining. Big drops fell on my face. There was something queer about the sound of the wind in the wet trees, and when I drove through the poort where the Government road skirts the line of the Dwarsberge the place looked very dark to me. I thought of death and things like that. I thought of pale strange ghosts that come upon you from behind ... suddenly. I felt sorry, then, that I had not brought a kafir along. It was not that I was afraid of being alone; but it would have been useful, on the return, to have a kafir sitting in the back of the mule-cart to look after the wagon-sail for me.

The rain stopped.

I came to the farm's graveyard, where had been buried members of the Lemmer family and of other families who had lived there before the Lemmers, and I knew that I was near the house. It seemed to me to be a very silly sort of thing to make a graveyard so close to the road. There's no sense in that. Some people, for instance, who are ignorant and a bit superstitious are liable, perhaps, to start shivering a little, especially if the night is dark and there is a wind and the mule-cart is bumpy.

There were no lights in the Lemmers' house when I got there. I knocked a long time before the door was opened, and then it was Krisjan Lemmer standing in the doorway with a lantern held above his head. He looked agitated at first, until he saw who it was and then he smiled.

"Come in, Neef Schalk," he said, "I am pleased you are here. I was beginning to feel lonely - you know, the rain and the wind and ..."

"But you are not alone," I replied. "What about Susannah?"

"Oh, Susannah has gone back to her mother," Krisjan answered. "She went yesterday."

We went into the voorkamer and sat down. Krisjan Lemmer lit a candle and we talked and smoked. The window-panes looked black against the night. The wind blew noisily through openings between the wall and the thatched roof. The candle flame flickered unsteadily. It could not be pleasant for Krisjan Lemmer alone in that house without his wife. He looked restless and uncomfortable. I tried to make a joke about it.

"What's the matter with you, Krisjan?" I asked. "You're looking so unhappy, anybody would think you've still got your wife here with you."

Krisjan laughed, and I wished he hadn't. His laughter did not sound natural; it was too loud. Somehow I got a cold kind of feeling in my blood. It was rather a frightening thing, the wind blowing incessantly outside the house, and inside the house a man laughing too loudly.

"Let us play the gramophone, Krisjan," I said.

By that time I knew how to work the thing myself. So I put in one of the little pins and started it off. But before doing that I had taken the gramophone off its table and placed it on the floor in front of my chair, where I could get at it more easily.

It seemed different without Susannah's being there. Also, it looked peculiar to me that she should leave so suddenly. And there was no doubt about it that Krisjan was acting in a strange way that I didn't like. He was restless. When he lit his pipe he had to strike quite a number of matches. And all that time round the house the wind blew very loudly.

The gramophone began to play.

The plate was "O Brandewyn laat my staan".

I thought of Susannah and of the way she had listened three months before to that same song. I glanced quickly at Krisjan, and as soon as he caught my eye he looked away. I was glad when the gramophone finished playing. And there was something about Krisjan that made me feel that he was also pleased. He seemed very queer about Susannah.

Then an awful thought occurred to me.

You know sometimes you get a thought like that and you know that it is true.

I got up unsteadily and took my hat. I saw that all round the place where the gramophone stood the dung floor of the voorkamer had been loosened and then stamped down again. The candle threw flickering shadows over the floor and over the clods of loose earth that had not been stamped down properly.

I drove back without the bucksail.

MAMPOER

The berries of the karee-boom (Oom Schalk Lourens said, nodding his head in the direction of the tall tree whose shadows were creeping towards the edge of the stoep) may not make the best kind of mampoer that there is. What I mean is that karee brandy is not as potent as the brandy you distil from moepels or maroelas. Even peach brandy, they say, can make you forget the rust in the corn quicker than the mampoer you make from karee berries.

But karee-mampoer is white and soft to look at, and the smoke that comes from it when you pull the cork out of the bottle is pale and rises up in slow curves. And in time of drought, when you have been standing at the borehole all day, pumping water for the cattle, so that by the evening water has got a bitter taste for you, then it is very soothing to sit on the front stoep, like now, and to get somebody to pull the cork out of a bottle of this kind of mampoer. Your hands will be sore and stiff from the pump-handle, so that if you try and pull it out the cork will seem as deep down in the bottle as the water is in the borehole.

Many years ago, when I was a young man, and I sat here, on the front stoep, and I saw that white smoke floating away slowly and gracefully from the mouth of the bottle, and with a far-off fragrance, I used to think that the smoke looked like a young girl walking veiled under the stars. And now that I have grown old, and I look at that white smoke, I imagine that it is a young girl walking under the stars, and still veiled. I have never found out who she is.

Hans Kriel and I were in the same party that had gone from this section of the Groot Marico to Zeerust for the Nagmaal. And it was a few evenings after our arrival, when we were on a visit to Kris Wilman's house on the outskirts of the town, that I learnt something of the first half of Hans Kriel's love story - that half at which I laughed. The

Peter Badcock

knowledge of the second half came a little later, and I didn't laugh then.

We were sitting on Krisjan Wilman's stoep and looking out in the direction of Sephton's Nek. In the setting sun the koppies were red on one side; on the other side their shadows were lengthening rapidly over the vlakte. Krisjan Wilman had already poured out the mampoer, and the glasses were going round.

"That big shadow there is rushing through the thorn-trees just like a black elephant," Adrian Bekker said, "in a few minutes' time it will be at Groot Marico station."

"The shorter the days are, the longer the shadows get," Frikkie Marais said. "I learnt that at school. There are also lucky and unlucky shadows."

"You are talking about ghosts, now, and not shadows," Adrian Bekker interrupted him, learnedly. "Ghosts are all the same length, I think, more or less."

"No, it is the ghost stories that are all the same length," Krisjan Wilman said. "The kind you tell."

It was good mampoer, made from karee berries that were plucked when they were still green and full of thick sap, just before they had begun to whiten, and we said things that contained much wisdom.

"It was like the shadow of a flower on her left cheek," I heard Hans Kriel say, and immediately I sat up to listen, for I could guess of whom it was that he was talking.

"Is it on the lower part of the cheek?" I asked. "Two small purple marks?"

Because in that case I would know for sure that he was talking about the new waitress in the Zeerust café. I had seen her only once, through the plate-glass window, and because I had liked her looks I had gone up to the counter and asked for a roll of Boer tobacco, which she said they did not stock. When she said they didn't stock kudu biltong, either, I had felt too embarrassed to ask for anything else. Only afterwards I remembered that I could have gone in and sat down and ordered a cup of coffee and some harde beskuit. But it was too late then. By that time I felt that she could see that I came from this part of the Marico, even though I was wearing my hat well back on my head.

"Did you - did you speak to her?" I asked Hans Kriel after a while.

"Yes," he said, "I went in and asked her for a roll of Boer tobacco. But she said they didn't sell tobacco by the roll, or kudu biltong either. She said this last with a sort of sneer. I thought it was funny, seeing that I hadn't asked her for kudu biltong. So I sat down in front of a little table and ordered some harde beskuit and a cup of coffee. She brought me a number of little dry, flat cakes with letters on them that I couldn't read very well. Her name is Marie Rossouw."

"You must have said quite a lot to her to have found out her name," I said, with something in my voice that must have made Hans Kriel suspicious.

"How do you know who I am talking about?" he demanded suddenly.

"Oh, never mind," I answered, "let us ask Krisjan Wilman to refill our glasses."

I winked at the others and we all laughed, because by that time Hans Kriel was sitting half sideways on the riempies bench, with his shoulders drawn up very high and his whole body seeming to be kept up by one elbow. It wasn't long after that that he moved his elbow, so that we had to pick him up from the floor and carry him into the voorkamer, where we laid him in a corner on some leopard skins.

But before that he had spoken more about Marie Rossouw, the new waitress in the café. He said he had passed by and had seen her through the plate-glass window and there had been a vase of purple flowers on the counter, and he had noticed those two marks on her cheek, and those marks had looked very pretty to him, like two small shadows from those purple flowers.

"She is very beautiful," Hans Kriel said. "Her eyes have got deep things in them, like those dark pools behind Abjaterskop. And when she smiled at me once - by mistake, I think - I felt as though my heart was rushing over the vlaktes like that shadow we saw in the sunset."

"You must be careful of those dark pools behind Abjaterskop," I warned him, "we know those pools have got witches in them."

I felt it was a pity that we had to carry him inside, shortly afterwards. For the mampoer had begun to make Hans Kriel talk rather well.

As it happened, Hans Kriel was not the only one, that night, who encountered difficulties with the riempies bench. Several more of us were carried inside. And when I look back on that Nagmaal my most vivid memories are not of what the predikant said at the church service, or of Krisjan Wilman's mampoer, even, but of how very round the black spots were on the pale yellow of the leopard skin. They were so round that every time I looked at them they were turning.

In the morning Krisjan Wilman's wife woke us up and brought us coffee. Hans Kriel and I sat up side by side on the leopard skins, and in between drinking his coffee Hans Kriel said strange things. He was still talking about Marie Rossouw.

"Just after dark I got up from the front stoep and went to see her in the café," Hans Kriel said.

"You may have got up from the front stoep," I answered, "but you never got up from these leopard skins. Not from the moment we carried you here. That's the truth."

"I went to the café," Hans Kriel said, ignoring my interruption, "and it was very dark. She was there alone. I wanted to find out how she got those marks on her cheeks. I think she is very pretty even without them. But with those marks Marie Rossouw is the most wild and most beautiful thing in the whole world."

"I suppose her cheek got cut there when she was a child," I suggested. "Perhaps when a bottle of her father's mampoer exploded."

"No," Hans Kriel replied, very earnestly. "No. It was something else. I asked her where the marks came from. I asked her there, in the café, where we were alone together, and it suddenly seemed as though the whole place was washed with moonlight, and there was no counter between us any more, and there was a strange laughter in her eyes when she brought her face very close to mine. And she said, 'I know you won't believe me. But that is where the devil kissed me. Satan kissed me there when we were behind Abjaterskop. Shall I show you?'"

"That was what she said to me," Hans Kriel continued, "and I knew, then, that she was a witch. And that it was a very sinful thing to be in love with a witch. And so I caught her up, in my arms, and I whispered, trembling all the time, 'Show me,' and our heads rose up very tall through the shadows. And everything moved very fast, faster than the shadows move from Abjaterskop in the setting of the sun. And I knew that we were behind Abjaterskop, and that her eyes were indeed the dark pools there, with the tall reeds growing on the edges. And then I saw Satan come in between us. And he had hooves and a forked tail. And there were flames coming out of him. And he stooped down and kissed Marie Rossouw on her cheek, where those marks were. And she laughed. And her eyes danced with merriment. And I found that it was all the time I who was kissing her. Now, what do you make of this, Schalk?"

I said, of course, that it was the mampoer. And that I knew, now, why I had been sleeping in such discomfort. It wasn't because the spots on the leopard skin were turning like round wheels; but because I had Satan sleeping next to me all night. And I said that this discovery wasn't new, either. I had always suspected something like that about him.

But I got an idea. And while the others were at breakfast I went out, on the pretext that I had to go and help Manie Burghers with his oxen at the church square outspan. But instead, I went into the café, and because I knew her name was Marie Rossouw, when the waitress came for my order I could ask her whether she was related to the Rossouws of Rysmierbult, and I could tell her that I was distantly related to that family, also. In the daylight there was about that café none of the queerness that Hans Kriel had spoken about. It was all very ordinary. Even those purple flowers were still on the counter. They looked slightly faded.

And then, suddenly, while we were talking, I asked her the thing that I was burning to know.

"That mark on your cheek, juffrou," I said, "will you tell me where you got it from?"

Marie Rossouw brought her face very close to mine, and her eyes were like dark pools with dancing light in them.

"I know you won't believe me," she said, "but that is where Satan kissed me. When we were at the back of Abjaterskop together. Shall I show you?"

It was broad daylight. The morning lay yellow on the world and the sun shone in brightly through the plate-glass window, and there were quite a number of people in the street. And yet as I walked out of the café quickly, and along the pavement, I was shivering.

With one thing and another, I did not come across Hans Kriel again until three or four days later, when the Nagmaal was over and we were trekking to the other side of the Dwarsberge once more.

We spoke of a number of things, and then, trying to make my voice sound natural, I made mention of Marie Rossouw.

"That was a queer sort of dream you had," I said.

"Yes," he answered, "it was queer."

"And did you find out," I asked, again trying to sound casual, "about those marks on her cheek?"

"Yes," Hans Kriel answered, "I asked Marie and she told me. She said that when she was a child a bottle of mampoer burst in the voorkamer. Her cheek got cut by a splinter of glass. She is an unusual kind of girl, Marie Rossouw."

"Yes," I agreed, moving away. "Oh, yes."

But I also thought there are things about mampoer that you can't understand very easily.

PINK ROSES AND BROWN WATER

It was a visit that I remembered for the rest of my life (Oom Schalk Lourens said).

I was a small child, then. My father and his brother took me along in the back seat of the Cape-cart when they went to see an old man with a white beard. And when this old man stooped down to shake hands with me they told me to say, "Goeie dag, Oom Gysbert." I thought Oom Gysbert had something to do with God. I thought so from his voice and from Bible pictures I had seen of holy men, like prophets, who wore the same kind of beards.

My father and uncle went to see Oom Gysbert about pigs, which it seemed that he bred. And afterwards, when we drove home again, and my father and uncle spoke of Oom Gysbert, they both said he was a real old Pharisee. From that I was satisfied that I had been right in thinking of Oom Gysbert as a Bible person.

"Saying that those measled animals he sent us were the same prize pigs we had bought and paid for," my uncle went on, while we were riding back in the Cape-cart. "Does he not know how Ananias was smitten by the Lord?"

But that was not the reason why I remembered our visit to Oom Gysbert. For while I was on his farm I saw no pigs, measled or otherwise. And later on in life I was to come across many more people that I have heard compared to Bible characters. To Judas, for instance.

After I had shaken hands with Oom Gysbert, the three men walked off together in the direction of the pigsties. I was left alone there, at the side of the house, where there was a stream of brown water flowing over rounded stones. This in itself was a sufficiently strange circumstance. You know how dry it is in these parts. I had until then seen water only in a dam or being pumped out of a borehole into a cattle-trough. I had never before in my life seen a stream of water flowing away over stones.

I learnt afterwards that Oom Gysbert's farm was near the Malopo, and that he was thus enabled to lead off furrows of water, except in the times of most severe drought, to irrigate his tilled lands. My father and uncle had left me by one of those water-furrows.

That was something I did not know then, of course.

I walked for some little distance downstream, paddling in the water, since I was barefooted. Then it was that I came across a sight that I have never since forgotten. I had, of course, before then seen flowers. Veld flowers. And the moepel and the maroela in bloom. But that was the first time in my life that I had seen such pink and white flowers, growing in such amazing profusion, climbing over and covering a fence of wire-netting that seemed very high and that stretched away as far as I could see.

I could not explain then, any more than I can now, the feelings of joy that came to me when I stood by that fence where rambling roses clustered.

At intervals, from the direction of the pigsties, came the voices of my father and my uncle and Oom Gysbert, who were conversing. They were quite far away, for I could not see them. But they were conversing with each other very clearly, as though each thought that the other could perhaps not hear very well. Oom Gysbert was saying mostly "Prize Large Whites", and my father and my uncle were saying mostly, "Measled walking rubbish".

Afterwards it seemed that Oom Gysbert's wife had gone across to the pigsties, too. For I could hear a woman's voice starting to converse as well. She conversed even more distinctly than the men. So much so, that when a kafir passed where I was standing by the roses, he shook his head at me. For Oom Gysbert's wife had likewise begun by saying mostly, "Prize Large Whites". But she also ended up by saying, "Measled walking rubbish". And from the way the kafir shook his head it appeared that she wasn't talking about the pigs that Oom Gysbert had sold to my father and uncle.

Meanwhile, I stood there by the fence, in childhood wonderment at all that loveliness. It was getting on towards evening. And all the air was filled with the fragrance of the roses. And there was the feeling that goes with wet earth. And a few pink and white petals floated in the brown water that rippled about my feet.

I was thrilled at this new strangeness and freshness of the world. And I thought that I would often again know the same kind of thrill.

But I never did.

Perhaps it is as we grow older our senses do not get swayed by the perfume of flowers as much as they did when we were young. Or maybe it is that flowers just haven't got the same perfume any more.

I realized that when I met Magda Burgers.

I should explain that my father gave up farming in that part of the Marico a few years after his conversation with Oom Gysbert. My father said that the bushveld was suited only for pigs. Hypocritical pigs with long white beards, my father took pains to make clear. So we went to the highveld. Afterwards we trekked back to the Marico.

For in the meantime my father had found that the highveld was good only for snakes. Snakes in the grass, who said one thing to you when they meant another, my father pointed out.

And years later I went to settle north of the Dwarsberge. Everything had changed a great deal, however, from when I had lived there as a child. People had died or trekked away. Strangers had come in and taken their places. Landmarks had grown unrecognizable.

Then, one day, I met Magda Burgers. I had gone over to Willem Burgers' farm with the intention of staying only long enough to borrow some mealie sacks. When I saw his daughter Magda I forgot what I had come about. This was all the more remarkable since the colour of Magda Burgers' hair kept on reminding me over and over again of ripe mealies. I stayed until quite late, and before leaving I had promised Willem Burgers that I would vote for him at the next Dwarsberge school committee elections.

I went to call on Willem Burgers often after that. My pretext was that I wanted to know still better why I should not vote for the other school committee candidates.

He told me. And I thought it was a pity that my father was not still alive to hear Willem Burgers talk. It would have done my father's heart good for him to know that he had been right when he said of the bush country that it was fit only for pigs with white beards. Willem Burgers also brought in pigs with brown beards and black beards, as well as a sprinkling of pigs that were clean-shaven. Willem Burgers also compared several of his rival candidates with persons in the Bible. I felt glad, then, that I had not also allowed my name to go forward the time they were taking nominations for the school committee.

Magda Burgers was in her early twenties. She was gay. There was something in her prettiness that in a strange way eluded me, also. And for this reason, I suppose, I was attracted to her more than ever.

But my real trouble was that I had little opportunity of talking to Magda alone.

I felt that she was not completely indifferent to me. I could tell that in a number of ways. There was, for instance, the afternoon when she allowed me to turn the handle of the cream separator for her in the milk-shed. That was very pleasant. The only difficulty was that I had to stand sideways. For it was a small shed. And Willem Burgers took up most of the room, sitting on an upturned bucket. He was busy telling me that Gerhardus Oosthuizen was like a hyena.

Another time, Magda allowed me to dry the cups for her in the kitchen when she washed up after we had had coffee. But the kitchen was also small, and her father took up a lot of space, sitting on an upturned paraffin box. He was then engaged in explaining to me that Flip Welman was like a green tree-snake with black spots on his behind. Nevertheless, each time Magda Burgers passed me a spoon to dry, I was able to hold her hand for a few moments. Once she was so absent-minded as to pass me her hand even when there wasn't a spoon in it.

But during all these weeks I was never able to speak to Magda Burgers on her own. And always there was something in her prettiness that eluded me.

Then, one afternoon, when Magda's father was telling me that "Rooi" Francois Hanekom was like a crocodile with laced-up top boots and a gold chain on his belly, two men came to the door. They were strangers to me. I could not remember Willem Burgers having mentioned them to me, either, as resembling some of the more unsatisfactory sort of bushveld animal. From this I concluded that they were not candidates for the school committee.

Magda told me that the visitors were the Van Breda brothers.

"The tall one with the cleft in his chin is Joost van Breda," she said.

Willem Burgers walked off with the two men along a footpath that led to the back of the house.

That was how, for the first time, I came to find myself alone with Magda. And because she looked so beautiful to me, then, with a light in her eyes that I thought to have seen there before, I told her of my visit to a farm, long ago, in the company of my father and my uncle. I told her of how I stood by a fence covered in roses, where there was a stream of brown water. I spoke of the rose perfume that had enchanted me as a child, and that I had not known since. It seems queer to me, now, that I was able to say so much to her, all in a few minutes.

I also said a few more words to her in a voice that I could not keep steady.

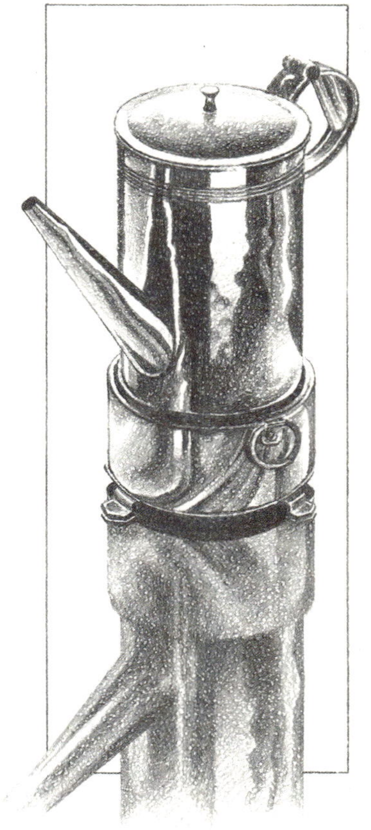

"Oom Gysbert?" Magda asked. "Why, it must be this same farm. Years ago this farm belonged to an old Gysbert Steenkamp. Come, I will show you."

Magda led me out of the house along a path which was different from the footpath her father and the Van Breda brothers had taken, and which was not the way, either, to the milk-shed.

It was getting on towards sunset. In the west the sky was gaudy with stripes like a kafir blanket. In the distance we could hear the voices of Magda's father and the Van Breda brothers raised in conversation. It was all just like long ago. Before I realized it I found I had taken Magda's hand.

"I suppose they are talking about pigs," I said to Magda. And I laughed, remembering that other day, which did not seem so far off, then, when I was a child.

"Yes," Magda answered. "Joost van Breda – the one with the cleft in his chin – bought some pigs from my father last month."

Even before we got there, I knew it was the same place. I could sense it all in a single moment, and without knowing how.

A few yards further on I came across that fence. It did not look at all high, any more. But it was clustered about with pink and white roses that grew in great profusion, climbing over and covering the netting for almost as far as I could see.

Before I reached the fence, however, Magda Burgers had left me. She had slipped her small white hand out of mine and had sped off through the trees into the gathering dusk – and in the direction from which came the voices of her father and the two Van Breda brothers. The three men were conversing very clearly, by then, as though each thought the others were deaf. The Van Breda brothers were also laughing very distinctly. They laughed every time Magda's father said "Prize Large Whites". And after they laughed they used rough language.

A little later a girl's voice started joining in the conversation. And I did not need a kafir to come by and shake his head at me. It was a sad enough thing for me, in any case, to have to listen to a young girl taking the part of two strangers against her father. She sided particularly with one of the two strangers. I knew, without having to be told, that the stranger was tall and had a cleft in his chin.

I stood for a long time watching the brown water flowing along the furrow. And I thought of how much water had flowed down all the rivers and under all the bridges of the world since I had last stood on that spot, as a child.

The roses clambering over the wire-netting shed no heady perfume.

Peter Backcock

THE HOME-COMING

Laughter (Oom Schalk Lourens said). Well, there's a queer thing for you, now, and something not so easy to understand. And the older you get, the more things you seem to find to laugh at. Take old Frans Els, for instance. I can still remember the way he laughed, that time at Zeerust, when we were coming around the church building and we saw one of the tents from the Nagmaal camping-ground being carried away by a sudden gust of wind.

"It must be the ouderling's tent," Frans Els called out. "Well he never was any good at fixing the ground-pegs. Look kêrels, there it goes right across the road." And he laughed so much that his beard, which was turning white in places, flapped about almost like that tent in the wind.

Shortly afterwards, what was left of the tent got caught round the wooden poles of somebody's verandah, and several adults and a lot of children came running out of the house, shouting. By that time Frans Els was standing bent almost double over a fence. The tears were streaming down his cheeks and he had difficulty in getting his breath. I don't think I ever saw a man laugh so much in my life.

I don't think I ever saw a man stop laughing as quickly, either, as Frans Els did when some people from the camping-ground came up and spoke to him. They had to say it over twice before he could get the full purport of the message, which was to the effect that it was not the ouderling's tent at all, that had got blown away, but his.

I suppose you could describe the way in which Frans Els carried on that day while he still thought that it was the ouderling's tent, as one kind of laughter. The fact is that there are more kinds of laughter than just that one sort, and it seems to me that this is the cause of a lot of regrettable awkwardness in the world.

Another thing I have noticed is that when a woman laughs it usually means a good deal of trouble for a man. Not at that very moment, maybe, but afterwards. And more especially when it is a musical sort of laugh.

There is still another kind of laughter that you have also come across in your time, I am sure. That is the way we laugh when there are a number of us together in the Indian store at Ramoutsa, and Hendrik Moolman tells a funny story that he has read in the *Goede Hoop*. What is so entertaining about his way of telling these stories is that Hendrik Moolman always forgets what the point is. Then when we ask, "But what's so funny about it?" he tries to make up another story as he goes along. And because he's so weak at that, it makes us laugh more than ever.

So when we talk about Hendrik Moolman's funny stories, it is not the stories themselves that we find amusing, but his lack of skill in telling them. But I suppose it's all the same to Hendrik Moolman. He joins heartily in our laughter and waves his crutch about. Sometimes he even gets so excited that you almost expect him to rise up out of his chair without help.

It all happened very long ago, the first part of this story of Hendrik Moolman and his wife Malie. And in those days, when they had just married, you would not, if the idea of laughter had come into your mind, have thought first of Hendrik Moolman telling jokes in the Indian store.

They were just of an age, the young Moolman couple and they were both good to look at. And when they arrived back from Zeerust after the wedding, Hendrik made a stirring show of the way he lifted Malie from the mule-cart, to carry her across the threshold of the little farmhouse in which their future life was to be cast. Needless to say, that was many years before Hendrik Moolman was to acquire the nickname of Crippled Hendrik, as the result of a fall into a diamond claim when he was drunk. Some said that his fall was an accident. Others saw in the occurrence the hand of the Lord.

What I remember most vividly about Malie, as she was in those early days of her marriage, are her eyes, and her laughter that was in strange contrast to her eyes. Her laughter was free and clear and ringing. Each time you heard it, it was like a sudden bright light. Her laughter was like a summer's morning. But her eyes were dark and did not seem to belong with any part of the day at all.

It was the women who by-and-by started to say about the marriage of Hendrik and Malie this thing, that Malie's love for Hendrik was greater than his love for her. You could see it all, they said, by that look that came on her face when Hendrik entered the voorkamer, called in from the lands because there were visitors. You could tell it too, they declared, by that unnatural stillness that would possess her when she was left alone on the farm for a few days, as would happen each time her husband went with cattle or mealies to the market town.

With the years, also, that gay laugh of Malie Moolman's was heard more seldom, until in the end she seemed to have forgotten how to laugh at all. But there was never any suggestion of Malie having been unhappy. That was the queerest part of it – that part of the marriage of Malie and Hendrik that confuted all the busybodies. For it proved that Malie's devotion to Hendrik had not been just one-sided.

They had been married a good many years before that day when it became known to Malie – as a good while before that it had become known to the rest of the white people living on this side of the Dwarsberge – that Hendrik's return from the market town of Zeerust would be indefinitely delayed.

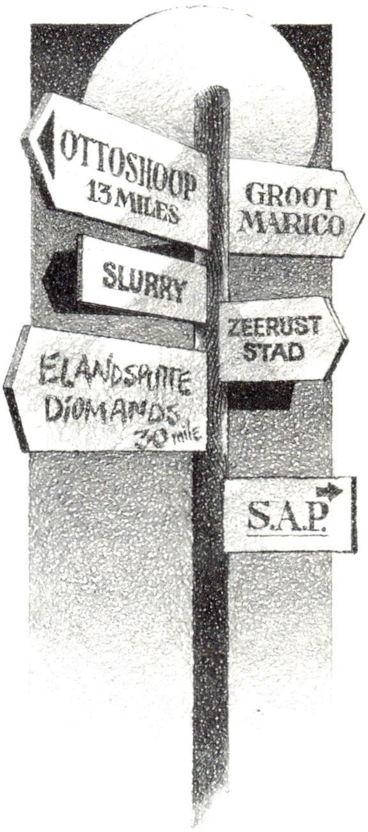

Those were prosperous times, and it was said that Hendrik had taken a considerable sum with him in gold coins for his journey to the Elandsputte diamond diggings, whither he had gone in the company of the Woman of Zeerust. Malie went on staying on the farm, and saw to it that the day-to-day activities in the kraal and on the lands and in the homestead went on just as though Hendrik were still there. Instead of in the arms of the Woman of Zeerust.

This went on for a good while, with Hendrik Moolman throwing away, on the diggings, real gold after visionary diamonds.

There were many curious features about this thing that had happened with Hendrik Moolman. For instance, it was known that he had written to his wife quite a number of times. Jurie Bekker, who kept the post office at Drogedal, had taken the trouble on one occasion to deliver into Malie's hands personally a letter addressed to her in her husband's handwriting. He had taken over the letter himself, instead of waiting for Malie to send for it. And Jurie Bekker said that Malie had thanked him very warmly for the letter, and had torn open the envelope in a state of agitation, and had wept over the contents of the letter, and had then informed Jurie Bekker that it was from her sister in Kuruman, who wrote about the drought there.

"It seemed to be a pretty long drought," Jurie Bekker said to us afterwards in the post office, "judging from the number of pages."

It was known, however, that when a woman visitor had made open reference to the state of affairs on the Elandsputte diggings, Malie had said that her husband was suffering from a temporary infatuation for the Woman of Zeerust, of whom she spoke without bitterness. Malie said she was certain that Hendrik would grow tired of that woman, and return to her.

Meanwhile, many rumours of what was happening with Hendrik Moolman on the Elandsputte diggings were conveyed to this part of the Marico by one means and another – mainly by donkey-cart. Later on it became known that Hendrik had sold the wagon and the oxen with which he had trekked from his farm to the diggings. Still later it became known why Malie was sending so many head of cattle to market. Finally, when a man with a waxed moustache and a notebook appeared in the neighbourhood, the farmers hereabouts, betokening no surprise, were able to direct him to the Moolman farm, where he went to take an inventory of the stock.

By that time the Woman of Zeerust must have discovered that Hendrik Moolman was about at the end of his resources. But nobody knew for sure when she deserted him – whether it was before or after that thing had happened to him which paralysed the left side of his body.

And that was how it came about that in the end Hendrik Moolman did return to his wife, Malie, just as she had during all that time maintained that he would. In reply to a message from Elandsputte diggings she had sent a kafir in the mule-cart to fetch Baas Hendrik Moolman back to his farm.

Hendrik Moolman was seated in a half-reclining posture against the kafir who held the reins, that evening when the mule-cart drew up in front of the home into which, many years before on the day of their wedding, he had carried his wife, Malie. There was something not unfitting about his own home-coming in the evening, in the thought that Malie would be helping to lift him off the mule-cart, now.

Some such thought must have been uppermost in Malie's mind also. At all events, she came forward to greet her errant husband. Apparently she now comprehended for the first time the true extent of his incapacitation. Malie had not laughed for many years. Now the sound of her laughter, gay and silvery, sent its infectious echoes ringing through the farmyard.

MARICO MOON

I buttoned up my jacket because of the night wind that came whistling through the thorn-trees (Oom Schalk Lourens said); my fingers on the reins were stiff with the cold.

There were four of us in the mule-cart, driving along the Government road on our way back from the dance at Withaak. I sat in front with Dirk Prinsloo, a young schoolteacher. In the back were Petrus Lemmer and his sister's stepdaughter, Annie.

Petrus Lemmer was an elder in the Dutch Reformed Church. He told us that he was very strongly opposed to parties, because people got drunk at parties, and all sorts of improper things happened. He had only gone to the dance at Withaak, he said, because of Annie. He explained that he had to be present to make quite sure that nothing unseemly took place at a dance that his sister's stepdaughter went to.

We all thought that it was very fine of Petrus Lemmer to sacrifice his own comfort in that way. And we were very glad when he said that this was one of the most respectable dances he had ever attended.

He said that at two o'clock in the morning. But before that he had said a few other things of so unusual a character that all the women walked out. And they only came back a little later on, after a number of young men had helped Petrus Lemmer out through the front door. One of the young men was Dirk Prinsloo, the schoolteacher, and I noticed that there was quite a lot of peach brandy on his clothes. The peach brandy had come out of a big glass that Petrus Lemmer had in his hand, and when he went out of the door he was still saying how glad he was that this was not an improper party, like others he had seen.

Shortly afterwards Petrus Lemmer fell into the dam, backwards. And when they pulled him out he was still holding onto the big glass, very tightly. But when he put the glass to his mouth he said that what was in it tasted to him a lot like water. He threw the glass away then.

So it came about that, in the early hours of the morning, there were four of us driving along the road back from Withaak. Petrus Lemmer had wanted to stay longer at the dance, after they had pulled him out of the dam and given him a dry pair of trousers and a shirt. But they said, no, it wasn't right that he should go on sacrificing himself like that. Petrus Lemmer said that was nothing. He was willing to sacrifice himself a lot more. He said he would go on sacrificing himself until the morning, if necessary, to make quite sure that nothing disgraceful took place at the dance. But the people said there was no need for him to stay any longer. Nothing more disgraceful could happen than what had already happened, they said.

At first, Petrus Lemmer seemed pleased at what they said. But afterwards he grew a bit more thoughtful. He still appeared to be thinking about it when a number of young men, including Dirk Prinsloo, helped him onto my mule-cart, heavily. His sister's stepdaughter, Annie, got into the back seat beside him. Dirk Prinsloo came and sat next to me.

It was a cold night, and the road through the bush was very long. The house where Dirk Prinsloo boarded was the first that we would come to. It was a long way ahead. Then came Petrus Lemmer's farm, several miles farther on. I had the longest distance to go of us all.

In between shivering, Petrus Lemmer said how pleased he was that nobody at the dance had used really bad language.

"Nobody except you, Uncle," Annie said then.

Petrus Lemmer explained that anybody was entitled to forget himself a little, after having been thrown into the dam, like he was.

"You weren't thrown, Uncle," Annie said. "You fell in."

"Thrown," Petrus persisted.

"Fell," Annie repeated firmly.

Petrus said that she could have it her way, if she liked. It was no use arguing with a woman, he explained. Women couldn't understand reason, anyway. But what he maintained strongly was that, if you were wet right through, and standing in the cold, you might perhaps say a few things that you wouldn't say ordinarily.

"But even before you fell in the dam, Uncle," Annie went on, "you used bad language. The time all the women walked out. It was awful language. And you said it just for nothing, too. You ought to be ashamed of yourself, Uncle. And you an elder in the Reformed Church."

But Petrus Lemmer said that was different. He said that if he hadn't been at the dance he would like to know what would have happened. That was all he wanted to know. Young girls of today had no sense of gratitude. It was only for Annie's sake that he had come to the dance in the first place. And then they went and threw him into the water.

The moon was big and full above the Dwarsberge; and the wind grew colder; and the stars shone dimly through the thorn-trees that overhung the road.

Then Petrus Lemmer started telling us about other dances he had attended in the Bushveld, long ago. He was a young man, then, he said. And whenever he went to a dance there was a certain amount of trouble. "Just like tonight," he said. He went to lots of dances, and it was always the same thing. They were the scandal of the Marico, those dances he went to. And he said it was no use his exercising his influence, either; people just wouldn't listen to him.

"Influence," Annie said, and I could hear her laughter above the rattling of the mule-cart.

"But there was one dance I went to," Petrus Lemmer continued, "on a farm near Abjaterskop. That was very different. It was a quiet sort of dance. And it was different in every way."

Annie said that perhaps it was different because they didn't have a dam on that farm. But Petrus Lemmer replied, in a cold kind of voice, that he didn't know what Annie was hinting at, and that, anyway, she was old enough to have more sense.

"It was mainly because of Grieta," Petrus Lemmer said, "that I went to that dance at Abjaterskop. And I believed that it was because she hoped to see me there that Grieta went."

Annie said something about this, also. I couldn't hear what it was. But this time Petrus Lemmer ignored her.

"There were not very many people at this dance," he went on. "A large number who had been invited stayed away."

"It seems that other people besides Grieta knew you were going to that dance, Uncle," Annie remarked then.

"It was because of the cold," Petrus Lemmer said shortly. "It was a cold night, just like it is tonight. I wore a new shirt with stripes and I rubbed sheep-fat on my veldskoens, to make them shine. At first I thought it was rather foolish, my taking all this trouble over my appearance, for the sake of a girl whom I had seen only a couple of times. But when I got to the farmhouse at Abjaterskop, where the dance was, and I saw Grieta in the voorkamer, I no longer thought it was foolish of me to get all dressed up like that."

Petrus Lemmer fell silent for a few moments, as though waiting for one of us to say what an interesting story it was, and would he tell us what happened next. But none of us said anything. So Petrus just coughed and went on with his story without being asked. That was the sort of man Petrus Lemmer was.

"I saw Grieta in the voorkamer," Petrus Lemmer repeated, "and she had on a pink frock. She was very pretty. Even now, after all those years, when I look back on it, I can still picture to myself how pretty she was. For a long time I stood in the far end of the room and just watched her. Another young fellow was wasting her time, talking to her. Afterwards he wasted still more of her time by dancing with her. If it wasn't that I knew that I was the only one in that voorkamer that Grieta cared for, I would have got jealous of the way in which that young fellow carried on. And he kept getting more and more foolish. But afterwards I got tired of standing up against that wall and watching Grieta from a distance. So I sat down on a chair, next to the two men with the guitar and the concertina. For some time I sat and watched Grieta from the chair. By then that fellow was actually wasting her time to the extent of tickling her under the chin with a piece of grass."

Petrus Lemmer stopped talking again, and we listened to the bumping of the mule-cart and the wind in the thorn-trees. The moon was large and full above the Dwarsberge.

"But how did you know that this girl liked you, Oom Petrus?" Dirk Prinsloo asked. It seemed as though the young schoolteacher was getting interested in the story.

"Oh, I just knew," Petrus Lemmer replied. "She never said anything to me about it, but with these things you can always tell."

"Yes, I expect you can," Annie said softly, in a far-away sort of voice. And she asked Petrus Lemmer to tell us what happened next.

"It was just like I said it was," Petrus Lemmer continued. "And shortly afterwards Grieta left that foolish young man, with his piece of grass and all, and came past the chair where I was sitting, next to the musicians. She walked past me quickly, and what she said wasn't much above a whisper. But I heard all right. And I didn't even bother to look up and see whether that other fellow had observed anything. I felt so superior to him, at that moment."

Once again Petrus Lemmer paused. But it was obvious that Annie wanted him to get to the end of the story quickly.

"Then did you go and meet Grieta, Oom Petrus?" she asked.

"Oh, yes," Petrus answered. "I was there at the time she said."

"By the third withaak," Annie asked again, "under the moon?"

"By the third withaak," Petrust Lemmer replied. "Under the moon."

I wondered how Annie knew all that. In some ways there seemed little that a woman didn't know.

"There's not much more to tell," Petrus Lemmer said. "And I could never understand how it happened, either. It was just that, when I met Grieta there, under the thorn-tree, it suddenly seemed that there was nothing I wanted to say to her. And I could see that she felt the same way about it. She seemed just an ordinary woman, like lots of other women. And I felt rather foolish, standing there beside her, wearing a new striped shirt, and with sheep-fat on my veldskoens. And I knew just how she felt, also. At first I tried to pretend to myself that it was the fault of the moon. Then I blamed that fellow with the piece of grass. But I knew all the time that it was nobody's fault. It just happened like that.

"As I have said," Petrus Lemmer concluded sombrely, "I don't know how it came about. And I don't think Grieta knew, either. We stood there wondering – each of us – what it was that had been, a little while before, so attractive about the other. But whatever it was, it had gone. And we both knew that it had gone for good. Then I said that it was getting cold. And Grieta said that perhaps we had better go inside. So we went back to the voorkamer. It seemed an awfully quiet party, and I didn't stay much longer. And I remember how, on my way home, I looked at the moon under which Grieta and I had stood by the thorn-tree. I watched the moon until it went down behind the Dwarsberge."

Petrus Lemmer finished his story, and none of us spoke.

Some distance farther on we arrived at the place where Dirk Prinsloo stayed. Dirk got off the mule-cart and said good night. Then he turned to Annie.

"It's funny," he said, "this story of your uncle's. It's queer how things like that happen."

"He's not my uncle," Annie replied. "He's only my stepmother's brother. And I never listen to his stories, anyway."

So we drove on again, the three of us, down the road, through the thorn-trees, with the night wind blowing into our faces. And a little later, when the moon was going down behind the Dwarsberge it sounded to me as though Annie was crying.

THE LOVE-POTION

You mention the juba-plant (Oom Schalk Lourens said). Oh, yes, everybody in the Marico knows about the juba-plant. It grows high up on the krantzes, and they say you must pick off one of its little red berries at midnight, under the full moon. Then, if you are a young man, and you are anxious for a girl to fall in love with you, all you have to do is to squeeze the juice of the juba-berry into her coffee.

They say that after the girl has drunk the juba-juice she begins to forget all sorts of things. She forgets that your forehead is rather low, and that your ears stick out, and that your mouth is too big. She even forgets having told you, the week before last, that she wouldn't marry you if you were the only man in the Transvaal.

All she knows is that the man she gazes at, over her empty coffee-cup, has grown remarkably handsome. You can see from this that the plant must be very potent in its effects. I mean, if you consider what some of the men in the Marico look like.

One young man I knew, however, was not very enthusiastic about juba-juice. In fact, he always said that before he climbed up the krantz one night, to pick one of those red berries, he was more popular with the girls than he was afterwards. This young man said that his decline in favour with the girls of the neighbourhood might perhaps be due to the fact that, shortly after he had picked the juba-berry, he lost more of his front teeth.

This happened when the girl's father, who was an irascible sort of fellow, caught the young man in the act of squeezing juba-juice into his daughter's cup.

And afterwards, while others talked of the magic properties of this love-potion, the young man would listen in silence, and his lip would curl in a sneer over the place where his front teeth used to be.

"Yes, kêrels," he would lisp at the end, "I suppose I must have picked that juba-berry at the wrong time. Perhaps the moon wasn't full enough, or something. Or perhaps it wasn't just exactly midnight. I am only glad now that I didn't pick off two of those red berries while I was about it."

We all felt it was a sad thing that the juba-plant had done to that young man.

But with Gideon van der Merwe it was different.

One night I was out shooting in the veld with a lamp fastened on my hat. You know that kind of shooting: in the glare of the lamplight you can see only the eyes of the thing you are aiming at, and you get three months if you are caught. They made it illegal to hunt by lamplight since the time a policeman got shot in the foot, this way, when he was out tracking cattle-smugglers on the Bechuanaland border.

The magistrate at Zeerust, who did not know the ways of the cattle-smugglers, found that the shooting was an accident. This verdict satisfied everybody except the policeman, whose foot was still bandaged when he came into court. But the men in the Volksraad, some of whom had been cattle-smugglers themselves, knew better than the magistrate did as to how the policeman came to have a couple of buckshot in the soft part of his foot, and accordingly they brought in this new law.

Therefore I walked very quietly that night on the krantz. Frequently I put out my hand and stood very still amongst the trees, and waited long moments to make sure I was not being followed. Ordinarily, there would have been little to fear, but a couple of days before two policemen had been seen disappearing into the bush. By their looks they seemed young policemen, who were anxious for promotion, and who didn't know that it is more becoming for a policeman to drink an honest farmer's peach brandy than to arrest him for hunting by lamplight.

I was walking along, turning the light from side to side, when suddenly, about a hundred paces from me, in the full brightness of the lamp, I saw a pair of eyes. When I also saw, above the eyes, a policeman's khaki helmet, I remembered that a moonlight night, such as that was, was not good for finding buck.

So I went home.

I took the shortest way, too, which was over the side of the krantz - the steep side - and on my way down I clutched at a variety of branches, tree-roots, stone ledges and tufts of grass. Later on, at the foot of the krantz , when I came to and was able to sit up, there was that policeman bending over me.

"Oom Schalk," he said, "I was wondering if you would lend me your lamp."

I looked up. It was Gideon van der Merwe, a young policeman who had been stationed for some time at Derdepoort. I had met him on several occasions and had found him very likeable.

"You can have my lamp," I answered, "but you must be careful. It's worse for a policeman to get caught breaking the law than for an ordinary man."

Gideon van der Merwe shook his head.

"No, I don't want to go shooting with the lamp," he said, "I want to..."

And then he paused.

He laughed nervously.

"It seems silly to say it, Oom Schalk," he said, "but perhaps you'll understand. I have come to look for a juba-plant. I need it for my studies. For my third-class sergeant's examination. And it will soon be midnight, and I can't find one of those plants anywhere."

I felt sorry for Gideon. It struck me that he would never make a good policeman. If he couldn't find a juba-plant, of which there were thousands on the krantz, it would be much harder for him to find the spoor of a cattle-smuggler.

So I handed him my lamp and explained where he had to go and look. Gideon thanked me and walked off.

About half an hour later he was back.

He took a red berry out of his tunic pocket and showed it to me. For fear he should tell any more lies about needing that juba-berry for his studies, I spoke first.

"Lettie Cordier?" I asked.

Gideon nodded. He was very shy, though, and wouldn't talk much at the start. But I had guessed long ago that Gideon van der Merwe was not calling at Krisjan Cordier's house so often just to hear Krisjan relate the story of his life.

Nevertheless, I mentioned Krisjan Cordier's life story.

"Yes," Gideon replied, "Lettie's father has got up to what he was like at the age of seven. It has taken him a month, so far."

"He must be glad to get you to listen," I said, "the only other man who listened for any length of time was an insurance agent. But he left after a fortnight. By that time Krisjan had reached to only a little beyond his fifth birthday."

"But Lettie is wonderful, Oom Schalk," Gideon went on. "I have never spoken more than a dozen words to her. And, of course, it is ridiculous to expect her even to look at a policeman. But to sit there, in the voorkamer, with her father talking about all the things he could do before he was six - and Lettie coming in now and again with more coffee - that is love, Oom Schalk."

I agreed with him that it must be.

"I have worked it out," Gideon explained, "that at the rate he is going now, Lettie's father will have come to the end of his life story in two years' time, and after that I won't have any excuse for going there. That worries me."

I said that no doubt it was disconcerting.

"I have tried often to tell Lettie how much I think of her," Gideon said, "but every time, as soon as I start, I get a foolish feeling. My uniform begins to look shabby. My boots seem to curl up at the toes. And my voice gets shaky, and all I can say to her is that I will come round again, soon, as I have simply got to hear the rest of her father's life story."

"Then what is your idea with the juba-juice?" I asked.

"The juba-juice," Gideon van der Merwe said wistfully, "might make her say something first."

We parted shortly afterwards. I took up my lamp and gun, and as I saw Gideon's figure disappear among the trees I thought of what a good fellow he was. And very simple. Still, he was best off as a policeman, I reflected. For if he was a cattle-smuggler it seemed to me that he would get arrested every time he tried to cross the border.

Next morning I rode over to Krisjan Cordier's farm to remind him about a tin of sheep-dip that he still owed me from the last dipping season.

As I stayed for only an hour, I wasn't able to get in a word about the sheep-dip, but Krisjan managed to tell me quite a lot about the things he did at the age of nine. When Lettie came in with the coffee I made a casual remark to her father about Gideon van der Merwe.

"Oh, yes, he's an interesting young man," Krisjan Cordier said, "and very intelligent. It is a pleasure for me to relate to him the story of my life. He says the incidents I describe to him are not only thrilling, but very helpful. I can quite understand that. I wouldn't be surprised if he is made a sergeant one of these days. For those reasons I always dwell on the more helpful parts of my story."

I didn't take much notice of Krisjan's remarks, however. Instead, I looked carefully at Lettie when I mentioned Gideon's name. She didn't give much away, but I am quick at these things, and I saw enough. The colour that crept into her cheeks. The light that came in her eyes.

On my way back I encountered Lettie. She was standing under a thorn-tree. With her brown arms and her sweet, quiet face and her full bosom, she was a very pretty picture. There was no doubt that Lettie Cordier would make a fine wife for any man. It wasn't hard to understand Gideon's feelings about her.

"Lettie," I asked, "do you love him?"

"I love him, Oom Schalk," she answered.

It was as simple as all that.

Lettie guessed I meant Gideon van der Merwe, without my having spoken his name. Accordingly, it was easy for me to acquaint Lettie with what had happened the night before, on the krantz, in the moonlight. At least, I only told her the parts that mattered to her, such as the way I explained to Gideon where the juba-plant grew. Another man might have wearied her with a long and unnecessary description of the way he fell down the krantz, clutching at branches and tree-roots. But I am different. I told her that it was Gideon who fell down the krantz.

After all, it was Lettie's and Gideon's love affair, and I didn't want to bring myself into it too much.

"Now you'll know what to do, Lettie," I said. "Put your coffee on the table within easy reach of Gideon. Then give him what you think is long enough to squeeze the juba-juice into your cup."

"Perhaps it will be even better," Lettie said, "if I watch through a crack in the door."

I patted her head approvingly.

"After that you come into the voorkamer and drink your coffee," I said.

"Yes, Oom Schalk," she answered simply.

"And when you have drunk the coffee," I concluded, "you'll know what to do next. Only don't go too far."

It was pleasant to see the warm blood mount to her face. As I rode off I said to myself that Gideon van der Merwe was a lucky fellow.

There isn't much more to tell about Lettie and Gideon.

When I saw Gideon some time afterwards, he was very elated, as I had expected he would be.

"So the juba-plant worked?" I enquired.

"It was wonderful, Oom Schalk," Gideon answered, "and the funny part of it was that Lettie's father was not there, either, when I put that juba-juice into her coffee. Lettie had brought him a message, just before then, that he was wanted in the mealie-lands."

"And was the juba-juice all they claim for it?" I asked.

"You'd be surprised how quickly it acted," he said, "Lettie just took one sip at the coffee and then jumped straight onto my lap."

But then Gideon van der Merwe winked in a way that made me believe that he was not so very simple, after all.

"I was pretty certain that the juba-juice would work, Oom Schalk," he said, "after Lettie's father told me that you had been there that morning."

THE ROOINEK

Rooineks, said Oom Schalk Lourens, are queer. For instance, there was that day when my nephew Hannes and I had dealings with a couple of Englishmen near Dewetsdorp. It was shortly after Sanna's Post, and Hannes and I were lying behind a rock watching the road. Hannes spent odd moments like that in what he called a useful way. He would file the points of his Mauser cartridges on a piece of flat stone until the lead showed through the steel, in that way making them into dumdum bullets.

I often spoke to my nephew Hannes about that.

"Hannes," I used to say. "That is a sin. The Lord is looking at you."

"That's all right," Hannes replied. "The Lord knows that this is the Boer War, and in wartime He will always forgive a little foolishness like this, especially as the English are so many."

Anyway, as we lay behind that rock we saw, far down the road, two horsemen come galloping up. We remained perfectly still and let them approach to within four hundred paces. They were English officers. They were mounted on first-rate horses and their uniforms looked very fine and smart. They were the most stylish-looking men I had seen for some time, and I felt quite ashamed of my own ragged trousers and veldskoens. I was glad that I was behind a rock and they couldn't see me. Especially as my jacket was also torn all the way down the back, as a result of my having had, three days before, to get through a barbed-wire fence rather quickly. I just got through in time, too. The veldkornet, who was a fat man and couldn't run so fast, was about twenty yards behind me. And he remained on the wire with a bullet through him. All through the Boer War I was pleased that I was thin and never troubled with corns.

Hannes and I fired just about the same time. One of the officers fell off his horse. He struck the road with his shoulders and rolled over

Peter Badcock

twice, kicking up the red dust as he turned. Then the other soldier did a queer thing. He drew up his horse and got off. He gave just one look in our direction. Then he led his horse up to where the other man was twisting and struggling on the ground. It took him a little while to lift him onto his horse, for it is no easy matter to pick up a man like that when he is helpless. And he did all this slowly and calmly, as though he was not concerned about the fact that the men who had just shot his friend were lying only a few hundred yards away. He managed in some way to support the wounded man across the saddle, and walked on beside the horse. After going a few yards he stopped and seemed to remember something. He turned round and waved at the spot where he imagined we were hiding, as though inviting us to shoot. During all that time I had simply lain watching him, astonished at his coolness.

But when he waved his hand I thrust another cartridge into the breach of my Martini and aimed. I aimed very carefully and was just on the point of pulling the trigger when Hannes put his hand on the barrel and pushed up my rifle.

"Don't shoot, Oom Schalk," he said. "That's a brave man."

I looked at Hannes in surprise. His face was very white. I said nothing, and allowed my rifle to sink down onto the grass, but I couldn't understand what had come over my nephew. It seemed that not only was that Englishman queer, but that Hannes was also queer. That's all nonsense not killing a man just because he's brave. If he's a brave man and he's fighting on the wrong side, that's all the more reason to shoot him.

I was with my nephew Hannes for another few months after that. Then one day, in a skirmish near the Vaal River, Hannes with a few dozen other burghers, was cut off from the commando and had to surrender. That was the last I ever saw of him. I heard later on that, after taking him prisoner, the English searched Hannes and found dum-dum bullets in his possession. They shot him for that. I was very much grieved when I heard of Hannes's death. He had always been full of life and high spirits. Perhaps Hannes was right in saying that the Lord didn't mind about a little foolishness like dum-dum bullets. But the mistake he made was in forgetting that the English did mind.

I was in the veld until they made peace. Then we laid down our rifles and went home. What I knew my farm by, was the hole under the koppie where I quarried slate stones for the threshing-floor. That was about all that remained as I left it. Everything else was gone. My home was burnt down. My lands were laid waste. My cattle and sheep were slaughtered. Even the stones I had piled for the kraals were pulled down. My wife came out of the concentration camp and we went together to look at our old farm. My wife had gone into the concentration camp with our two children, but she came out alone. And when I saw her again and noticed the way she had changed, I knew that I, who had been through all the fighting, had not seen the Boer War.

Neither Sannie nor I had the heart to go on farming again on that same place. It would be different without the children playing about the house and getting into mischief. We got paid out some money by the new Government for part of our losses. So I bought a wagon and oxen and we left the Free State, which was not even the Free State any longer. It was now called the Orange River Colony.

We trekked right through the Transvaal into the northern part of the Marico Bushveld. Years ago, as a boy, I had trekked through that same country with my parents. Now that I went there again I felt that it was still a good country. It was on the far side of the Dwarsberge, near Derdepoort, that we got a Government farm. Afterwards other farmers trekked in there as well. One or two of them had also come from the Free State, and I knew them. There were also a few Cape rebels whom I had seen on commando. All of us had lost relatives in the war. Some had died in the concentration camps or on the battlefield. Others had been shot for going into rebellion. So, taken all in all, we who trekked into that part of the Marico that lay nearest the Bechuanaland border were bitter against the English.

Then it was that the rooinek came.

It was in the first year of our having settled around Derdepoort. We heard that an Englishman had bought a farm next to Gerhardus Grobbelaar. This was when we were sitting in the voorkamer of Willem Odendaal's house, which was used as a post office. Once a week the post-cart came up with letters from Zeerust, and we came together at Willem Odendaal's house and talked and smoked and drank coffee. Very few of us ever got letters, and then it was mostly demands to pay for the boreholes that had been drilled on our farms or for cement and fencing materials. But every week regularly we went for the post. Sometimes the post-cart didn't come, because the Groen River was in flood, and we would most of us have gone home without noticing it, if somebody didn't speak about it.

When Koos Steyn heard that an Englishman was coming to live amongst us he got up from the riempies-bank.

"No, kêrels," he said, "always when the Englishman comes, it means that a little later the Boer has got to shift. I'll pack up my wagon and make coffee, and just trek first thing tomorrow morning."

Most of us laughed then. Koos Steyn often said funny things like that. But some didn't laugh. Somehow, there seemed to be too much truth in Koos Steyn's words.

We discussed the matter and decided that if we Boers in the Marico could help it the rooinek would not stay amongst us too long. About half an hour later one of Willem Odendaal's children came in and said that there was a strange wagon coming along the big road. We went to the door and looked out. As the wagon came nearer we saw that it was piled up with all kinds of furniture and also sheets of iron and farming implements. There was so much stuff on the wagon that the tent had to be taken off to get everything on.

The wagon rolled along and came to a stop in front of the house. With the wagon there was one white man and two kafirs. The white man shouted something to the kafirs and threw down the whip. Then he walked up to where we were standing. He was dressed just as we were, in shirt and trousers and veldskoens, and he had dust all over him. But when he stepped over a thorn-bush we saw that he had got socks on. Therefore we knew that he was an Englishman.

Koos Steyn was standing in front of the door.

The Englishman went up to him and held out his hand.

"Good afternoon," he said in Afrikaans. "My name is Webber."

Koos shook hands with him.

"My name is Prince Lord Alfred Milner," Koos Steyn said.

That was when Lord Milner was Governor of the Transvaal, and we all laughed. The rooinek also laughed.

"Well, Lord Prince," he said, "I can speak your language a little, and I hope that later on I'll be able to speak it better. I'm coming to live here, and I hope that we'll all be friends."

He then came round to all of us, but the others turned away and refused to shake hands with him. He came up to me last of all; I felt sorry for him, and although his nation had dealt unjustly with my nation, and I had lost both my children in the concentration camp, still it was not so much the fault of this Englishman. It was the fault of the English Government, who wanted our gold mines. And it was also the fault of Queen Victoria, who didn't like Oom Paul Kruger, because they say that when he went over to London Oom Paul spoke to her only once for a few minutes. Oom Paul Kruger said that he was a married man and he was afraid of widows.

When the Englishman Webber went back to his wagon Koos Steyn and I walked with him. He told us that he had bought the farm next to Gerhardus Grobbelaar and that he didn't know much about sheep and cattle and mealies, but he had bought a few books on farming, and he was going to learn all he could out of them. When he said that I looked away towards the poort. I didn't want him to see that I was laughing. But with Koos Steyn it was otherwise.

"Man," he said, "let me see those books."

Webber opened the box at the bottom of the wagon and took out about six big books with green covers.

"These are very good books," Koos Steyn said. "Yes, they are very good for the white ants. The white ants will eat them all in two nights."

As I have told you, Koos Steyn was a funny fellow, and no man could help laughing at the things he said.

Those were bad times. There was drought, and we could not sow mealies. The dams dried up, and there was only last year's grass on the veld. We had to pump water out of the boreholes for weeks at a time. Then the rains came and for a while things were better.

Now and again I saw Webber. From what I heard about him it seemed that he was working hard. But of course no rooinek can make a living out of farming, unless they send him money every month from England. And we found out that almost all the money Webber had was what he paid on the farm. He was always reading in those green books what he had to do. It's lucky that those books are written in English, and that the Boers can't read them. Otherwise many more farmers would be ruined every year. When his cattle had the heart-water, or his sheep had the blue-tongue, or there were cutworms or stalkborers in his mealies, Webber would look it all up in his books. I suppose that when the kafirs stole his sheep he would look that up, too.

Still, Koos Steyn helped Webber quite a lot and taught him a number of things, so that matters did not go as badly with him as they would have if he had only acted according to the lies that were printed in those green books. Webber and Koos Steyn became very friendly. Koos Steyn's wife had had a baby just a few weeks before Webber came. It was the first child they had after being married seven years, and they were very proud of it. It was a girl. Koos Steyn said that he would sooner it had been a boy; but that, even so, it was better than nothing. Right from the first Webber had taken a liking to that child, who was christened Jemima after her mother. Often when I passed

Koos Steyn's house I saw the Englishman sitting on the front stoep with the child on his knees.

In the meantime the other farmers around there became annoyed on account of Koos Steyn's friendship with the rooinek. They said that Koos was a handsopper and a traitor to his country. He was intimate with a man who had helped to bring about the downfall of the Afrikaner nation. Yet it was not fair to call Koos a handsopper. Koos had lived in the Graaff-Reinet district when the war broke out, so that he was a Cape Boer and need not have fought. Nevertheless, he joined up with a Free State commando and remained until peace was made, and if at any time the English caught him they would have shot him as a rebel, in the same way they shot Scheepers and many others.

Gerhardus Grobbelaar spoke about this once when we were in Willem Odendaal's post office.

"You are not doing right," Gerhardus said; "Boer and Englishman have been enemies since after Slagtersnek. We've lost this war, but someday we'll win. It's the duty we owe to our children's children to stand against the rooineks. Remember the concentration camps."

There seemed to me to be truth in what Gerhardus said.

"But the English are here now, and we've got to live with them," Koos answered. "When we get to understand one another perhaps we won't need to fight any more. This Englishman Webber is learning Afrikaans very well; and someday he might almost be one of us. The only thing I can't understand about him is that he has a bath every morning. But if he stops that and if he doesn't brush his teeth any more you will hardly be able to tell him from a Boer."

Although he made a joke about it, I felt that in what Koos Steyn said there was also truth.

Then, the year after the drought, the miltsiek broke out. The miltsiek seemed to be in the grass of the veld, and in the water of the dams, and even in the air the cattle breathed. All over the place I would find cows and oxen lying dead. We all became very discouraged. Nearly all of us in that part of the Marico had started farming again on what the Government had given us. Now that the stock died we had nothing. First the drought had put us back to where we were when we started. Now with the miltsiek we couldn't hope to do anything. We couldn't even sow mealies, because, at the rate at which the cattle were dying, in a short while we would have no oxen left to pull the plough. People talked of selling what they had and going to look for work on the mines. We sent a petition to the Government, but that did no good.

It was then that somebody got hold of the idea of trekking. In a few days we were talking of nothing else. But the question was where we could trek to. They would not allow us into Rhodesia for fear we might spread the miltsiek there as well. And it was useless going to any other part of the Transvaal. Somebody mentioned German West Africa. We had none of us been there before, and I suppose that really was the reason why, in the end, we decided to go there.

"The blight of the English is over South Africa," Gerhardus Grobbelaar said. "We'll remain here only to die. We must go away somewhere where there is not the Englishman's flag."

In a few weeks' time we arranged everything. We were going to trek across the Kalahari into German territory. Everything we had we loaded up. We drove the cattle ahead and followed behind on our wagons. There were five families: the Steyns, the Grobbelaars, the Odendaals, the Ferreiras and Sannie and I. Webber also came with us. I think it was not so much that he was anxious to leave as that he and Koos Steyn had become very much attached to one another, and the Englishman did not wish to remain alone behind.

The youngest person in our trek was Koos Steyn's daughter Jemima, who was then about eighteen months old. Being the baby, she was a favourite with all of us.

Webber sold his wagon and went with Koos Steyn's trek.

When at the end of the first day we outspanned several miles inside the Bechuanaland Protectorate, we were very pleased that we were done with the Transvaal, where we had had so much misfortune. Of course, the Protectorate was also British territory, but all the same we felt happier there than we had done in our country. We saw Webber every day now, and although he was a foreigner with strange ways, and would remain an Uitlander until he died, yet we disliked him less than before for being a rooinek.

It was on the first Sunday that we reached Malopolole. For the first part of our way the country remained bushveld. There were the same kind of thorn-trees that grew in the Marico, except that they became fewer the deeper into the Kalahari that we went. Also, the ground became more and more sandy, until even before we came to Malopolole it was all desert. But scattered thorn-bushes remained all the way. That Sunday we held a religious service. Gerhardus Grobbelaar read a chapter out of the Bible and offered up a prayer. We sang a number of psalms, after which Gerhardus prayed again. I shall always remember that Sunday and the way we sat on the ground beside one of the wagons, listening to Gerhardus. That was the last Sunday that we were all together.

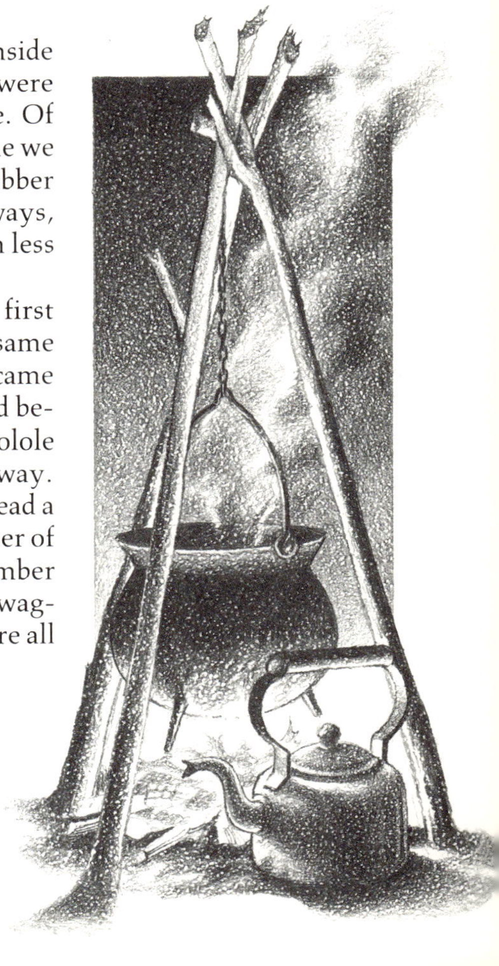

The Englishman sat next to Koos Steyn and the baby Jemima lay down in front of him. She played with Webber's fingers and tried to bite them. It was funny to watch her. Several times Webber looked down at her and smiled. I thought then that although Webber was not one of us, yet Jemima certainly did not know it. Maybe in a thing like that the child was wiser than we were. To her it made no difference that the man whose fingers she bit was born in another country and did not speak the same language as she did.

There are many things that I remember about that trek into the Kalahari. But one thing that now seems strange to me is the way in which, right from the first day, we took Gerhardus Grobbelaar for our leader. Whatever he said we just seemed to do without talking very much about it. We all felt that it was right simply because Gerhardus wished it. That was a strange thing about our trek. It was not simply that we knew Gerhardus had got the Lord with him - for we did know that - but it was rather that we believed in Gerhardus as well as in the Lord. I think that even if Gerhardus Grobbelaar had been an ungodly man we would still have followed him in exactly the same way. For when you are in the desert and there is no water and the way back is long, then you feel that it is better to have with you a strong man who does not read the Book very much, than a man who is good and religious, and yet does not seem sure how far to trek each day and where to outspan.

But Gerhardus Grobbelaar was a man of God. At the same time there was something about him that made you feel that it was only by acting as he advised that you could succeed. There was only one other man I have ever known who found it so easy to get people to do as he wanted. And that was Paul Kruger. He was very much like Gerhardus Grobbelaar, except that Gerhardus was less quarrelsome. But of the two Paul Kruger was the bigger man.

Only once do I remember Gerhardus losing his temper. And that was with the Nagmaal at Elandsberg. It was on a Sunday and we were camped out beside the Crocodile River. Gerhardus went round early in the morning from wagon to wagon and told us that he wanted everybody to come over to where his wagon stood. The Lord had been good to us at that time, so that we had had much rain and our cattle were fat. Gerhardus explained that he wanted to hold a service, to thank the Lord for all His good works, but more especially for what He had done for the farmers on the northern part of the Groot Marico District. This was a good plan, and we all came together with our Bibles and hymn-books. But one man, Karel Pieterse, remained behind at his wagon. Twice Gerhardus went to call him, but Karel Pieterse lay down on the grass and would not get up to come to the service. He said it was all right thanking the Lord now that there had been rains, but what about all those seasons when there had been drought and the cattle had died of thirst. Gerhardus Grobbelaar shook his head sadly, and said there was nothing he could do then as it was Sunday. But he prayed that the Lord would soften brother Pieterse's heart, and he finished off his prayer by saying that in any case, in the morning, he would help to soften the brother's heart himself.

The following morning Gerhardus walked over with a sjambok and an ox-riem to where Karel Pieterse sat before his fire, watching the kafir making coffee. They were both of them men who were big in the body. But Gerhardus got the better of the struggle. In the end he won. He fastened Karel to the wheel of his own wagon with the ox-riem. Then he thrashed him with the sjambok while Karel's wife and children were looking on.

That had happened years before. But nobody had forgotten. And now, in the Kalahari, when Gerhardus summoned us to a service, it was noticed that no man stayed away.

Just outside Malopolole is a muddy stream that is dry part of the year and part of the year has a foot or so of brackish water. We were lucky in being there just at the time when it had water. Early the following morning we filled up the water-barrels that we had put on our wagons before leaving Marico. We were going right into the desert, and we did not know where we would get water again. Even the Bakwena kafirs could not tell us for sure.

"The Great Dorstland Trek," Koos Steyn shouted as we got ready to move off. "Anyway, we won't fare as badly as the Dorstland Trekkers. We'll lose less cattle than they did because we've got less to lose. And seeing that we are only five families, not more than about a dozen of us will die of thirst."

I thought it was bad luck for Koos Steyn to make jokes like that about the Dorstland Trek, and I think that others felt the same about it. We trekked through the day, and it was all desert. By sunset we had not come across a sign of water anywhere. Abraham Ferreira said towards evening that perhaps it would be better if we went back to Malopolole and tried to find out for sure which was the best way of getting through the Kalahari. But the rest said that there was no need to do that, since we would be sure to come across water the next day. And, anyway, we were Doppers and, having once set out, we were not going to turn back. But after we had given the cattle water our barrels did not have too much left in them.

By the middle of the following day all our water had given out except a little that we kept for the children. But still we pushed on. Now that we had gone so far we were afraid to go back because of the long way we would have to go without water to get back to Malopolole. In the evening we were very anxious. We all knelt down in the sand and prayed. Gerhardus Grobbelaar's voice sounded very deep and earnest when he besought God to have mercy on us, especially for the sake of the little ones. He mentioned the baby Jemima by name.

It was moonlight. All around us was the desert. Our wagons seemed very small and lonely; there was something about them that looked very mournful. The women and the children put their arms round one another and wept a long while. Our kafirs stood some distance away and watched us. My wife Sannie put her hand in mine, and I thought of the concentration camp. Poor woman, she had suffered much. And I knew that her thoughts were the same as my own: that after all it was perhaps better that our children should have died then than now.

We had got so far into the desert that we began telling one another that we must be near the end. Although we knew that German West was far away, and that in the way we had been travelling we had got little more than into the beginning of the Kalahari, yet we tried to tell one another lies about how near water was likely to be. But, of course, we told those only to one another. Each man in his own heart knew what the real truth was. And later on we even stopped telling one another lies about what a good chance we had of getting out alive. You can understand how badly things had gone with us when you know that we no longer troubled about hiding our position from the women and children. They wept, some of them. But that made no difference then. Nobody tried to comfort the women and children who cried. We knew that tears were useless, and yet somehow at that hour we felt that the weeping of the women was not less useless than the courage of the men. After a while there was no more weeping in our camp. Some of the women who lived through the dreadful things of the days that came after, and got safely back to the Transvaal, never again wept. What they had seen appeared to have hardened them. In this respect they had become as men. I think that is the saddest thing that ever happens in this world, when women pass through great suffering that makes them become as men.

That night we hardly slept. Early the next morning the men went out to look for water. An hour after sun-up Ferreira came back and told us that he had found a muddy pool a few miles away. We all went there, but there wasn't much water. Still, we got a little, and that made us feel better. It was only when it came to driving our cattle towards the mudhole that we found our kafirs had deserted us during the night. After we had gone to sleep they had stolen away. Some of the weaker cattle couldn't get up to go to the pool. So we left them. Some were trampled to death or got choked in the mud, and we had to pull them out to let the rest get to the hole. It was pitiful.

Just before we left, one of Ferreira's daughters died. We scooped a hole in the sand and buried her.

So we decided to trek back.

After his daughter was dead Abraham Ferreira went up to Gerhardus and told him that if we had taken his advice earlier on and gone back, his daughter would not have died.

"Your daughter is dead now, Abraham," Gerhardus said. "It is no use talking about her any longer. We all have to die someday. I refused to go back earlier. I have decided to go back now."

Abraham Ferreira looked Gerhardus in the eyes and laughed. I shall always remember how that laughter sounded on the desert. In Abraham's voice there was the hoarseness of the sand and thirst. His voice was cracked with what the desert had done to him; his face was lined and his lips were blackened. But there was nothing about him that spoke of grief for his daughter's death.

"Your daughter is still alive, Oom Gerhardus," Abraham Ferreira said, pointing to the wagon wherein lay Gerhardus's wife, who was weak, and the child to whom she had given birth two years before. "Yes, she is still alive ... so far."

Ferreira turned away laughing, and we heard him a little later explaining to his wife in cracked tones about the joke he had made.

Gerhardus Grobbelaar watched the other man walk away without saying anything. So far we had followed Gerhardus through all things, and our faith in him had been great. But now that he had decided to trek back we lost our belief in him. We lost it suddenly, too. We knew that it was best to turn back, and that to continue would mean that we would all die on the Kalahari. And yet, if Gerhardus had said we must still go on we would have done so. We would have gone through with him right to the end. But now that he as much as said he was beaten by the desert we had no more faith in Gerhardus. That is why I have said that Paul Kruger was a greater man than Gerhardus. Because Paul Kruger was that kind of man whom we still worshipped even when he decided to retreat. If it had been Paul Kruger who told us that we had to go back we would have returned with strong hearts. We would have retained exactly the same love for our leader, even if we knew that he was beaten. But from the moment that Gerhardus said we must go back we all knew that he was no longer our leader. Gerhardus knew that also.

We knew what lay between us and Malopolole and there was grave doubt in our hearts when we turned our wagons round. Our cattle were very weak, and we had to inspan all that could walk. We hadn't enough yokes, and therefore we cut poles from the scattered bushes and tied them to the trek-chains. As we were also without skeis we had to fasten the necks of the oxen straight onto the yokes with strops, and several of the oxen got strangled.

Then we saw that Koos Steyn had become mad. For he refused to return. He inspanned his oxen and got ready to trek on. His wife sat silent in the wagon with the baby; wherever her husband went she would go, too. That was only right, of course. Some women kissed her goodbye and cried. But Koos Steyn's wife did not cry. We reasoned with Koos about it, but he said that he had made up his mind to cross the Kalahari, and he was not going to turn back for just nonsense.

"But, man," Gerhardus Grobbelaar said to him, "you've got no water to drink."

"I'll drink coffee then," Koos Steyn answered, laughing as always, and took up the whip and walked away beside the wagon. And Webber went off with him, just because Koos Steyn had been good to him, I suppose. That's why I have said that Englishmen are queer. Webber must have known that if Koos Steyn had not actually gone wrong in the head, still what he was doing now was madness, and yet he stayed with him.

We separated. Our wagons went slowly back to Malopolole. Koos Steyn's wagon went deeper into the desert. My wagon went last. I looked back at the Steyns. At that moment Webber also looked round. He saw me and waved his hand. It reminded me of that day in the Boer War when that other Englishman, whose companion we had shot, also turned round and waved.

Eventually we got back to Malopolole with two wagons and a handful of cattle. We abandoned the other wagons. Awful things happened on that desert. A number of children died. Gerhardus Grobbelaar's wagon was in front of me. Once I saw a bundle being dropped through the side of the wagon-tent. I knew what it was. Gerhardus would not trouble to bury his dead child, and his wife lay in the tent too weak to move. So I got off the wagon and scraped a small heap of sand over the body. All I remember of the rest of the journey to Malopolole is the sun and the sand. And the thirst. Although at one time we thought we had lost our way, yet that did not matter much to us. We were past feeling. We could neither pray nor curse, our parched tongues cleaving to the roofs of our mouths.

Until today I am not sure how many days we were on our way back, unless I sit down and work it all out, and then I suppose I get it wrong. We got back to Malopolole and water. We said we would never go away from there again. I don't think that even those parents who had lost children grieved about them then. They were stunned with what they had gone through. But I knew that later on it would all come back again. Then they would remember things about shallow graves in the sand, and Gerhardus Grobbelaar and his wife would think of a little bundle lying out in the Kalahari. And I knew how they would feel.

Afterwards we fitted out a wagon with fresh oxen; we took an abundant supply of water and went back into the desert to look for the Steyn family. With the help of the Bechuana kafirs, who could see tracks that we could not see, we found the wagon. The oxen had been outspanned; a few lay dead beside the wagon. The kafirs pointed out to us footprints on the sand, which showed which way those two men and that woman had gone.

In the end we found them.

Koos Steyn and his wife lay side by side in the sand; the woman's head rested on the man's shoulder; her long hair had become loosened, and blew softly in the wind. A great deal of fine sand had drifted over their bodies. We never found the baby Jemima. She must have died somewhere along the way and Koos Steyn must have buried her. But we agreed that the Englishman Webber must have passed through terrible things; he could not even have had any understanding left as to what the Steyns had done with their baby. He probably thought, up to the moment when he died, that he was carrying the child. For, when we lifted his body, we found, still clasped in his dead and rigid arms, a few old rags and a child's clothes.

It seemed to us that the wind that always stirs in the Kalahari blew very quietly and softly that morning.

Yes, the wind blew very gently.

SOLD DOWN THE RIVER

We had, of course, heard of Andre Maritz's play and his company of play-actors long before they got to Zeerust (Oom Schalk Lourens said).

For they had travelled a long road. Some of the distance they went by train. Other parts of the way they travelled by mule-cart or ox-wagon. They visited all the dorps from the Cape – where they had started from – to Zeerust in the Transvaal, where Hannekie Roodt left the company. She had an important part in the play, as we knew even before we saw her name in big letters on the posters.

Andre Maritz had been somewhat thoughtless, that time, in his choice of a play for his company to act in. The result was that there were some places that he had to go away from at a pace rather faster than could be made by even a good mule-team. Naturally, this sort of thing led to Andre Maritz's name getting pretty well known throughout the country – and without his having to stick up posters, either.

The trouble did not lie with the acting. There was not very much wrong with that. But anybody could have told Andre Maritz that he should never have toured the country with that kind of a play. There was a negro in it, called Uncle Tom, who was supposed to be very good and kind-hearted. Andre Maritz, with his face blackened, took that part. And there was also a white man in the play, named Simon Legree. He was the kind of white man who, if he was your neighbour, would think it funny to lead the Government tax-collector to the aardvark-hole that you were hiding in.

It seems that Andre Maritz had come across a play that had been popular on the other side of the sea; and he translated it into Afrikaans and adapted it to fit in with South African traditions. Andre Maritz's fault was that he hadn't adapted the play enough.

The company made this discovery in the very first Free State dorp

SLURRY
-STASIE-
ZASM
100
ZAS
Peter Badcock

they got to. For, when they left that town, Andre Maritz had one of his eyes blackened, and not just with burnt cork.

Andre Maritz adapted his play a good deal more, immediately after that. He made Uncle Tom into a much less kind-hearted negro. And he also made him steal chickens.

The only member of the company that the public of the backveld seemed to have any time for was the young man who acted Simon Legree.

Thus it came about that we heard of Andre Maritz's company when they were still far away, touring the highveld. Winding their play-actors' road northwards, past koppies and through vlaktes, and by blue gums and willows.

After a few more misunderstandings with the public, Andre Maritz so far adapted the play to South African conditions as to make Uncle Tom threaten to hit Topsy with a brandy bottle.

The result was that, by the time the company came to Zeerust, even the Church elder, Theunis van Zyl, said that there was much in the story of Uncle Tom that could be considered instructive.

True, there were still one or two little things, Elder van Zyl declared, that did not perhaps altogether accord with what was best in our outlook. For instance, it was not right that we should be made to feel so sentimental about the slave-girl as played by Hannekie Roodt. The elder was referring to that powerful scene in which Hannekie Roodt got sold down the river by Simon Legree. We couldn't understand very clearly what it meant to be sold down the river. But from Hannekie Roodt's acting we could see that it must be the most awful fate that could overtake anybody.

She was so quiet. She did not speak in that scene. She just picked up the small bundle containing her belongings. Then she put her hand up to her coat collar and closed over the lapel in front, even though the weather was not cold.

Yet there were still some people in Zeerust who, after they had attended the play on the first night, thought that that scene could be improved on. They said that when Hannekie Roodt walked off the stage for the last time, sold down the river, and carrying the bundle of her poor possessions tied up in a red-spotted rag, a few of her mistress's knives and forks could have been made to drop out of the bundle.

As I have said, Andre Maritz's company eventually arrived in Zeerust. They came by mule-cart from Slurry, where the railway ended in those days. They stayed at the Marico Hotel which was a few doors from Elder van Zyl's house. It was thus that Andre Maritz met Deborah, the daughter of the elder. That was one thing that occasioned a good deal of talk. Especially as we believed that even if Hannekie Roodt was not actually married to Andre Maritz in the eyes of the law, the two of them were nevertheless as nearly husband and wife as it is possible for play-actors to be, since they are known to be very unenlightened in such matters.

The other things that gave rise to much talk had to do with what happened on the first night of the staging of the play in Zeerust. Andre Maritz hired the old hall adjoining the mill. The hall had last been used two years before.

The result was that, after the curtain had gone up for the first act of Andre Maritz's play, it was discovered that a wooden platform above the stage was piled high with fine flour that had sifted through the ceiling from the mill next door. The platform had been erected by the stage company that had given a performance in the hall two years previously. That other company had used the platform to throw down bits of paper from to look like snow, in a scene in which a girl gets thrust out into the world with her baby in her arms.

At the end of the first act, when the curtain was lowered, Andre Maritz had the platform swept. But until then, with all that flour coming down, it looked as though he and his company were moving about the stage in a Cape mist. Each time an actor took a step forward or spoke too loudly – down would come a shower of fine meal. Afterwards the players took to standing in one place as much as possible, to avoid shaking down the flour – and in fear of losing their way in the mist, too, by the look of things.

Naturally, all this confused the audience a good deal. For, with the flour sifting down onto the faces of the actors, it became difficult, after a little while, to tell which were the white people in the play and which the negroes. Towards the end of the first act Uncle Tom, with a layer of flour covering his make-up, looked just as white as Simon Legree.

During the time that the curtain was lowered, however, the flour was swept from the platform and the actors repaired their faces very neatly, so that when the next act began there was nothing any more to remind us of that first unhappy incident.

Later on I was to think that it was a pity that the consequences of that *second* unhappy incident, that of Andre Maritz's meeting with the daughter of Elder van Zyl, could not also have been brushed away so tidily.

The play was nevertheless very successful. And I am sure that in the crowded hall that night there were few dry eyes when Hannekie

Roodt played her great farewell scene. When she picked up her bundle and got ready to leave, having been sold down the river, you could see by her stillness that her parting from her lover and her people would be forever. No one who saw her act that night would ever forget the tragic moment when she put her hand up to her coat collar and closed over the lapels in front, even though – as I have said – the weather was not cold.

The applause at the end lasted for many minutes.

The play got the same enthusiastic reception night after night. Meanwhile, off the stage, there were many stories linking Deborah van Zyl's name with Andre Maritz's.

"They say that Deborah van Zyl is going to be an actress now," Flip Welman said when several of us were standing smoking in the hardware store. "She is supposed to be getting Hannekie Roodt's part."

"We all know that Deborah van Zyl has been talking for a long while about going on the stage," Koos Steyn said. "And maybe this is the chance she has been waiting for. But I can't see her in Hannekie Roodt's part for very long. I think she will rather be like the girl in that other play we saw here a few years ago – the one with the baby."

Knowing what play-actors were, I could readily picture Deborah van Zyl being pushed out into the world, carrying a child in her arms, and with white paper-snow fluttering about her.

As for Hannekie Roodt, she shortly afterward left Andre Maritz's company of play-actors. She arranged with Koos Steyn to drive her, with her suitcases, to Slurry station. Koos explained to me that he was a married man and so he could not allow it to be said of him, afterwards, that he had driven alone in a cart with a play-actress. That was how it came about that I rode with them.

But Koos Steyn need have had no fears of the kind that he hinted at. Hannekie Roodt spoke hardly a word. At close hand she looked different from what she had done on the stage. Her hair was scraggy. I also noticed that her teeth were uneven and that there was loose skin at her throat.

Yet, there was something about her looks that was not without a strange sort of beauty. And in her presence there was that which made me think of great cities. There were also marks on her face from which you could tell that she had travelled a long road. A road that was longer than just the thousand miles from the Cape to the Marico.

Hannekie Roodt was going away from Andre Maritz. And during the whole of that long journey by mule-cart she did not once weep. I could not help but think that it was true what people said about play-actors. They had no real human feelings. They could act on the stage and bring tears to your eyes, but they themselves had no emotions.

We arrived at Slurry station. Hannekie Roodt thanked Koos Steyn and paid him. There was no platform there in those days. So Hannekie had to climb up several steps to get onto the balcony of the carriage. It was almost as though she were getting onto the stage. We lifted up her suitcases for her.

Koos Steyn and I returned to the mule-cart. Something made me look back over my shoulder. That was my last glimpse of Hannekie Roodt. I saw her put her hand up to her coat collar. She closed over the lapels in front. The weather was not cold.

GOD
IS
LIEFDE
Peter Bardcock

A BEKKERSDAL MARATHON

At Naudé, who had a wireless set, came into Jurie Steyn's voorkamer, where we were sitting waiting for the Government lorry from Bekkersdal, and gave us the latest news. He said that the newest thing in Europe was that young people there were going in for non-stop dancing. It was called marathon dancing, At Naudé told us, and those young people were trying to break the record for who could remain on their feet longest, dancing.

We listened for a while to what At Naudé had to say, and then we suddenly remembered a marathon event that had taken place in the little dorp of Bekkersdal - almost in our midst, you could say. What was more, there were quite a number of us sitting in Jurie Steyn's post office who had actually taken part in that non-stop affair, and without knowing that we were breaking records, and without expecting any sort of a prize for it, either.

We discussed that affair at considerable length and from all angles, and we were still talking about it when the lorry came. And we agreed that it had been in several respects an unusual occurrence. We also agreed that it was questionable whether we could have carried off things so successfully that day if it had not been for Billy Robertse.

You see, our organist at Bekkersdal was Billy Robertse. He had once been a sailor and had come to the Bushveld some years before, travelling on foot. His belongings, fastened in a red handkerchief, were slung over his shoulder on a stick. Billy Robertse was journeying in that fasion for the sake of his health. He suffered from an unfortunate complaint for which he had at regular intervals to drink something out of a black bottle that he always carried handy in his jacket pocket.

Billy Robertse would even keep that bottle beside him in the organist's gallery in case of a sudden attack. And if the hymn the predikant gave out had many verses, you could be sure that about halfway through Billy Robertse would bring the bottle up to his mouth, leaning sideways towards what was in it. And he would put several extra twirls into the second part of the hymn.

When he first applied for the position of organist in the Bekkersdal church, Billy Robertse told the meeting of deacons that he had learnt to play the organ in a cathedral in Northern Europe. Several deacons felt, then, that they could not favour his application. They said that the cathedral sounded too Papist, the way Billy Robertse described it, with a dome 300 ft. high and with marble apostles. But it was lucky for Billy Robertse that he was able to mention, at the following combined meeting of elders and deacons, that he had also played the piano in a South American dance-hall, of which the manager had been a Presbyterian. He asked the meeting to overlook his unfortunate past, saying that he had had a hard life, and anybody could make mistakes. In any case, he had never cared much for the Romish atmosphere of the cathedral, he said, and had been happier in the dance-hall.

In the end, Billy Robertse got the appointment. But in his sermons for several Sundays after that the predikant, Dominee Welthagen, had spoken very strongly against the evils of dance-halls. He described those places of awful sin in such burning words that at least one young man went to see Billy Robertse, privately, with a view to taking lessons in playing the piano.

But Billy Robertse was a good musician. And he took a deep interest in his work. And he said that when he sat down on the organist's stool behind the pulpit, and his fingers were flying over the keyboards, and he was pulling out the stops, and his feet were pressing down the notes that sent the deep bass tones through the pipes - then he felt that he could play all day, he said.

I don't suppose he guessed that he would one day be put to the test, however.

It all happened through Dominee Welthagen one Sunday morning going into a trance in the pulpit. And we did not realize that he was in a trance. It was an illness that overtook him in a strange and sudden fashion.

At each service the predikant, after reading a passage from the Bible, would lean forward with his hand on the pulpit rail and give out the number of the hymn we had to sing. For years his manner of conducting the service had been exactly the same. He would say, for instance: "We will now sing Psalm 82, verses 1 to 4." Then he would allow his head to sink forward onto his chest and he would remain rigid, as though in prayer, until the last notes of the hymn died away in the church.

Now, on that particular morning, just after he had announced the number of the psalm, without mentioning what verses, Dominee Welthagen again took a firm grip on the pulpit rail and allowed his head to sink forward onto his breast. We did not realize that he had fallen into a trance of a peculiar character that kept his body standing upright while his mind was a blank. We learnt that only later.

In the meantime, while the organ was playing over the opening bars, we began to realize that Dominee Welthagen had not indicated how many verses we had to sing. But he would discover his mistake, we thought, after we had been singing for a few minutes.

All the same, one or two of the younger members of the congregation did titter, slightly, when they took up their hymn-books. For Dominee Welthagen had given out Psalm 119. And everybody knows that Psalm 119 has 176 verses.

This was a church service that will never be forgotten in Bekkersdal.

We sang the first verse and then the second and then the third. When we got to about the sixth verse and the minister still gave no sign that it would be the last, we assumed that he wished us to sing the first eight verses. For, if you open your hymn-book, you'll see that Psalm 119 is divided into sets of eight verses, each ending with the word *"Pouse"*.

We ended the last notes of verse eight with more than an ordinary number of turns and twirls, confident that at any moment Dominee Welthagen would raise his head and let us know that we could sing *"Amen"*.

It was when the organ started up very slowly and solemnly with the music for verse nine that a real feeling of disquiet overcame the congregation. But, of course, we gave no sign of what went on in our minds. We held Dominee Welthagen in too much veneration.

Nevertheless, I would rather not say too much about our feelings, when verse followed verse and *Pouse* succeeded *Pouse*, and still Dominee Welthagen made no sign that we had sung long enough, or that there was anything unusual in what he was demanding of us.

After they had recovered from their first surprise, the members of the church council conducted themselves in a most exemplary manner. Elders and deacons tiptoed up and down the aisles, whispering words of reassurance to such members of the congregation, men as well as women, who gave signs of wanting to panic.

At one stage it looked as though we were going to have trouble from the organist. That was when Billy Robertse, at the end of the 34th verse, held up his black bottle and signalled quietly to the elders to indicate that his medicine had finished. At the end of the 35th verse he made signals of a less quiet character, and again at the end of the 36th verse. That was when Elder Landsman tiptoed out of the church and went round to the Konsistorie, where the Nagmaal wine was kept. When Elder Landsman came back into the church he had a long black bottle half-hidden under his *manel*. He took the bottle up to the organist's gallery, still walking on tiptoe.

At verse 61 there was almost a breakdown. That was when a message came from the back of the organ, where Koster Claassen and the assistant verger, whose task it was to turn the handle that kept the organ supplied with wind, were in a state near to exhaustion. So it was Deacon Cronje's turn to go tiptoeing out of the church. Deacon Cronje was head-warder at the local gaol. When he came back it was with three burly Native convicts in striped jerseys, who also went through the church on tiptoe. They arrived just in time to take over the handle from Koster Claassen and the assistant verger.

At verse 98 the organist again started making signals about his medicine. Once more Elder Landsman went round to the Konsistorie. This time he was accompanied by another elder and a deacon, and they stayed away somewhat longer than the time when Elder Landsman had gone on his own. On their return the deacon bumped into a small hymn-book table at the back of the church. Perhaps it was because the deacon was a fat, red-faced man, and not used to tiptoeing.

At verse 124 the organist signalled again, and the same three members of the church council filed out to the Konsistorie, the deacon walking in front this time.

It was about then that the pastor of the Full Gospel Apostolic Faith Church, about whom Dominee Welthagen had in the past used almost as strong language as about the Pope, came up to the front gate of the church to see what was afoot. He lived near our church and, having heard the same hymn-tune being played over and over for about eight hours, he was a very amazed man. Then he saw the door of the Konsistorie open, and two elders and a deacon coming out, walking on tiptoe - they having apparently forgotten that they were not in church, then. When the pastor saw one of the elders hiding a black bottle under his *manel*, a look of understanding came over his features. The pastor walked off, shaking his head.

At verse 152 the organist signalled again. This time Elder Landsman and the other elder went out alone. The deacon stayed behind in the deacon's bench, apparently in deep thought. The organist signalled again, for the last time, at verse 169. So you can imagine how many visits the two elders made to the Konsistorie altogether.

The last verse came, and the last line of the last verse. This time it had to be *Amen*. Nothing could stop it. I would rather not describe the state that the congregation was in. And by then the three Native convicts, red stripes and all, were, in the Bakhatla tongue, threatening mutiny. "Aa-m-e-e-n" came from what sounded like less than a score of voices, hoarse with singing.

The organ music ceased.

Maybe it was the sudden silence that at last brought Dominee Welthagen out of his long trance. He raised his head and looked slowly about him. His gaze travelled over his congregation, and then, looking at the windows, he saw that it was night. We understood right away what was going on in Dominee Welthagen's mind. He thought he had just come into the pulpit, and that this was the beginning of the evening service. We realized that, during all the time we had been singing, the predikant had been in a state of unconsciousness.

Once again Dominee Welthagen took a firm grip on the pulpit rail. His head again started drooping forward onto his breast. But before he went into a trance for the second time, he gave the hymn for the evening service.

"We will," Dominee Welthagen announced, "sing Psalm 119."

NEWS STORY

"The way the world is today," At Naudé said, shaking his head, "I don't know what is going to happen."

From that it was clear that At Naudé had been hearing news over the wireless again that made him fear for the future of the country. We did not exactly sit up, then. There was never any change, even in the kind of news he would bring us. Every time it was about stone-throwings in Johannesburg locations and about how many new kinds of bombs the Russians had got, and about how many people had gone to gaol for telling the Russians about still other kinds of bombs they could make. Although it did not look as though the Russians *needed* to be educated much in that line.

And we could never really understand why At Naudé listened at all. We hardly ever listened to *him*, for that matter. We would rather hear from Gysbert van Tonder if it was true that the ouderling at Pilansberg really forgot himself in the way that Jurie Steyn's wife had heard about from a kraal Mtosa at the kitchen door. The Mtosa had come to buy halfpenny stamps to stick on his forehead for the yearly Ndlolo dance. Now, there was news for you. About the ouderling, I mean. And even to hear that the Ndlolo dance was being held soon again was at least something. And if it should turn out that what was being said about the Pilansberg ouderling was not true, well, then, the same thing applied to a lot of what At Naudé heard over the wireless also.

"I don't know what is going to happen," At Naudé repeated, "the way the world is today. I just heard over the wireless ..."

"That's how the news we got in the old days was better," Oupa Bekker said. "I mean in the real old days, when there was no wireless, and there was not the telegraph, either. The news you got then you could do something with. And you didn't have to go to the post office and get it from a newspaper. The post office is the curse of the Transvaal ..."

Jurie Steyn said that Oupa Bekker was quite right, there. He himself would never have taken on the job of postmaster at Drogevlei if he had as much as guessed that there were four separate forms that he would have to fill in, each of them different, for a simple five-shilling money order. It would be so much brainier *en* neater, Jurie Steyn said, for people who wanted to send five shillings somewhere, if they would just wrap up a couple of half-crowns in a thick wad of brown paper and then post them in the ordinary way, like a letter. That was what the new red pillar-box in front of his door was *for*, Jurie Steyn explained. The authorities had gone to the expense of that new pillar-box in order to help the public. And yet you still found people coming in for postal orders and money orders. The other day a man even came in and asked could he telegraph some money somewhere.

"I gave that man a piece of brown paper and showed him the pillar-box," Jurie Steyn said. "It seemed, until then, that he did not know what kind of progress we had been making here. I therefore asked him if I could show him some more ways in regard to how advanced the Groot Marico was getting. But he said, no, the indications I had already given him were plenty."

Jurie Steyn said that he thought it was handsome of the man to have spoken up for the Marico like that, seeing that he was quite a new-comer to these parts.

Because we never knew how long Jurie Steyn would be when once he got on the subject of his work, we were glad when Johnny Coen asked Oupa Bekker to explain some more to us about how they got news in the old days. We were all pleased, that is, except At Naudé, who had again tried to get in a remark but had got no further than to say that if we knew something we would all shiver in our veldskoens.

"How did we get news?" Oupa Bekker said, replying to another question of Johnny Coen's. "Well, you would be standing in the lands, say, and then one of the Bechuanas would point to a small cloud of dust in the poort, and you would walk across to the big tree by the dam, where the road bends, and the traveller would come past there, with two *vos* horses in front of his Cape-cart, and he would get off from the cart and shake hands and say he was Du Plessis. And you would say you were Bekker, and he would say, afterwards, that he couldn't stay the night on your farm, because he had to get to Tsalala's Kop. Well, there was *news*. You could talk about if for days. For weeks even. You have got no idea how often my wife and I discussed it. And we knew everything that there was to know about the man. We knew his name was Du Plessis."

At Naudé said, then, that he did not think much of that sort of news. People must have been a bit 'simpel' in the head, in those old times that Oupa Bekker was talking about, if they thought anything of that sort of news. Why, if you compared it with what the radio announcer said, only yesterday ...

Jurie Steyn's wife came in from the kitchen at that moment. There was a light of excitement in her eyes. And when she spoke it was to none of us in particular.

"It has just occurred to me," Jurie Steyn's wife said, "that is, if it's *true* what they are saying about the Pilansberg ouderling, of course. Well, it has just struck me that, when he forgot himself in the way they say - provided that he *did* forget himself like that, mind you - well, perhaps the ouderling didn't know that anybody was looking."

That was a possibility that had not so far occurred to us, and we discussed it at some length. In between our talk At Naudé was blurting out something about the rays from a still newer kind of bomb that would kill you right in the middle of the veld and through fifty feet of concrete. So we said, of course, that the best thing to do would be to keep a pretty safe distance away from concrete, with those sort of rays about, if concrete was as dangerous as all that.

We were in no mood for foolishness. Oupa Bekker took this as an encouragement for him to go on.

"Or another day," Oupa Bekker continued, "you would again be standing in your lands, say, or sitting, even, if there was a long day of ploughing ahead, and you did not want to tire yourself out unnecessarily. You would be sitting on a stone in the shade of a tree, say, and you would think to yourself how lazy those Bechuanas look, going backwards and forwards, backwards and forwards, with the plough and the oxen, and you would get quite sleepy, say, thinking to yourself how lazy those Bechuanas are. If it wasn't for the oxen to keep them going, they wouldn't do any work at all, you might perhaps think.

"And then, without your in the least expecting it, you would again have news. And the news would find a stone for himself and come along and sit down right next to you. It would be the new veldkornet, say. And why nobody saw any dust in the poort, that time, was because the veldkornet didn't come along the road. And you would make a joke with him and say: 'I suppose that's why they call you a *veld*-kornet, because you don't travel along the road, but you come by the veld-*langers.*' And the veldkornet would laugh and ask you a few questions, and he would tell you that they had had good rains at Derdepoort ... Well, there was something that I could tell my wife over and over again, for weeks. It was news. For weeks I had that to think about. The visit of the veldkornet. In the old days it was real news."

We could see from the way At Naudé was fidgeting in his chair that he guessed we were just egging the old man on to talk, in order to scoff at all the important European news that he, At Naudé, regularly retailed to us, and that we were getting tired of.

After a while At Naudé could no longer contain himself.

"This second-childhood drivel that Oupa Bekker is talking," At Naudé announced, not looking at anybody in particular, but saying it to all of us, in the way Jurie Steyn's wife had spoken when she came out of the kitchen. "Well, I would actually sooner listen to scandal about the Pilansberg ouderling. There is at least some sort of meaning to it. I am not being unfriendly to Oupa Bekker, of course. I know it's just that he's old. But it's also quite clear to me that he doesn't know what news *is*, at all."

Jurie Steyn said that Oupa Bekker's news was at least more sensible than a man lying on the veld under fifty feet of concrete because of some rays. If a man were to lie under fifty feet of concrete he wouldn't be able to breathe, leave alone anything else.

In the meantime, Johnny Coen had been asking Oupa Bekker to tell us some more.

"On another day, say," Oupa Bekker would go on, "you would not be in your lands at all, but you would be sitting on your front stoep, drinking coffee, say. And the Cape-cart with the two *vos* horses in front would be coming down the road again, but in the opposite direction, going *towards* the poort, this time. And you would not see much of Du Plessis's face, because his hat would be pulled over his eyes. And the veldkornet would be sitting on the Cape-cart next to him, say."

Oupa Bekker paused. He paused for a while, too, holding a lighted match cupped over his pipe as though he was out in the veld where there was wind, and puffing vigorously.

"And my wife and I would go on talking about it for years afterwards, say," Oupa Bekker went on. "For years after Du Plessis was hanged, I mean."

STARLIGHT ON THE VELD

It was a cold night (Oom Schalk Lourens said), the stars shone with that frosty sort of light that you see on the wet grass some mornings, when you forget that it is winter, and you get up early, by mistake. The wind was like a girl sobbing out her story of betrayal to the stars.

Jan Ockerse and I had been to Derdepoort by donkey-cart. We came back in the evening. And Jan Ockerse told me of a road round the foot of a koppie that would be a short cut back to Drogevlei. Thus it was that we were sitting on the veld, close to the fire, waiting for the morning. We would then be able to ask a kafir to tell us a short cut back to the foot of that koppie.

"But I know that it was the right road," Jan Ockerse insisted, flinging another armful of wood on the fire.

"Then it must have been the wrong koppie," I answered, "or the wrong donkey-cart. Unless you also want me to believe that I am at this moment sitting at home, in my voorkamer."

The light from the flames danced frostily on the spokes of a cart-wheel, and I was glad to think that Jan Ockerse must be feeling as cold as I was.

"It is a funny sort of night," Jan Ockerse said, "and I am very miserable and hungry."

I was glad of that, too. I had begun to fear that he was enjoying himself.

"Do you know how high up the stars are?" Jan asked me next.

"No, not from here," I said, "but I worked it all out once, when I had a pencil. That was on the Highveld, though. But from where we are now, in the Lowveld, the stars are further away. You can see that they look smaller, too."

"Yes, I expect so," Jan Ockerse answered, "but a schoolteacher told me a different thing in the bar at Zeerust. He said that the star-gazers

Peter Badcock
Bottle?
BECAUSE THEY WILL HAVE
OHLSSON'S

work out how far away a star is by the number of years that it takes them to find it in their telescopes. This schoolteacher dipped his finger in the brandy and drew a lot of pictures and things on the bar counter, to show me how it was done. But one part of his drawings always dried up on the counter before he had finished doing the other part with his finger. He said that was the worst of that dry sort of brandy. Yet, he didn't finish his explanation, because the barmaid came and wiped it all off with a rag. Then the schoolteacher told me to come with him and he would use the blackboard in the other classroom. But the barmaid wouldn't allow us to take our glasses into the private bar, and the schoolteacher fell down just about then, too."

"He seems to be one of that new kind of schoolteacher," I said, "the kind that teaches the children that the earth turns round the sun. I am surprised they didn't sack him."

"Yes," Jan Ockerse answered, "they did."

I was glad to hear that also.

It seemed that there was a water-hole near where we were outspanned. For a couple of jackals started howling mournfully. Jan Ockerse jumped up and piled more wood on the fire.

"I don't like these wild animal noises," he said.

"They are only jackals, Jan," I said.

"I know," he answered, "but I was thinking of our donkeys. I don't want our donkeys to get frightened."

Suddenly a deep growl came to us from out of the dark bush. And it didn't sound a particularly mournful growl, either. Jan Ockerse worked very fast then with the wood.

"Perhaps it would be even better if we made two fires, and lay down between them," Jan Ockerse said, "our donkeys will feel less frightened if they see that you and I are safe. You know how a donkey's mind works."

The light of the fire shone dimly on the skeletons of the tall trees that the white ants had eaten, and we soon had two fires going. By the time that the second deep roar from the bush reached us, I had made an even bigger fire than Jan Ockerse, for the sake of the donkeys.

Afterwards it got quiet again. There was only the stirring of the wind in the thorn branches, and the rustling movement of things that you hear in the bushveld at night.

Jan Ockerse lay on his back and put his hands under his head, and once more looked up at the stars.

"I have heard that these stars are worlds, just like ours," he said, "and that they have got people living on them even."

"I don't think they would be good for growing mealies on, though," I answered, "they look too high up. Like the range of the Sneeuberge, in the Cape. But I suppose they would make quite a good horse and cattle country. That's the trouble with these low-lying districts, like the Marico and the Waterberg: there is too much horse-sickness and tsetse-fly here."

"And butterflies," Jan Ockerse said sleepily, "with gold wings."

I also fell asleep shortly afterwards. And when I woke up again the fires were almost dead. I got up and fetched more wood. It took me quite a while to wake Jan Ockerse, though. Because the veldskoens I was wearing were the wrong kind, and had soft toes. Eventually he sat up and rubbed his eyes; and he said, of course, that he had been lying awake all night. What made him so certain that he had not been asleep, he said, was that he was imagining all the time that he was chasing blue-bottles amongst the stars.

"And I would have caught up with them, too," he added, "only a queer sort of thing happened to me while I was jumping from one star to another. It was almost as though somebody was kicking me."

Jan Ockerse looked at me in a suspicious kind of way.

So I told him that it was easy to see that he had been dreaming.

When the fires were piled high with wood, Jan Ockerse again said that it was a funny night, and once more started talking about the stars.

"What do you think sailors do at sea, Schalk," he said, "if they don't know the way and there aren't any other ships around from whom they can ask?"

"They have got it all written down on a piece of paper with a lot of red and blue on it," I answered, "and there are black lines that show you the way from Cape Town to St. Helena. And figures to tell you how many miles down the ship will go if it sinks. I went to St. Helena during the Boer War. You can live in a ship just like an ox-wagon. Only, a ship isn't so comfortable, of course. And it is further between outspans."

"I heard, somewhere, that sailors find their way by the stars," Jan Ockerse said, "I wonder what people want to tell me things like that for."

He lay silent for a while, looking up at the stars and thinking.

"I remember one night when I stood on Annie Steyn's stoep and spoke to her about the stars," Jan Ockerse said later, "I was going to trek with the cattle to the Limpopo because of the drought. I told Annie that I would be away until the rains came, and I told her that every night when I was gone, she had to look at a certain star and think of me. I showed her which star. Those three stars there, that are close together in a straight line. She had to remember me by the middle one, I said. But Annie explained that Willem Mostert, who had trekked to the Limpopo about a week before, had already picked that middle star for her to remember him by. So I said, all right, the top star would do. But Annie said that one already belonged to Stoffel Brink. In the end I agreed that she could remember me by the bottom star, and Annie was still saying that she would look at the lower one of those three stars every night and think of me, when her father, who seemed to have been listening behind the door, came onto the stoep and said: 'What about cloudy nights?' in what he supposed was a clever sort of way."

"What happened then?" I asked Jan Ockerse.

"Annie was very annoyed," he replied, "she told her father that he was always spoiling things. She told him that he wasn't a bit funny, really, especially as I was the third young man to whom he had said the same thing. She said that no matter how foolish a young man might be, her father had no right to make jokes like that in front of him. It was good to hear the way that Annie stood up for me. Anyway, what followed was a long story. I came across Willem Mostert and Stoffel Brink by the Limpopo. And we remained together there for several months. And it must have been an unusual sight for a stranger to see three young men sitting round the camp fire, every night, looking up at the stars. We got friendly, after a while, and when the rains came the three of us trekked back to Marico. And I found, then, that Annie's father had been right. About the cloudy nights I mean. For I understood that it was on just such a sort of night that Annie had run off to Johannesburg with a bywoner who was going to look for work on the mines."

Jan Ockerse sighed and returned to his thinking.

But with all the time that we had spent in talking and sleeping, most of the night had slipped away. We kept only one fire going now, and Jan Ockerse and I took turns in putting on the wood. It gets very cold just before dawn, and we were both shivering.

"Anyway," Jan Ockerse said after a while, "now you know why I am interested in stars. I was a young man when this happened. And I have told very few people about it. About seventeen people, I should say. The others wouldn't listen. But always, on a clear night, when I see those bright stars in a row, I look for a long time at the lowest star, and there seems to be something very friendly about the way it shines. It seems to be my star, and its light is different from the light of the other stars ... and you know, Schalk, Annie Steyn had such red lips. And such long, soft hair, Schalk. And there was that smile of hers."

Afterwards the stars grew pale and we started rounding up the donkeys and got ready to go. And I wondered what Annie Steyn would have thought of it, if she had known that during all those years there was this man, looking up at the stars on nights when the sky was clear, and dreaming about her lips and her hair and her smile. But as soon as I reflected about it, I knew what the answer was also. Of course, Annie Steyn would think nothing of Jan Ockerse. Nothing at all. And, no doubt, Annie Steyn was right.

But it was strange to think that we had passed a whole night in talking about the stars. And I did not know, until then, that it was all on account of a love story of long ago.

We climbed onto the cart and set off to look for the way home.

"I know that schoolteacher in the Zeerust bar was all wrong," Jan Ockerse said finally, "when he tried to explain how far away the stars are. The lower of those three stars - ah, it has just faded – is very near to me. Yes, it is near."

THE SELONS-ROSE

Any story (Oom Schalk Lourens said) about that half-red flower, the selons-rose, must be an old story. It is the flower that a Marico girl most often pins in her hair to attract her lover. The selons-rose is also the flower that here, in the Marico, we customarily plant upon a grave.

One thing that certain thoughtless people sometimes hint at about my stories is that nothing ever seems to happen in them. Then there is another kind of person who goes even further, and he says that the stories I tell are all stories that he has heard before, somewhere long ago – he can't remember when, exactly, but somewhere at the back of his mind he knows that it is not a new story.

I have heard that remark passed quite often – which is not surprising, seeing that I really don't know any new stories. But the funny part of it is that these very people will come around, say, ten years later, and ask me to tell them another story. And they will say, then, because of what they have learnt of life in between, that the older the better.

Anyway, I have come to the conclusion that with an old story it is like with an old song. People tire of a new song readily. I remember how it was when Marie Dupreez came back to the Bushveld after her parents had sent her overseas to learn singing, because they had found diamonds on their farm, and because Marie's teacher said she had a nice singing voice. Then, when Marie came back from Europe – through the diamonds on the Dupreez farm having given out suddenly – we on this side of the Dwarsberge were keen to have Marie sing for us.

There was a large attendance, that night, when Marie Dupreez gave a concert in the Drogedal schoolroom. She sang what she called arias from Italian opera. And at first things didn't go at all well. We didn't

Peter Badcock

care much for those new songs in Italian. One song was about the dawn being near, goodbye beloved and about being under somebody's window – that was what Marie's mother told us, in quick whispers, it was. Marie Dupreez's mother came from the Cape and had studied at the Wellington seminary. Another song was about mother see these tears. The Hollander schoolmaster told me the meaning of that one. But I don't know if it was Marie's mother that was meant.

We didn't actually dislike those songs that Marie Dupreez sang. It was only that we weren't moved by them.

Accordingly, after the interval, when Marie was again stepping up onto the low platform before the blackboard on which the teacher wrote sums on school-days, Philippus Bonthuys, a farmer who had come all the way from Nietverdiend to attend the concert, got up and stood beside Marie Dupreez. And because he was so tall and broad it seemed almost as though he stood half in front of her, elbowing her a little, even.

Philippus Bonthuys said he was just a plain Dopper. And we all cheered. Then Philippus Bonthuys said that his grandfather was also just a plain Dopper, who wore his pipe and his tobacco-bag on a piece of string fastened at the side of his trousers. We cheered a lot more, then. Philippus Bonthuys went on to say that he liked the old songs best. They could keep those new songs about laugh because somebody has stolen your clown. We gathered from that that Marie's mother had been explaining to Philippus Bonthuys, also in quick whispers, the meanings of some of Marie's songs.

And before we knew where we were, the whole crowd in the schoolroom was singing, with Philippus Bonthuys beating time, "My Oupa was 'n Dopper, en 'n Dopper was hy". You've got no idea how stirring that old song sounded, with Philippus Bonthuys beating time, in the night, under the thatch of that Marico schoolroom, and with Marie Dupreez looking slightly bewildered but joining in all the same – since it was her concert, after all – and not singing in Italian, either.

We sang many songs, after that, and they were all old songs. We sang "Die Vaal Hare en die Blou Oge" and "Daar Waar die Son en die Maan Ondergaan" and "Vat Jou Goed en Trek, Ferreira" and "Met My Rooi Rok Voor Jou Deur". It was very beautiful.

We sang until late into the night. Afterwards, when we congratulated Marie Dupreez's mother, who had arranged it all, on the success of her daughter's concert, Mevrou Dupreez said it was nothing, and she smiled. But it was a peculiar sort of a smile.

I felt that she must have smiled very much in the same way when she was informed that the diamond mine on the Dupreez farm was only an alluvial gravel-bed, and not a pipe, like in Kimberley.

Now, Marie Dupreez had not been out of the Marico very long. All told, I don't suppose she had been in Europe for more than six months before the last shovelful of diamondiferous gravel went through Dupreez's sieve. By the time she got back, her father was so desperate that he was even trying to sift ordinary Transvaal red clay. But Marie's visit overseas had made her restive.

That, of course, is something that I can't understand. I have also been to foreign parts. During the Boer War I was a prisoner on St. Helena. And I was twice in Johannesburg. And one thing about St. Helena is that there were no Uitlanders on it. There were just Boers and English and Coloureds and Indians, like you come across here in the Marico. There were none of those all-sorts that you've got to push past on Johannesburg pavements. And each time I got back to my own farm, and I could sit on my stoep and fill my pipe with honest Magaliesberg tobacco, I was pleased to think I was away from all that sin that you read about in the Bible.

But with Marie Dupreez it was different.

Marie Dupreez, after she came back from Europe, spoke a great deal about how unhappy a person with a sensitive nature could be over certain aspects of life in the Marico.

We were not unwilling to agree with her.

"When I woke up that morning at Nietverdiend," Willie Prinsloo said to Marie during a party at the Dupreez homestead, "and found I couldn't inspan my oxen because during the night the Mlapi kafirs had stolen my trek-chain – well, to a person with a sensitive nature, I can't tell you how unhappy I felt about the Marico."

Marie said that was the sort of thing that made her ill, almost.

"It's always the same kind of conversation that you have to listen to, day in and day out," Marie Dupreez said. "A farmer outspans his oxen for the night. And next morning, when he has to move on, the kafirs have stolen his trek-chain. I don't know how often I have heard that same story. Why can't something different ever happen? Why can't the kafirs think of stealing something else, for a change?"

"Yes," Jurie Bekker interjected, quickly, "why can't they steal a clown, say?"

Thereupon Marie explained that it was not a clown that had got stolen in the Italian song that she sang in the schoolroom, but a girl who had belonged to a clown. And so several of us said, speaking at the same time, that she couldn't have been much of a girl, anyway, belonging to a clown. We said we might be behind the times and so forth, here in the Bushveld, but we had seen clowns in the circus in Zeerust, and we could imagine what a clown's girl must be like, with her nose painted all red.

I must admit, however, that we men enjoyed Marie's wild talk. We preferred it to her singing, anyway. And the women also listened quite indulgently.

Shortly afterwards Marie Dupreez made a remark that hurt me, a little.

"People here in the Marico say all the same things over and over again," Marie announced. "Nobody ever says anything new. You all talk just like the people in Oom Schalk Lourens' stories. Whenever we have visitors it's always the same thing. If it's a husband and wife, it will be the man who first starts talking. And he'll say that his Afrikaner cattle are in a bad way with the heart-water. Even though he drives his cattle straight out onto the veld with the first frost, and he keeps to regular seven-day dipping, he just can't get rid of the heart-water ticks."

Marie Dupreez paused. None of us said anything, at first. I only know that for myself I thought this much: I thought that, even though I dip my cattle only when the Government inspector from Onderstepoort is in the neighbourhood, I still lose just as many Afrikaner beasts from the heart-water as any of the farmers hereabouts who go in for the seven-day dipping.

"They should dip the Onderstepoort inspector every seven days," Jurie Bekker called out suddenly, expressing all our feelings.

"And they should drive the Onderstepoort inspector straight out onto the veld with the first frost," Willie Prinsloo added.

We got pretty well worked up, I can tell you.

"And it's the same with the women," Marie Dupreez went on. "Do they ever discuss books or fashions or music? No. They also talk just like those simple Boer women that Oom Schalk Lourens' head is so full of. They talk about the amount of Kalahari sand that the Indian in the store at Ramoutsa mixed with the last bag of yellow sugar they bought off him. You know, I have heard that same thing so often, I am surprised there is any sand at all left in the Kalahari desert, the way that Indian uses it all up."

Those of us who were in the Dupreez voorkamer that evening, in spite of our amusement, also felt sad at the thought of how Marie Dupreez had altered from her natural self, like a seedling that has been transplanted too often in different kinds of soil.

But we felt that Marie should not be blamed too much. For one thing, her mother had been taught at that woman's college at the Cape. And her father had also got his native knowledge of the soil pretty well mixed up, in his own way. It was said that he was by now even trying to find diamonds in the *turfgrond* on his farm. I could just imagine how that must be clogging up his sieves.

"One thing I am glad about, though," Marie said after a pause, "is that since my return from Europe I have not yet come across a Marico girl who wears a selons-rose in her hair to make herself look more attractive to a young man – as happens time after time in Oom Schalk's stories."

This remark of Marie's gave a new turn to the conversation, and I felt relieved. For a moment I had feared that Marie Dupreez was also becoming addicted to the kind of Bushveld conversation that she complained about, and that she, too, was beginning to say the same thing over and over again.

Several women started talking, after that, about how hard it was to get flowers to grow in the Marico, on account of the prolonged droughts. The most they could hope for was to keep a bush of selons-roses alive near the kitchen door. It was a flower that seemed, if anything, to thrive on harsh sunlight and soapy dish-water and Marico earth, the women said.

Some time later we learnt that Theunis Dupreez, Marie's father, was giving up active farming, because of his rheumatics. Through having spent so much time in all kinds of weather, we said, walking about the vlei in search of a new kind of sticky soil to put through his sieves.

Consequently, Theunis Dupreez engaged a young fellow, Joachem Bonthuys, to come and work on his farm as a bywoner. Joachem was a nephew of Philippus Bonthuys, and I was at the post office when he arrived at Drogedal, on the lorry from Zeerust, with Theunis Dupreez and his daughter, Marie, there to meet him.

Joachem Bonthuys's appearance was not very prepossessing, I thought. He shook hands somewhat awkwardly with the farmers who had come to meet the lorry to collect their milk-cans. Joachem did not seem to have much to say for himself, either, until Theunis Dupreez, his new employer, asked him what his journey up from Zeerust had been like.

"The veld is dry all the way," he replied. "And I've never seen so much heart-water in Afrikaner herds. They should dip their cattle every seven days."

Joachem Bonthuys spoke at great length, then, and I could not help smiling to myself when I saw Marie Dupreez turn away. In that moment my feelings also grew warmer towards Joachem. I felt that, at all events, he was not the kind of young man who would go and sing foreign songs under a respectable Boer girl's window.

All this brings me back to what I was saying about an old song and an old story. For it was quite a while before I again had occasion to visit the Dupreez farm. And when I sat smoking on the stoep with Theunis Dupreez it was just like an old story to hear him talk about his rheumatics.

Marie came out onto the stoep with a tray to bring us our coffee. – Yes, you've heard all that before, the same sort of thing. The same stoep. The same tray. – And for that reason, when she held the glass bowl out towards me, Marie Dupreez apologised for the yellow sugar.

"It's full of Kalahari sand, Oom Schalk," she said. "It's that Indian at Ramoutsa."

And when she turned to go back into the kitchen, leaving two old men to their stories, it was not difficult for me to guess who the young man was for whom she was wearing a half-red flower in her hair.

DOPPER AND PAPIST

It was a cold night (Oom Schalk Lourens said) on which we drove with Gert Bekker in his Cape-cart to Zeerust. I sat in front, next to Gert, who was driving. In the back seat were the predikant, Rev. Vermooten, and his ouderling, Isak Erasmus, who were on their way to Pretoria for the meeting of the synod of the Dutch Reformed Church. The predikant was lean and hawk-faced; the ouderling was fat and had broad shoulders.

Gert Bekker and I did not speak. We had been transport-drivers together in our time, and we had learnt that when it is two men alone, travelling over a long distance, it is best to use few words, and those well chosen. Two men, alone in each other's company, understand each other better the less they speak.

The horses kept up a good, steady trot. The lantern, swinging from side to side with the jogging of the cart, lit up stray patches of the uneven road and made bulky shadows rise up among the thorn-trees. In the back seat the predikant and the ouderling were discussing theology.

"You never saw such a lot of brand-siek sheep in your life," the predikant was saying, "as what Chris Haasbroek brought along as tithe."

We then came to a stony part of the road, and so I did not hear the ouderling's reply; but afterwards, above the rattling of the cart-wheels, I caught other snatches of God-fearing conversation, to do with the raising of pew rents.

From there the predikant started discussing the proselytizing activities being carried on among the local Bapedi kafirs by the Catholic mission at Vleisfontein. The predikant dwelt particularly on the ignorance of the Bapedi tribes and on the idolatrous form of the Papist Communion service, which was quite different from the Protestant

Peter Badcock

Peter Badcock

Nagmaal, the predikant said, although to a Bapedi, walking with his buttocks sticking out, the two services might, perhaps, seem somewhat alike.

Rev. Vermooten was very eloquent when he came to denouncing the heresies of Catholicism. And he spoke loudly, so that we could hear him on the front seat. And I know that both Gert Bekker and I felt very good, then, deep inside us, to think that we were Protestants. The coldness of the night and the pale flickering of the lantern-light among the thorn-trees gave an added solemnity to the predikant's words.

I felt that it might perhaps be all right to be a Catholic if you were walking on a Zeerust sidewalk in broad daylight, say. But it was a different matter to be driving through the middle of the bush on a dark night, with just a swinging lantern fastened to the side of a Cape-cart with baling-wire. If the lantern went out suddenly, and you were left in the loneliest part of the bush, striking matches, then it must be a very frightening thing to be a Catholic, I thought.

This led me to thinking of Piet Reilly and his family, who were Afrikaners, like you and me, except that they were Catholics. Piet Reilly even brought out his vote for General Lemmer at the last Volksraad election, which we thought would make it unlucky for our candidate. But General Lemmer said no, he didn't mind how many Catholics voted for him. A Catholic's vote was, naturally, not as good as a Dopper's, he said, but the little cross that had to be made behind a candidate's name cast out the evil that was of course otherwise lurking in a Catholic's ballot paper. And General Lemmer must have been right, because he got elected, that time.

While I was thinking on those lines, it suddenly struck me that Piet Reilly was now living on a farm about six miles on the bushveld side of Sephton's Nek, and that we would be passing his farmhouse, which was near the road, just before daybreak. It was comforting to think that we would have the predikant and the ouderling in the Cape-cart with us, when we passed the homestead of Piet Reilly, a Catholic, in the dark.

I tried to hear what the predikant was saying, in the back seat, to the ouderling. But the predikant was once more dealing with an abstruse point of religion, and had lowered his voice accordingly. I could catch only fragments of the ouderling's replies.

"Yes, dominie," I heard the ouderling affirm, "you are quite right. If he again tries to overlook your son for the job of anthrax inspector, then you must make it clear to the Chairman of the Board that you have all that information about his private life ..."

I realized then that you could find much useful guidance for your everyday problems in the conversation of holy men.

The night got colder and darker.

The palm of my hand, pressed tight around the bowl of my pipe, was the only part of me that felt warm. My teeth began to chatter. I wished that, next time we stopped to let the horses blow, we could light a fire and boil coffee. But I knew that there was no coffee left in the chest under the back seat.

While I sat silent next to Gert Bekker, I continued to think of Piet Reilly and his wife and children. With Piet, of course, I could understand it. He himself had merely kept up the religion – if you could call what the Catholics believe in a religion – that he had inherited from his father and his grandfather. But there was Piet Reilly's wife, Gertruida, now. She had been brought up a respectable Dopper girl. She was one of the Drogedal Bekkers, and was, in fact, distantly related to Gert Bekker, who was sitting on the Cape-cart next to me. There was something for you to ponder about, I thought to myself, with the cold all the time looking for new places in my skin through which to strike into my bones.

The moment Gertruida met Piet Reilly she forgot all about the sacred truths she had learnt at her mother's knee. And on the day she got married she was saying prayers to the Virgin Mary on a string of beads, and was wearing a silver cross at her throat that was as soft and white as the roses she held pressed against her. Here was now a sweet Dopper girl turned Papist.

As I have said, I knew that there was no coffee left in the box under the back seat; but I did know that under the front seat there was a full bottle of raw peach brandy. In fact, I could see the neck of the bottle protruding from between Gert Bekker's ankles.

I also knew, through all the years of transport-driving that we had done together, that Gert Bekker had already, over many miles of road, been thinking how we could get the cork off the bottle without the predikant and the ouderling shaking their heads reprovingly. And the way he managed it in the end was, I thought, highly intelligent.

For, when he stopped the cart again to rest the horses, he alighted beside the road and held out the bottle to our full view.

"There is brandy in this bottle, dominie," Gert Bekker said to the predikant, "that I keep for the sake of the horses on cold nights, like now. It is an old Marico remedy for when horses are in danger of getting the *floute*. I take a few mouthfuls of the brandy, which I then blow into the nostrils of the horses, who don't feel the cold so much, after that. The brandy revives them."

Gert commenced blowing brandy into the face of the horse on the near side, to show us.

Then he beckoned to me, and I also alighted and went and stood next to him, taking turns with him in blowing brandy into the eyes and nostrils of the offside horse. We did this several times.

The predikant asked various questions, to show how interested he was in this old-fashioned method of overcoming fatigue in draught animals. But what the predikant said at the next stop made me perceive that he was more than a match for a dozen men like Gert Bekker in point of astuteness.

When we stopped the cart, the predikant held up his hand.

"Don't you and your friend trouble to get off this time," the predikant called out when Gert Bekker was once more reaching for the bottle, "the ouderling and I have decided to take turns with you in blowing brandy into the horses' faces. We don't want to put all the hard work onto your shoulders."

We made several more halts after that, with the result that daybreak found us still a long way from Sephton's Nek. In the early dawn we saw the thatched roof of Piet Reilly's house through the thorn-trees some distance from the road. When the predikant suggested that we call at the homestead for coffee, we explained to him that the Reillys were Catholics.

"But isn't Piet Reilly's wife a relative of yours?" the predikant asked of Gert Bekker. "Isn't she your second cousin, or something?"

"They are Catholics," Gert answered.

"Coffee," the predikant insisted.

"Catholics," Gert Bekker repeated stolidly.

The upshot of it was, naturally enough, that we outspanned shortly afterwards in front of the Reilly homestead. That was the kind of man that the predikant was in an argument.

"The coffee will be ready soon," the predikant said as we walked up to the front door. "There is smoke coming out of the chimney."

Almost before we had stopped knocking, Gertruida Reilly had opened both the top and bottom doors. She started slightly when she saw, standing in front of her, a minister of the Dutch Reformed Church. In spite of her look of agitation, Gertruida was still pretty, I thought, after ten years of being married to Piet Reilly.

When she stepped forward to kiss her cousin, Gert Bekker, I saw him turn away, sadly; and I realized something of the shame that she had brought on her whole family through her marriage to a Catholic.

"You looked startled when you saw me, Gertruida," the predikant said, calling her by her first name, as though she was still a member of his congregation.

"Yes," Gertruida answered. "Yes – I was – surprised."

"I suppose it was a Catholic priest that you wanted to come to your front door," Gert Bekker said, sarcastically. Yet there was a tone in his voice that was not altogether unfriendly.

"Indeed, I was expecting a Catholic priest," Gertruida said, leading us into the voorkamer. "But if the Lord has sent the dominie and his ouderling, instead, I am sure it will be well, also."

It was only then, after she had explained to us what had happened, that we understood why Gertruida was looking so troubled. Her eight-year-old daughter had been bitten by a snake; they couldn't tell from the fang-marks if it was a ringhals or a bakkop. Piet Reilly had driven off in the mule-cart to Vleisfontein, the Catholic Mission Station, for a priest.

They had cut open and cauterized the wound and had applied red permanganate. The rest was a matter for God. And that was why, when she saw the predikant and the ouderling at her front door, Gertruida believed that the Lord had sent them.

I was glad that Gert Bekker did not at that moment think of mentioning that we had really come for coffee.

"Certainly, I shall pray for your little girl's recovery," the predikant said to Gertruida. "Take me to her."

Gertruida hesitated.

"Will you – will you pray for her the Catholic way, dominie?" Gertruida asked.

Now it was the predikant's turn to draw back.

"But, Gertruida," he said, "you, you whom I myself confirmed in the Enkel-Gereformeerde Kerk in Zeerust – how can you now ask me such a thing? Did you not learn in the catechism that the Romish ritual is a mockery of the Holy Ghost?"

"I married Piet Reilly," Gertruida answered simply, "and his faith is my faith. Piet has been very good to me, Father. And I love him."

We noticed that Gertruida called the predikant "Father", now, and not "Dominie". During the silence that followed, I glanced at the candle burning before an image of the Mother Mary in a corner of the voorkamer. I looked away quickly from that unrighteousness.

The predikant's next words took us by complete surprise.

"Have you got some kind of a prayer-book," the predikant asked, "that sets out the – the Catholic form for a ..."

"I'll fetch it from the other room," Gertruida answered.

When she had left, the predikant tried to put our minds at ease.

"I am only doing this to help a mother in distress," he explained to the ouderling. "It is something that the Lord will understand. Gertruida was brought up a Dopper girl. In some ways she is still one of us. She does not understand that I have no authority to conduct this Catholic service for the sick."

The ouderling was going to say something.

But at that moment Gertruida returned with a little black book that you could almost have taken for a Dutch Reformed Church psalm-book. Only, I knew that what was printed inside it was as iniquitous as the candle burning in the corner.

Yet I also began to wonder if, in not knowing the difference, a Bapedi really was so very ignorant, even though he walked with his buttocks sticking out.

"My daughter is in this other room," Gertruida said, and started in the direction of the door. The predikant followed her. Just before entering the bedroom he turned round and faced the ouderling.

"Will you enter with me, Brother Erasmus?" the predikant asked.

The ouderling did not answer. The veins stood out on his forehead. On his face you could read the conflict that went on inside him. For what seemed a very long time he stood quite motionless. Then he stooped down to the rusbank for his hat – which he did not need – and walked after the predikant into the bedroom.

THE PICTURE OF GYSBERT JONKER

This tobacco-bag, now (Oom Schalk Lourens said, producing a four-ounce linen bag with the picture on it of a leaping blesbuck – the trade-mark of a well-known tobacco company), well, it is very unusual, the way this tobacco-bag picture fits into the life story of Gysbert Jonker.

I had occasion to think of that only the other day, when at the Zeerust bioscope during the last Nagmaal they showed a film about an English lord who had his portrait painted. And it seemed that after that only the portrait changed, with the years, as the lord grew older and more sinful.

Some of the young people, when they got back from the bioscope, came and called on me, on the kerk-plein, and told me what a good film it was. A few of them hinted that I ought also to go to the bioscope, now and again – say, once in two years, or so – to get new ideas for my stories.

Koos Steyn's younger son, Frikkie, even went so far as to say, straight out, that I should go oftener than just once every two years. A good deal oftener. And that I shouldn't see the same film through more than once, either.

"Important things are happening in the world, Oom Schalk," young Frikkie said. "You know, culture and all that. That's why you should go to a film like the one we have just seen. A film with artists in it, and all."

"Yes, artists," another young fellow said. "Like an artist that got pointed out to me last time I was in Johannesburg. With his wide hat and his corduroy trousers, he looked just like a Marico farmer, except that his beard was too wild. We don't grow our beards so long in these parts, any more, since that new threshing-machine with the wide hopper came in. That machine is so quick."

"That is the trouble with your stories, Oom Schalk," Frikkie Steyn continued. "The Boers in them all grew their beards too long. And the uppers of their veldskoens have got an old-fashioned look. Why can't you bring into your next story a young man with a pair of brown shop boots on, and" – hitching his pants up and looking down – "yellow and pink striped socks with a –"

"And a waistcoat with long points coming over the top part of the trousers," another young man interrupted him. "And braces with clips that you can make longer or shorter, just as you like."

Anyway, after Theunis Malan had demonstrated to me the difference between a loose and an attached collar, and then couldn't find his stud, and after an ouderling had come past just when another young man was using bad language because he couldn't get his head out through his shirt again – through somebody else having thoughtfully tied the shirt-tails together while the young man was explaining about a new kind of underwear – well, there wasn't much about their new Nagmaal clothes that these young men wanted me to leave out of my next story. And the ouderling, without knowing what was going on, and without trying to find out, even, merely shook his head solemnly as he went past.

And, of course, Frikkie Steyn, just to make sure I had it right, told the bioscope story of the English lord all over again – all the time that I was filling my pipe from a quarter-pound bag of Magaliesberg tobacco; the sort with the picture of the high-bounding blesbuck on it.

So I thought, well, maybe Gysbert was not an English lord. But I could remember the time when his portrait, painted in the most beautiful colours, hung in his voorkamer. And I also thought of the way in which Gysbert's portrait was on display on every railway platform and in every Indian shop in the country. And almost until the very end the portrait remained unchanged. It was only Gysbert Jonker who, despite all his efforts, altered with the years. But when the portrait did eventually change, it was a much more incredible transformation than anything that could have happened to the portrait of that lord in the bioscope story.

It was while we were sitting in the Indian store at Ramoutsa drinking coffee and waiting for the afternoon to get cool enough for us to be able to drive back home by mule and donkey-cart, that we first noticed the resemblance.

Our conversation was, as usual, of an edifying character. We spoke about how sensible we were to go on sitting in the Indian store, hour after hour, like that, and drinking coffee, instead of driving out in the hot sun, and running the risk of getting sunstroke. Later on when some clouds came up, we were even more glad that we had not ventured out in our open carts, because everybody knows that the worst kind of sunstroke is what you get when the sun shines onto the back of your head through the clouds.

Of course, there were other forms of conveyance, such as Cape-carts, we said. But that sort of thing only undermined you. Naturally, we did not wish to be undermined. We spoke about how the younger generation was losing its self-reliance through – and we started naming some of the things we saw on the shelves around us. Gramophones, we said. And paraffin candles in packets, we said, instead of making our own. And tubes with white grease that you squeeze at the end to polish your plates and spoons with, one of us said. No, it was to brush your teeth with, somebody else interrupted him. And we said that, well, whatever it was for, it was undermining. And we said that our own generation was being sapped, also.

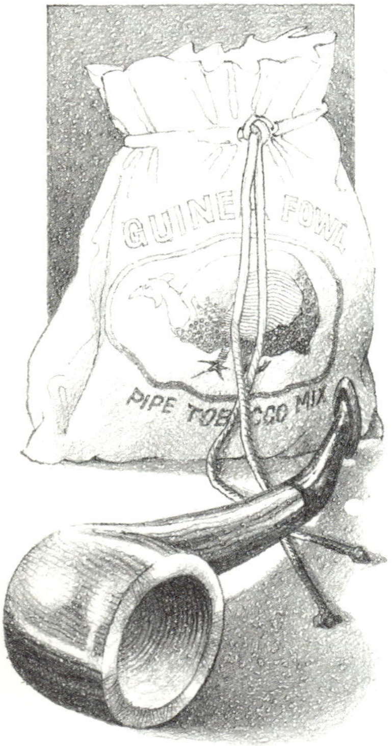

After we had asked the Indian behind the counter to stand to one side, so that we could see better how we were being undermined, Hans Bekker pointed to a shelf holding tins of coffee. "Formerly we burnt and ground our own coffee," Hans Bekker said. "Today –"

"Before I could walk," Andries Claassens said, "I used to shred my own tobacco from a black roll. I could cut up plug tobacco for my pipe before I could sharpen a slate-pencil. But now I have to sit with this little bag –"

I don't know who made the following observation, but we laughed at it for a long time. We looked from Andries Claassens' tobacco bag to the shelf on which dozens of similar bags were displayed. On each was the picture of a farmer with a black beard and a red-and-yellow checked shirt; and in his right hand, which was raised level with his shoulders, he held, elegantly, if somewhat stiffly, a pipe. Perhaps you remember that picture, which did not appear only on the tobacco bags, but was reproduced, also, in the newspapers, and stood on oblong metal sheets, enamelled in bright colours, in front of every store.

When our attention had been drawn to it, we saw the resemblance very clearly. In respect of both his features and his expression, the farmer on the tobacco bag was almost the exact image of Gysbert Jonker. Gysbert's beard was not so neatly trimmed, and his eyebrows were straighter; also, his mouth considerably larger than the man's on the picture. But in every other way – taking into consideration the difference in their dress – the likeness was astonishing.

Gysbert Jonker was there, in the Indian store, with us, when we made the discovery. He seemed very much interested.

"You will now have to push your ears in under the sweat-band of your hat, in the city fashion," Hans Bekker said to Gysbert. "You can't have them bent any more."

"And you will now have to hold your pipe up in the air, near to your shoulder, when you walk behind the plough," Andries Claassens added, "in your riding-breeches and leggings."

We were more than a little surprised at Gysbert's answer.

"It is absurd to think that I could do farmwork in that rigout," he replied. "But on Sundays, and some evenings after work, I shall wear riding-pants and top-boots. And it's a queer thing, but I have always wanted a shirt with red-and-yellow checks. In any case, it's the least I can do, in view of the fact that this tobacco company has honoured the Marico by making use of the portrait of the district's most progressive cattle-farmer in this way. I suppose the tobacco firm selected me for this purpose because of the improvements I made to my cement dip last year."

Gysbert Jonker added that next year he intended erecting another barbed-wire camp on the other side of the dam, and that he would bring this to the notice of the tobacco company as well.

We suddenly found that we had nothing more to say. And we were so taken aback at the way Gysbert responded to the purely accidental circumstance of his resembling the man in the picture that we were quite unable to laugh about it, even.

And I am sure that I was not the only Marico farmer, driving back home later that afternoon over the dusty road through the camelthorns, who reflected earnestly on the nature (and dangers) of sunstroke.

After a while, however, we got used to the change that had taken place in Gysbert Jonker's soul.

Consequently, with the passage of time, there was less and less said about the gorgeously-coloured shirts that Gysbert Jonker wore on Sundays, when he strolled about the front part of his homestead in riding-breeches and gaiters, apparently carefree and at ease, except that he held his pipe high up near his shoulder, somewhat stiffly. In time, too, the ouderling ceased calling on Gysbert in order to dissuade him from going about dressed as a tobacco advertisement on Sundays – a practice that the ouderling regarded as a desecration of the Sabbath.

In spite of everything, we had to admit that Gysbert Jonker had succeeded to a remarkable degree in imitating his portrait – especially when he started shaving the sides of his eyebrows to make them look more curved, and when he had cultivated a smile that wrinkled up his left cheek, halfway to his ear. And he used to smile carefully, almost as though he was afraid that some of the enamel would chip off him.

Jonker on one occasion announced to a number of acquaintances at a meeting of the Dwarsberge debating society, "Look at this shirt I have got on, for instance. Just feel the quality of it, and then compare it with the shirt on your tobacco bag. I had my photo taken last month in Zeerust, in these clothes. I sent the photograph to the head office of the tobacco company in Johannesburg – and would you believe it? The tobacco people sent me, by the following railway-lorry, one of those life-size enamelled pictures of myself painted on a sheet of iron. You know, the kind that you see on stations and in front of shops. I nailed it to the wall of my voorkamer."

Gysbert kept up his foolishness for a number of years. And it was, of course, this particular characteristic of his that we admired. We could see from this that he was a real Afrikaner, as obstinate as the Transvaal turf-soil. Even when, with the years, it became difficult for him to compete successfully with his portrait that did not age, so that he had to resort to artificial aids to keep his hair and beard black – then we did not laugh about it. We even sympathized with him in his hopeless struggle against the onslaughts of time. And we noticed that, the older Gysbert Jonker got, the more youthful his shirt seemed.

In the end, Gysbert Jonker had had to hands-up of course. But he gave in only after his portrait had changed. And it was so stupendous a change that it was beyond the capacity even of Gysbert to try to follow suit. One day suddenly – without any kind of warning from the tobacco firm – we noticed, when we were again in the Indian store at Ramoutsa, that the picture of the farmer in riding-pants had disappeared from the tobacco bags. Just like that. The farmer was replaced with the picture of the leaping blesbuck that you see on this bag, here. Afterwards, the blesbuck took the place of the riding-pants farmer on the enamelled iron sheets as well.

Meanwhile, however, when it dawned on us that the tobacco company was busy changing its advertisement, we made many carefully considered remarks about Gysbert Jonker. We said that he would now, in his old age, have to start practising the high jump, in order to be able to resemble his new portrait. We also said that he would now have to paint his belly white, like the blesbuck's. We also expressed the hope that a leopard wouldn't catch Gysbert Jonker when he walked about the veld on a Sunday morning, dressed up like his new portrait.

Nevertheless, I had the feeling that Gysbert Jonker did not altogether regret the fact that his portrait had been unrecognizably changed. For one thing he was now relieved of the strain of having all the time to live up to the opinion that the tobacco company had formed of him.

And although he removed the enamelled portrait from the wall of his voorkamer, and used it to repair a hole in the pigsty, and although he wore his gaudily-coloured shirts every day, now, and while doing the roughest kind of work, just so as to get rid of them – yet there were times, when I looked at Gysbert Jonker, that my thoughts were carried right back to the past. Most often this would happen when he was smoking. To the end, he retained something of his enamelled way by holding his pipe, his hand raised almost level with his shoulder, elegantly, but just a shade stiffly.

Some years later, when Gysbert Jonker was engaged in wearing out the last of his red-and-yellow checked shirts, I came across him at the back of his pigsty. He was standing near the spot where he had replaced a damaged sheet of corrugated iron with his tobacco-advertisement portrait.

And it struck me that in some mysterious way, Gysbert Jonker had again caught up his portrait. For they looked equally shabby and dilapidated, then, the portrait and Gysbert Jonker. They seemed to have become equally sullied – through the years and through sin. And so I turned away quickly from that rusted sheet of iron, with the picture on it of that farmer with his battered pipe, and his beard that was now greying and unkempt. And his shirt that looked as patched as Gysbert Jonker's own. And his eyes that had grown as wistful.

Peter Badcock

PEACHES RIPENING IN THE SUN

The way Ben Myburg lost his memory (Oom Schalk Lourens said) made a deep impression on all of us. We reasoned that that was the sort of thing that a sudden shock could do to you. There were those in our small section of General du Toit's commando who could recall similar stories of how people in a moment could forget everything about the past, just because of a single dreadful happening.

A shock like that can have the same effect on you even if you are prepared for it. Maybe it can be worse, even. And in this connection I often think of what it says in the Good Book, about that which you most feared having now at last caught up with you.

Our commando went as far as the border by train. And when the engine came to a stop on a piece of open veld, and it wasn't for water, this time, and the engine-driver and fireman didn't step down with spanners and use bad language, then we understood that the train stopping there was the beginning of the Second Boer War.

We were wearing new clothes and we had new equipment, and the sun was shining on the barrels of our Mausers. Our new clothes had been requisitioned for us by our veldkornets at stores along the way. All the veldkornet had to do was to sign his name on a piece of paper for whatever his men purchased.

In most cases, after we had patronized a store in that manner, the shopkeeper would put up his shutters for the day. And three years would pass and the Boer War would be over before the shopkeeper would display any sort of inclination to take the shutters down again.

Maybe he should have put them up before we came.

Only one "seksie" of General du Toit's commando entered Natal looking considerably dilapidated. This "seksie" looked as though it was already the end of the Boer War, and not just the beginning. Afterwards we found out that their veldkornet had never learnt to write his name. We were glad that in the first big battle these men kept well to the rear, apparently conscious of how sinful they looked. For, to make matters worse, a regiment of Indian troops was fighting on that front, and we were not anxious that an Eastern race should see white men at such a disadvantage.

"You don't seem to remember me, Schalk," a young fellow came up and said to me. I admitted that I didn't recognize him, straight away, as Ben Myburg. He did look different in those smart light-green riding pants and that new hat with the ostrich feather stuck in it. You could see he had patronized some mine concession store before the owner got his shutters down.

"But I would know you anywhere, Schalk," Ben Myburg went on. "Just from the quick way you hid that soap under your saddle a couple of minutes ago. I remembered where I had last seen something so quick. It was two years ago, at the Nagmaal in Nylstroom."

I told Ben Myburg that if it was that jar of brandy he meant, then he must realize that there had also been a good deal of misunderstanding about it. Moreover, it was not even a full jar, I said.

But I congratulated him on his powers of memory, which I said I was sure would yet stand the Republic in good stead.

And I was right. For afterwards, when the war of the big commandos was over, and we were in constant retreat, it would be Ben Myburg who, next day, would lead us back to the donga in which we had hidden some mealie-meal and a tin of cooking fat. And if the tin of cooking fat was empty, he would be able to tell us right away if it was kafirs or baboons. A kafir had a different way of eating cooking fat out of a tin from what a baboon had, Ben Myburg said.

Ben Myburg had been recently married to Mimi van Blerk, who came from Schweizer-Reneke, a district that was known as far as the Limpopo for its attractive girls. I remembered Mimi van Blerk well. She had full red lips and thick yellow hair. Ben Myburg always looked forward very eagerly to getting letters from his pretty young wife. He would also read out to us extracts from her letters, in which she encouraged us to drive the English into the blue grass – which was the name we gave to the sea in those days. For the English we had other names.

One of Mimi's letters was accompanied by a wooden candle-box filled with dried peaches. Ben Myburg was most proud to share out the dried fruit among our company, for he had several times spoken of the orchard of yellow cling peaches that he had laid out at the side of his house.

"We've already got dried peaches," Jurie Bekker said. Then he added, making free with our projected invasion of Natal: "In a few weeks' time we will be picking bananas."

It was in this spirit, as I have said, that we set out to meet the enemy. But nobody knew better than ourselves how much of this fine talk was to hide what we really felt. And I know, speaking for myself, that when we got the command "Opsaal", and we were crossing the border between the Transvaal and Natal, I was less happy at the thought that my horse was such a mettlesome animal. For it seemed to me that my horse was far more anxious to invade Natal than I was. I had to rein him in a good deal on the way to Spioenkop and Colenso. And I told myself that it was because I did not want him to go too fast downhill.

Eighteen months later saw the armed forces of the Republic in a worse case than I should imagine any army has ever been in, and that army still fighting. We were spread all over the country in small groups. We were in rags.

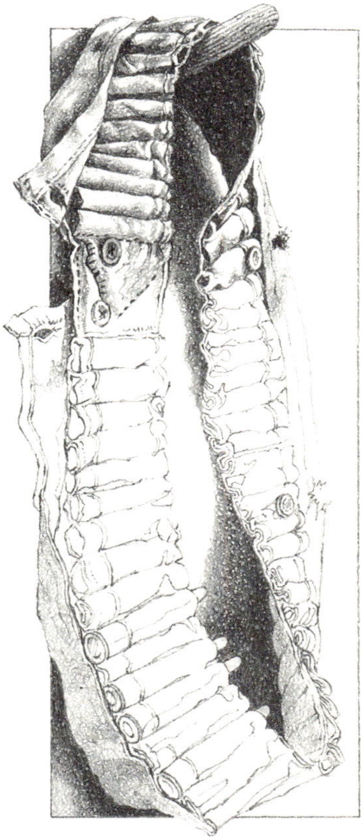

Many burghers had been taken prisoner. Others had yielded themselves up to British magistrates, holding not their rifles in their hands but their hats. There were a number of Boers, also, who had gone and joined the English.

For the Transvaal Republic it was near the end of a tale that you tell, sitting around the kitchen fire on a cold night. The story of the Transvaal Republic was at that place where you clear your throat before saying which of the two men the girl finally married. Or whether it was the cattle-smuggler or the Sunday school superintendent who stole the money. Or whether it was a real ghost or just her uncle with a sheet round him that Lettie van Zyl saw at the drift.

One night, when we were camped just outside Nietverdiend, and it was Ben Myburg's and my turn to go on guard, he told me that he knew that part well.

"You see that rant there, Schalk?" he asked. "Well, I have often stood on the other side of it, under the stars, just like now. You know, I've got a lot of peach-trees on my farm. Well, I have stood there, under the ripening peaches, just after dark, with Mimi at my side. There is no smell like the smell of young peach-trees in the evening, Schalk, when the fruit is ripening. I can almost imagine I am back there now.

And it is just the time for it, too."

I tried to explain to Ben Myburg, in a roundabout way, that although everything might be exactly the same on this side of the rant, he would have to be prepared for certain changes on the other side, seeing that it was war.

Ben Myburg agreed that I was probably right. Nevertheless, he began to talk to me at length about his courtship days. He spoke of Mimi with her full red lips and her yellow hair.

"I can still remember the evening when Mimi promised that she would marry me, Schalk," Ben Myburg said. "It was in Zeerust. We were there for the Nagmaal. When I walked back to my tent on the kerk-plein I was so happy that I just kicked the first three kafirs I saw."

I could see that, talking to me while we stood on guard, Ben Myburg was living through that time all over again. I was glad, for their sakes, that no kafirs came past at that moment. For Ben Myburg was again very happy.

I was pleased, too, for Ben Myburg's own sake, that he did at least have that hour of deep joy in which he could recall the past so vividly. For it was after that that his memory went.

By the following evening we had crossed the rant and had arrived at Ben Myburg's farm. We camped among the smoke-blackened walls of his former homestead, erecting a rough shelter with some sheets of corrugated iron that we could still use. And although he must have known only too well what to expect, what Ben Myburg saw there came as so much of a shock to his senses that from that moment all he could remember from the past vanished forever.

It was pitiful to see the change that had come over him. If his farm had been laid to ruins, the devastation that had taken place in Ben Myurg's mind was no less dreadful.

Perhaps it was that, in truth, there was nothing more left in the past to remember.

We noticed, also, that in singular ways, certain fragments of the bygone would come into Ben Myburg's mind; and that he would almost – but not quite – succeed in fitting these pieces together.

We observed that almost immediately. For instance, we remained camped on his farm for several days. And one morning, when the fire for our mealie-pap was crackling under one of the few remaining fruit-trees that had once been an orchard, Ben Myburg reached up and picked a peach that was, in advance of its season, ripe and yellow.

"It's funny," Ben Myburg said, "but I seem to remember, from long ago, reaching up and picking a yellow peach, just like this one. I don't quite remember where."

We did not tell him.

Some time later our "seksie" was captured in a night attack.

For us the Boer War was over. We were going to St. Helena. We were driven to Nylstroom, the nearest railhead, in a mule-wagon. It was a strange experience for us to be driving along the main road, in broad daylight, for all the world to see us. From years of wartime habit, our eyes still went to the horizon. A bitter thing about our captivity was that among our guards were men of our own people.

Outside Nylstroom we alighted from the mule-wagon and the English sergeant in charge of our escort got us to form fours by the roadside. It was queer – our having to learn to be soldiers at the end of a war instead of at the beginning.

Eventually we got into some sort of formation, the veldkornet, Jurie Bekker, Ben Myburg and I making up the first four. It was already evening. From a distance we could see the lights in the town. The way to the main street of Nylstroom led by the cemetery. Although it was dark, we could yet distinguish several rows of newly made mounds. We did not need to be told that they were concentration camp graves. We took off our battered hats and tramped on in a great silence.

Soon we were in the main street. We saw, then, what those lights were. There was a dance at the hotel. Paraffin lamps were hanging under the hotel's low, wide verandah. There was much laughter. We saw girls and English officers. In our unaccustomed fours we slouched past in the dark.

Several of the girls went inside then. But a few of the women-folk remained on the verandah, not looking in our direction. Among them I noticed particularly a girl leaning on an English officer's shoulder. She looked very pretty, with the light from a paraffin lamp shining on her full lips and yellow hair.

When we had turned the corner, and the darkness was wrapping us round again, I heard Ben Myburg speak.

"It's funny," I heard Ben Myburg say, "but I seem to remember, from long ago, a girl with yellow hair, just like that one. I don't quite remember where."

And this time, too, we did not tell him.

WEATHER PROPHET

That was after At Naudé had gone over the whole thing several times, telling us not only what he had heard over the wireless, but also what he had read in the newspapers. He made it clear to us what a weather wizard was. He also explained – although in this case not quite so clearly, perhaps – the functions and *raison d'être* of the meteorologist.

What made it more difficult for At Naudé was the fact that, while we already knew about weather prophecy, having met some prophets and having on occasion tried our hand at forecasting, ourselves - in time of sowing, say - the lengthy word, meteorologist, was a new one on us.

"All the same," Jurie Steyn persisted, after At Naudé had finished with his explanations, "I still don't see why you should speak in such an off-hand way about a weather prophet, just because he can prophesy a good while beforehand what the weather is going to be - and he gets it right. It shouldn't matter that he goes by just simple things like it's the last quarter of the moon on Wednesday and the wind changed last night."

Chris Welman expressed his agreement with Jurie Steyn.

"Well, I don't pretend to be a weather prophet or anything like," Chris Welman said, "but you'll remember how only last year I was right when I said, that time, that we'd have rain in three days. And when I said it there wasn't a cloud in the sky. But I just went by what my grandfather once said about when the wind blows from the Pilansberg with the new moon, what to expect."

And we said, yes, you could also tell if it was going to rain by other signs. "By the way swallows fly," Johnny Coen said. "And red ants walking around after sunset," Jurie Steyn said. "And by how the smoke comes out of the chimney," Gysbert van Tonder said. "And by spiders -" Oupa Bekker began.

At Naudé looked very superior, then, and he wore a thin smile.

"But you haven't any of you perhaps got a balloon going up on an island in the sea, have you?" he asked. "Or has any of you got a whole string of weather stations right through the Union? Just one weather station, even, maybe?"

With none of us answering, At Naudé looked more satisfied than ever with himself, then.

"That's where a meteorologist is different," At Naudé announced. "A meteorologist has got all those things." Although he realized then that he was beaten, Jurie Steyn could nevertheless not bring himself to yield straight away.

"It still doesn't make sense, quite," Jurie Steyn declared – but with less conviction than before – "that what you call a meteorologist doesn't say that next week there's going to be snow – and there *is* snow. Or that there is going to be a whirlwind – and then next week we've got no roofs left. It looks like it's only a weather prophet that comes and forecasts about that kind of thing. It looks like a meteorologist doesn't worry about it - or know of it, even."

"And does a meteorologist need to?" At Naudé asked, triumphantly. "Why should he trouble about working out when it's going to rain, say, seeing how he's got all those things for taking ground temperatures with, and for measuring the wind with, and he's got a balloon on an island in the sea? I mean, he's a scientist, a meteorologist is. You don't catch him walking outside to see what kind of smoke is coming out of his weather station chimney. Or going by red ants – no matter how many red ants may be walking around after supper-time. Or by spiders –" The absurdity of that last idea struck At Naudé so forcibly that he spluttered. We laughed a little ourselves, too, then. Yes, bringing in spiders seemed to be going just too far.

"After all, a meteorologist must be a man with a certain amount of learning," At Naudé finished up. "And so I don't suppose he'd be able to prophesy the weather right, even if he tried."

We could not but acknowledge, then, that what At Naudé said was indeed true. Such weather prophets as we knew to speak to were not people of great learning. And when one of ourselves, for instance, forecast correctly about did we have to put a bucksail over the wagon on the road to Bekkersdal, then we realized, also, that our way of working it out did not owe much to the letters we had been taught to write on our slates in the schoolroom. It was easy to see that a meteorologist would be far above a thing just like telling us when to put in

Autumn Giant cauliflowers. Our Hollander schoolmaster had been just as far above it, too.

"Of course, what helps you a lot in weather prophesying," Chris Welman said, "is mealies. I mean, after you've sown a patch of mealies, and they start coming up, then you know right away there's going to be a long piece of just absolute drought. And when a mealie gets to that size – if he ever gets to that size, I mean – where a head starts forming and you've *got* to have rain, then, or you won't get a crop at all, well, then you can be sure that for a whole month there's going to be just clear blue skies, so that you sit on your front stoep for day after day, working out in one of your children's school writing books how much you owe the Indian storekeeper at Ramoutsa.

"And when I see by my youngest son, Petrus's, quarterly report that he is good at sums, I think, yes, and I know what he's going to use all those sums for, one day, sitting on his front stoep with a pencil and a piece of paper, waiting for the rain. He'll need all the sums and more that they can teach him at school, I think to myself, then."

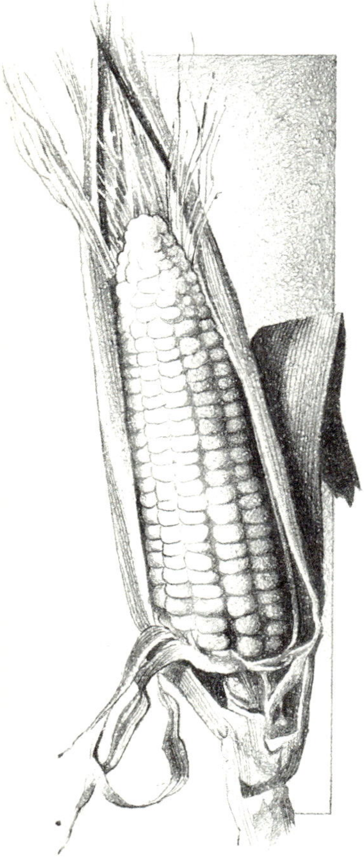

Thereupon Jurie Steyn, who was unacquainted with conditions prevailing years ago in the Cape Zwartland, said that if there was anything better than a mealie for prophesying the weather with, it was just a wheat plant.

"When a wheat plant," Jurie Steyn continued, "has got to there where you say to yourself that next week you'll start reaping and so you've got to see about getting all the sickles sharpened, then it's almost as though that wheat plant is himself so educated that he can tell you not to worry about it. For there's going to be the biggest hailstorm in years – it's like it's the wheat plant himself that's telling you that: an ordinary Hard Red wheat plant with no learning to speak of."

When it was a matter of hail, now, Oupa Bekker said, well, there was Klaas Rasmus. As a weather wizard Klaas Rasmus could have been said to specialize in hail, Oupa Bekker explained. Of course, nobody knew what methods Klaas Rasmus employed, exactly, Oupa Bekker said, although it was reasonable to suppose that it wasn't weather charts and graphs and rainfall figures and things like that. For one thing, it was unlikely that Klaas Rasmus would have known what rainfall figures were if you showed them to him, even.

"Not that he would ever have let on that he didn't know," Oupa Bekker continued. "Klaas Rasmus was not that kind of a man at all. If you had shown him the kind of rainfall figures, say, that At Naudé has been talking about, Klaas Rasmus would have nodded his head up and down solemnly quite a number of times.

"And he would have said, yes, that was just about how he would have worked it out himself, he thought, if he had had a piece of paper handy with lines drawn on it like that, and all. And then he would ask were you sure you were holding those rainfall figures the right way up, seeing that there were just one or two things there that he wasn't sure if he agreed with, quite.

"You see, that was Klaas Rasmus all over. If he understood a thing or not, it didn't make much difference to him. He would have something to say about it, all the same. But because he was so good at prophesying hail (being proved right time and again) there were a lot of little weaknesses he had that we could overlook."

Jurie Steyn said, then, that he thought he had heard that name, Klaas Rasmus, before, somewhere. Didn't he have some sort of nickname, Jurie Steyn asked.

Yes, that was quite right, Oupa Bekker said. They used to call him Klaas Baksteen, because of the size of the hailstones that used to fall each time that he prophesied hail. The hailstones would come down then the size of half-bricks.

"And I also seem to remember from something that I heard of long ago," Jurie Steyn went on, "that he - No, I can't recall it quite, now. But it was something that didn't seem to make sense, altogether, in a way."

Oupa Bekker said that he believed he knew what it was that Jurie Steyn was thinking about - something that Jurie Steyn had been told, about a happening in the Marico long ago.

"You see, like with all cases of real greatness," Oupa Bekker said, "there was some doubt, in some people's minds, about whether Klaas Baksteen was really as good at prophesying hail as he was held to be. There was talk that he was wrong, sometimes. And there was also talk that he would only forecast that there was going to be hail the size of half-bricks when the sky was already black and high up, and with awful white patches just above the horizon from which a child of four would know that after another half an hour there would be no harvest left that year.

"And so, one day, when he had worked out, to the hour, almost, when there was going to be a hailstorm the like of which this part of the Marico had rarely seen, and that hailstorm still a week ahead, Klaas Baksteen journeyed down to Bekkersdal so that the editor of the newspaper there could print it in his newspaper well before the hailstorm actually happened. And Klaas Baksteen put up at an hotel there, deciding to wait until his prophecy came out. And they say that everybody was very interested, of course. And quite a lot of people who didn't believe in Klaas Baksteen's powers said that that would show him up, all right, seeing that his prophecy was printed in the newspaper.

"And they say that it must have been pretty dreadful for Klaas Baksteen himself, waiting there in that hotel on the day when there was to be the hailstorm – more especially since up to quite late in the afternoon it was an absolutely cloudless sky. And Klaas Baksteen worried about it so much that afterwards he sent for a brandy, even, to try and calm himself. And afterwards he sent for another brandy. And when the waiter brought him the second brandy the sunlight shining on the glass was so bright that it blinded Klaas Baksteen, almost. That was how little chance there seemed to be of hail, then."

Oupa Bekker put a match to his pipe and puffed steadily for some moments.

"But before it was evening," he said, "there was such a hailstorm in Bekkersdal that hardly a window was left unbroken. Well, that was a proud moment for Klaas Baksteen, all right. Just with that he proved that he was the greatest hail prophet in the world. And before the sun had quite set a man who cultivated asparagus under glass frames just outside the town came and called on Klaas Baksteen at the hotel. And you've got no idea how proud Klaas Baksteen was that that man visited him. Even though Klaas Baksteen always used to wear a moustache after that. It was a thick, curling sort of moustache that Klaas Baksteen grew to cover up the place where his front teeth used to be before the asparagus man called round to see him."

But he couldn't understand that, Jurie Steyn said. It didn't make sense to him, Jurie Steyn said, quite. Although he had heard something about it, he seemed to remember.

"Well, why Klaas Baksteen was so happy about it," Oupa Bekker said, "was because that proved how great a weather prophet he was. The man who grew asparagus under glass frames *proved* it, by cutting up so rough. It made Klaas Baksteen king of hail prophets, that."

NEIGHBOURLY

A fence between the Union and the Bechuanaland Protectorate, At Naudé said. According to the radio, the two Governments were already discussing it.

"I hope they put gates in the fence, though, here and there," Chris Welman said, "otherwise how can we get to Ramoutsa siding?"

Yes, with a fence there, At Naudé agreed, goods we had ordered from Johannesburg could lie for years at the siding, and we none the wiser. "And likely as not we wouldn't even notice the difference," At Naudé added. "We'd think it was just the railways again a bit slow."

There was one queer thing about putting up a fence, Oupa Bekker said, that he himself had noticed long ago. And it was this. When you erected a fence around your farm, it never seemed to keep anybody out. All you were doing was to fence yourself in, and with barbed-wire.

In the meantime Gysbert van Tonder, with his somewhat extensive cattle-smuggling interests, had been doing a spot of thinking. When he spoke it was apparent that he had been indulging in no glad, carefree reveries. His reasoning had followed a severely practical line – as straight as the five-strand course, theodolite-charted, of the fence that would provide the Union and the Bechuanaland Protectorate with official frontiers.

"There should be a proper sort of a border: that I do believe in," Gysbert van Tonder announced piously. "It makes it a lot too hard, smuggling cattle from the Protectorate into the Transvaal, when there's no real line to smuggle them over. I'm glad the Government's doing something about it. These things have got to be correct. I've got discouraged more than once, I can tell you, asking myself well, what's the good. You see what I mean?

"Either you're in the Marico, or you aren't. And either you're in the Protectorate or you aren't. When there's no proper border you can be standing with a herd of cattle right on the Johannesburg market and not be feeling too sure are you in the Transvaal or in Bechuanaland. Even when the auctioneer starts calling for bids, you don't quite know is the answer going to come in pound notes or in rolls of brass wire.

"You almost expect somebody to shout out 'So many strings of beads'. So I can only say that the sooner they put up a decent kind of fence the better. The way things are, it's been going on too long. You've got to know if an ox is properly smuggled over or if it isn't. You've got to be legal."

The years he had put in at cattle-smuggling had imparted to Gysbert van Tonder's mind an unmistakably juridical slant. He liked arranging things by rule and canon, by precept and code. The next question he asked bore that out.

"In this discussion that our Government is having with the Protectorate Government," he asked, "did the broadcast say rightly what kind of fence it is that they are going to put up? Is it the steel posts with anchoring wires kind that you cut? Or will it have standards that you pull out and bend the fence down by the droppers for the cattle to walk over on bucksails? That's a thing they should get straight before anything else, I'm thinking."

The conversation at that point took, naturally enough, a technical turn. The talk had to do with strands and surveyors, and wrongly-positioned beacons and surveyors and rails, and the wire snapping and cutting Koos Nienaber's chin open in rebounding, and gauges and five-barb wires, and the language Koos Nienaber used afterwards, speaking with difficulty because of all that sticking plaster on his chin.

"And so the surveyor said to me," Chris Welman was declaring about half an hour later, "that if I didn't believe him about that spruit not coming on my side of the farm, then I could check through his figures myself. There were only eight pages of figures, he said, and those very small figures on some of the pages that didn't look too clear he would go over in ink for me, he said.

"And he would also lend me a book that was just all figures that would explain to me what the figures he had written down meant. And when I said that since my grandfather's time that spruit had been used on our farm and that we used to get water there, the surveyor just smiled like he was superior to my grandfather. And he said he couldn't understand it. On the other side of the bult, in a straight line, that spruit was a long way outside of our farm.

"What that other surveyor, many years ago, was up to, he just couldn't make out, he said. With all his books of figures, he said, he just couldn't figure that one. Well, I naturally couldn't go and tell him, of course. Although it's something that we all know in the family.

"Because my grandfather had the same kind of trouble, in his time, with a surveyor more years ago than I can remember. And when my grandfather said to the surveyor, 'How do you know that the line you marked out on the other side of the bult is in a straight line from here? Can you *see* through a bult – a bult about fifty paces high and half a mile over it?' – then the surveyor had to admit, of course, that no man could see through a bult. And the land surveyor felt very ashamed of himself, then, for being so ignorant. And he changed the plan just like my grandfather asked him to do.

"And the funny part of it is that my grandfather had no knowledge of figures. Indeed, I don't think my grandfather could even read figures. All my grandfather had, while he was talking to the land surveyor, was a shotgun, one barrel smooth and the other choke. And the barrels were sawn off quite short. And they say that when he went away from our farm – my grandfather having proved to him just where he went wrong in his figures – he was the politest surveyor that had ever come to this part of the Dwarsberge."

There would, he said, then, unquestionably be a good deal of that same sort of element in the erection of the boundary-wire between the Bechuanaland Protectorate and the Transvaal. More than one land surveyor would as likely as not raise his eyebrows, we said.

Or he would take a silk handkerchief out of his pocket and start dusting his theodolite, saying to himself that he shouldn't in the first place have entrusted so delicate an instrument to a raw Mchopi porter smelling of kafir-beer.

In the delimiting of the Transvaal-Bechuanaland Protectorate border we could see quite a lot of trouble sticking out for a number of people.

"I also hope," Jurie Steyn said, winking, "that when the Government sends up the poles and barbed-wire for the fence to the Ramoutsa siding, there isn't going to be the usual kind of misunderstanding that happens in these parts as to whom the fencing materials are *for*. I mean, you'll have farmers suddenly very busy putting up new cattle camps, and the fence construction workers will be sitting in little groups in the veld playing draughts, seeing they've got no barbed-wire and standards."

Anyway, so there was a fence going to come there, now, along the edge of the Marico, through the bush. Barbed-wire. A metal thread strung along the border. Sprouting at intervals, as befitted a bushveld tendril, thorns.

"A fence now," Chris Welman said. "Whenever I think of a fence I also call to mind a kindly neighbour standing on the other side of it, shaking his head and smiling in a brotherly-love sort of way at what he sees going on on my side of the fence. And all the time I am just about boiling at the advice he's giving me on how to do it better.

"Like when I was building my new house, once, that was to provide shelter for my wife and children. And a neighbour came and stood on the other side of the fence, shaking his head at the sun-dried bricks in a kind-hearted manner. Turf-clay was no good for sun-dried bricks, he told me, seeing that the walls of that kind of stable would collapse with the first rains. And I didn't have the strength of mind to tell him the truth. I mean, I was too ashamed to let him know that I had really meant those bricks for my house.

"So I just built another stable, instead, which I didn't need. And it was only a long time afterwards – through a good piece of the mud that he had smeared it up with in front crumbling away – that I found out that my neighbour's own house, which he always talked in such fashionable language about, was built of nothing more than turf-clay bricks, sun-dried."

Yes, Jurie Steyn said, or when you were putting up a *prieel* for a grapevine to trail over.

"And then that neighbour comes along and says, what, a shaky prieel like that – it'll never hold up a grapevine," Jurie Steyn continued. "And then you say, well, it's not *meant* for grapes, see? You're not that kind of a fool, you say. You're only making a trellis for the wife. She wants to grow a creeper with that feathery kind of leaves on it, you say.

"And then your neighbour says, well, he hopes it isn't very heavy feathers, because it won't take much weight on it to bring that whole thing down. By that time you feel about like a brown weevil crawling over one of the sideshoots of the grapevine you intended to plant there. And it's a funny thing, but you never really take to the blue flowers of the creeper that you put in there, instead."

It was significant, we said, how you would on occasion come across a stable that looked far too good for just an ordinary bushveld farm, with squares and triangles in plaster cut out above the door of the stable. And with a stoep that, if you didn't know it was a stable, why, you could almost picture people sitting drinking coffee on it. And spidery threads of creepers twining delicately if somewhat incongruously about solid scaffoldings with tarred uprights. Looking as though why the farmer made the pergola so sturdy was that the pale gossamer blooms shouldn't just float away. And it would all be because of the advice of a neighbour who at one time stood on the other side of the fence, kind-hearted, but with his eyes narrowed. Almost as though he couldn't believe what he was seeing there. And his one hand would be resting easily on the wire, as if at any instant he could jump clean over and come and take what you're busy with right away from you, and show you how it should be done. His other hand would be up to his forehead so that he could see better. And he would be shaking his head in a kindly fashion in between making recommendations.

That was what a fence represented to us, we said. Young Vermaak, the schoolmaster, made a remark, then. It was the first chance that he had had, so far, to talk.

As far as he could see, the schoolmaster said, the effect it was going to have – erecting a fence between the Union and the Bechuanaland Protectorate – was that it was going to make the Union and the Protectorate really *neighbourly*.

MAN TO MAN

The young mounted policeman, Bothma, explained of course, that why he had called round at Jurie Steyn's post office, that afternoon, was just because he was on his regular rounds. He hadn't picked that afternoon, particularly, he added. And he hadn't come to Jurie Steyn's post office specially, any more than he would visit any other post office or voorkamer in that part of the Groot Marico specially, he said.

It was only that he was carrying out his duties of patrolling the area, he explained, and it just so happened that in the course of routine he was patrolling over Jurie Steyn's farm, then.

He was new to the job of being a mounted policeman, young Bothma added.

Well, we realized that much about him, of course, without his having had to say it. And because he was new to his work we made a good deal of allowance for him. But we were also pretty sure that the time would come when Mounted Constable Bothma would learn a few more things.

And he would understand then that nothing could rouse people's suspicions more than that a policeman should come round and offer all sorts of excuses for his being there.

"I just sort of make a few notes in my notebook," Bothma went on, "to say at what time, and so on, I call at each farmhouse that I do call on, patrolling, like I said."

Gysbert van Tonder yawned.

You could see, from the policeman's taking out his notebook and pencil like that, right at the beginning of his visit, and before he had sat down properly, almost, that he would yet have a long way to go and would have to traverse many a mile of made bushveld road and bridle path, asking a multitude of questions and getting the same number of wrong answers, before his call at an isolated farmhouse

SAP
Peter Badcock

would make the farmer start thinking quickly to himself.

But the way Bothma was now, the farmer wouldn't ask him had he come through the vlakte – expecting the policeman to say, untruthfully, no, he had followed the Government road as far as the poort. The farmer's thoughts would not travel with lightning speed to his brandy still. Nor would the farmer wonder if those head of Bechuana cattle were safe in the truck to the Johannesburg market.

All those things we could sense about Constable Bothma in Jurie Steyn's voorkamer that afternoon. It was also apparent to us that, before arriving at where we were, he had called on more than one Bushveld farmer en route. That would account for something of the diffidence in his manner. It was easy to guess that he had asked a few stock questions along the road – not that there was anything specific that he wanted to *know*, really, as he would no doubt have explained, but just because asking those questions was a part of his patrol duties – and it was only reasonable to suppose that the answers some of the Marico farmers had given him were not characterized by a noteworthy degree of artlessness.

He had doubtless discovered that while a policeman's questions might be, in terms of standing orders, stereotyped, a farmer's replies, generally speaking, weren't. Especially when that farmer's answers were being written straight into a notebook.

Nevertheless, because Bothma was, after all, a mounted policeman and in khaki uniform, with brass letters on his shoulders, we did feel a measure of constraint in his company. This circumstance of our not feeling quite at ease manifested itself in the way that most of us sat on our riempies chairs – just a little more stiffly than usual, our shoulders not quite touching the backs of the chairs. It also manifested itself in the unconventional way in which Gysbert van Tonder saw fit to sprawl in his seat, in an affectation of a mental content that would have awakened mistrustful imaginings in the breast of a policeman who had been, say, two and a half years at the game.

It was then that Chris Welman made a remark that went a good way towards relieving the tension. Afterwards, in talking it over, we had to say that we could not but admire the manner in which Chris Welman had worked out the right words to use. Not that there was anything clever in the way that Chris Welman spoke, of course.

No, we all felt that the statement Chris Welman made then was something that was easily within the capacity of any one of us, if we had just sat back a little, and thought, and had then made use of the common sense that comes to anybody that has lived on a farm long enough.

"The man you should really ask questions of," Chris Welman said to Constable Bothma, "is Gysbert van Tonder. That's him there. Sitting with his legs taking up half the floor and his hands behind his head, with his elbows stretched out. Just from the way he's sitting, you can see he's the biggest cattle-smuggler in the whole of the Dwarsberg area."

Well, that gave us a good laugh, of course. We all *knew* that Gysbert van Tonder smuggled more cattle across the Konventie border than any other man in the Marico. What was more, we knew that Gysbert van Tonder's father had been regularly bringing in cattle over the line from Ramoutsa before there had ever been a proper barbed-wire fence there, even. And we also knew that, in the long years of the future, when we were all dead and gone, Gysbert van Tonder's sons would still be doing the same thing.

What was more, nothing would ever stop them, either. And not even if every policeman from Cape Town to the Limpopo knew about it. For the Bechuanas from whom he traded cattle felt friendly towards Gysbert van Tonder. And that was a sentiment they did not have for a border policeman, unreasonable though such an attitude of mind might perhaps seem. Moreover, this was an outlook on life, that, to a not inconsiderable degree, Gysbert van Tonder shared with the Bechuanas.

Consequently, in having spoken in the way he did, Chris Welman had cleared the air for all of us - for Gysbert van Tonder included. As a result, Gysbert van Tonder could for one thing sit more comfortably in his chair, relaxing as he sat. There was no longer any necessity for him to adopt a carefree pose which must have put quite a lot of strain on his neck and leg muscles, not even to talk of how hard it must have been for his spine to keep up that effortful bearing that was intended to suggest indifference.

Anyway, Gysbert van Tonder joined in the laughter that greeted Chris Welman's words. Constable Bothma laughed, also. It was clear from that that about the first thing the sergeant at the Bekkersdal headquarters must have told young Bothma was about how he had to keep an eye on Gysbert van Tonder.

It was good to feel that there was so much tension lifted from us then, after Chris Welman had spoken, and we had all laughed, and we understood that we need not pretend to each other any more.

"Of course, we know you haven't come here to spy on us," Jurie

Steyn said to Constable Bothma, after a pause. "I mean, you've told us all that yourself. The little odds and ends of things that you put in your notebook – well, it's your job, isn't it? If you didn't write those little things in your notebook you'd get the sack, as likely as not. And if you didn't come and patrol my voorkamer, too, like you're doing now, you'd as likely as not also get the sack. And if you wrote anything in your notebook that isn't so, why, for that, of course, you would just get the sack, too."

From the way Jurie Steyn spoke, it would appear that, looked at from any angle, whatever Constable Bothma did, the one thing staring him in the face was dismissal from the police force.

"And there aren't so many things a policeman – I mean, an ex-policeman – can find to do when once he's got the sack," Jurie Steyn continued. "Because when you go and look for a job, afterwards, almost the first thing the boss will ask you is why you got the sack from the police. And no matter what your answer is, it always seems as though there is more behind it than what you say. Seeing that you are an ex-policeman applying for work the boss can never be sure about how much of what you are telling him is lies."

Johnny Coen took a hand in the conversation, then, and he said to the policeman that seeing that he and the policeman were both young, he could feel for the policeman. And he didn't want Constable Bothma to misunderstand what Jurie Steyn had just been saying, Jonny Coen went on. It was known that Jurie Steyn was like that, Johnny Coen said, but everybody knew that Jurie Steyn meant nothing by it.

It was just that we were all respectable people, respectable farmers, and so on, Johnny Coen explained, and for that reason we all got a little upset when a policeman came round, especially when the policeman pulled out a pencil and notebook. If we weren't such respectable people, respectable farmers and so on, Johnny Coen said, we wouldn't mind if even a dozen mounted policemen in uniforms came marching into our voorkamers with S.A.P. on their shoulders and with their horses waiting outside.

But it was just because we were respectable people that we got a guilty sort of a conscience when a policeman came into our house, Johnny Coen proceeded. And for that reason he wanted Constable Bothma to bear with Jurie Steyn and not to get offended at anything that Jurie Steyn said in haste.

"Oh, no," Constable Bothma said. "That is quite in order. I would not even have thought that there was anything insulting in it, in what Meneer Steyn said."

So Johnny Coen said that that was just what he meant. Any man that was not a policeman would very likely have had his pride hurt, by the way that Jurie Steyn had spoken. But he could see that it would, of course, be different with a policeman, Johnny Coen said. It wasn't that he thought a policeman didn't have *pride* –

Johnny Coen looked pretty foolish, then. For he had been trying to stand up for Constable Bothma, but had only succeeded in making Jurie Steyn's disparaging references to the police force sound a lot worse.

After that it was, of course, Oupa Bekker's turn to talk. And although Oupa Bekker's story related to some period in the past when the functions of a police constable were exercised apparently not unsuccessfully by the local veldkornet, it seemed as though the difficulties that Constable Bothma was experiencing at present had some features in common with the vicissitudes that the young veldkornet in Oupa Bekker's story went through.

"Many a man would have been satisfied with that position," Oupa Bekker was saying, "just because of the honour that went with it in those days. For one thing, even if you didn't have a uniform or an office with a telephone in it to work in, like you have today, or even a mounted-policeman horse with a white star on his forehead that can keep time to the music at the Johannesburg Show – even if you had to ride just one of your own horses on a patched saddle, and you had a patch in the seat of your trousers, too, you still had a printed certificate signed by the President to say you were veldkornet, and that you could hang in a gold frame on the wall of your voorkamer."

But the glitter of rank and the nimbus of office were as nought to that young veldkornet, Oupa Bekker said. The thing that worried the young veldkornet, was that, because he was charged with the maintenance of law and order in his area, he was called upon, in however delicate a manner, to act as an informer on his neighbour. The thought that, through his job, he was cut off from intimate contact with his fellow men saddened him. He liked having friends, and he found he couldn't have any, any more – not real friends – now that he was veldkornet.

"In the end –" Oupa Bekker said.

But we had rather that Oupa Bekker had not continued to the end, which was at once stark and inexorable, pitiless and yet compelling. For the only true friend that the young veldkornet had in the end was Sass Koggel, a scoundrel the like of whom the Groot Marico district had had but few in its history. Only with Sass Koggel did the veldkornet find, in the end, that he could be as he really was.

Sass Koggel and the veldkornet took each other for what they were. Neither, in his relations with the other, had to put up any sort of pretence. They were on opposite sides of the law. The veldkornet was all out to lay Sass Koggel by the heels. Sass Koggel directed all his efforts to the end that the veldkornet should get nothing on him.

But, outside of that technicality, it would be hard to find, in the whole of the Marico, a couple of firmer friends than were those two.

It was a long story that Oupa Bekker told, and we listened to it with fluctuating degrees of attention.

But Constable Bothma and Gysbert van Tonder did not listen to Oupa Bekker at all. They were too engrossed in what each had to say to the other. And while talking to Gysbert van Tonder, the cattle-smuggler, it was only once necessary for the policeman, Constable Bothma, to open his notebook.

Constable Bothma opened his notebook at the back, somewhere, and extracted a photograph which he passed over to Gysbert van Tonder. Gysbert studied the likeness for some moments. "Takes after you, does he?" Gysbert van Tonder asked.

In his voice there was only sincerity.

LOST CITY

"It used to be different, in the Kalahari," Chris Welman said, commenting on At Naudé's announcement of what he had heard over the wireless. "You could go for miles and miles, and it would be just desert. All you'd come across, perhaps, would be a couple of families of Bushmen, and they'd be disappearing over the horizon. Then, days later, you'd again come across a couple of families of Bushmen. And *they'd* be disappearing over the horizon.

"And you wouldn't know if it was the same couple of families of Bushmen. Or the same horizon. And you wouldn't care either. I mean, in the Kalahari desert you wouldn't care. Maybe in other deserts it is different. I'm only talking about the Kalahari."

Yes, all you would be concerned about, in the Kalahari, Jurie Steyn said, was what the couple of families of Bushmen would be disappearing over the horizon *with*. For you might not always be able to check up quickly to find out what was missing out of your camp.

"But from what At Naudé has been telling us," Chris Welman went on, "it looks like you'd have no quiet in the Kalahari today. Or room to move. From Molepolole onwards it seems that there's just one expedition on top of another, each one searching for a lost city. And you can't slip out for a glass of pontac, even, in case when you come back somebody else has taken your place in the line."

It was apparent that Chris Welman was drawing on his memory of some past unhappy trip to Johannesburg.

It was not hard to think of how a city got lost in the first place, Jurie Steyn observed. "It must have been that the people that built the city didn't know what a couple of families of Bushmen were like. Still, I can't believe it, somehow, quite. Not a whole city, that is. I can't somehow imagine Bushmen disappearing over the horizon with all that. For one thing, it wouldn't be any use to them. Now if it wasn't so

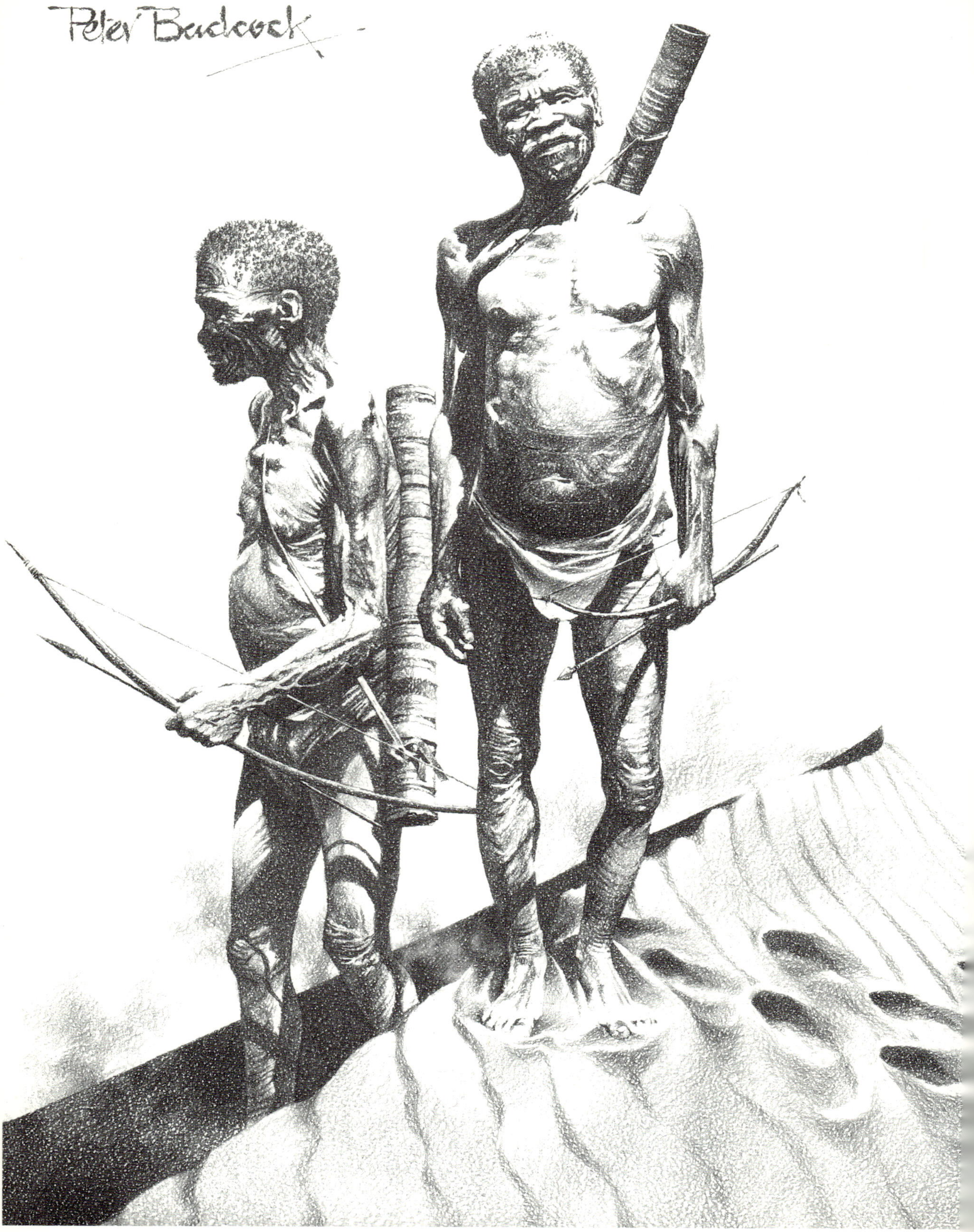
Peter Badcock

much a question of a whole lost city, but of some of the things that got lost *out* of the city - well, I could tell those expeditions just where to go and look."

But At Naudé said that we had perhaps misunderstood one or two of the less important details of the news he had communicated to us. There weren't quite as many expeditions as what Chris Welman seemed to think, out in the Kalahari looking for a lost city. Moreover, it wasn't a city that had got lost in the way that Jurie Steyn meant by lost. The city had just been built so many years ago that people had afterwards forgotten about it. Don't ask him how a thing like that could happen, now, At Naudé said. He admitted that he couldn't imagine it, himself.

"I mean, let's not take even a city -" At Naudé started to explain.

"No, let a few Bushman families take it," Jurie Steyn said, promptly, "with the washing hanging on the clothes-lines and all."

"Not a city, even," At Naudé continued, pointedly ignoring Jurie Steyn's second attempt that afternoon at being what he thought funny, "but if we think of quite a small town, like Bekkersdal, say ... Not that I won't agree that we've got a wider water-furrow in the main street of Bekkersdal than they've got in Zeerust, of course, but it's only that there are less people *in* the main street of Bekkersdal than they've got in Zeerust, if you understand what I mean ... Well, can you imagine anybody in Bekkersdal forgetting where they built the place? After all, anybody can see for himself how silly that sounds. It's like Dominee Welthagen, just before the Nagmaal, suddenly forgetting where the church is. Or David Policansky not remembering where his shop is, just after he's done it all up for the New Year."

We acknowledged that At Naudé was right there, of course. With Dominee Welthagen we might not perhaps be too sure. For it was known that in some respects the dominee could at times be pretty absent-minded. But with David Policansky At Naudé was on safe enough ground. Especially after that big new plate-glass window that David Policansky had put in. It was not reasonable to think that he would be able to forget it. Not with what he was still likely to be owing on it, we said. You just weren't allowed to forget anything you were owing on.

"So you see how much more silly it is with a city, then," At Naudé concluded. "Thinking that people would go and build a city, and then just lose it."

Thereupon young Vermaak, the schoolmaster, said that he had learnt in history of how for many centuries people believed that there was a foreign city called Monomotapa in these parts, and that numbers of expeditions had been sent out in the past to look for it. It was even marked on maps, long ago, the schoolmaster said. But if you saw that name on a map of Africa today, he said, well, then you would know that it wasn't a very up-to-date map of Africa.

As likely as not, there would not be the town of Vanderbijl Park marked on that map, young Vermaak said, laughing. Or the town of Odendaalsrus, even. There was supposed to be a lot of gold and diamonds in that city with the foreign name, the schoolmaster added.

Well, with those remarks young Vermaak broached a subject with which we were not altogether unfamiliar. More than one of us had, before today, held in his hand a map showing as clearly as anything with a cross the exact spot where the hidden treasure would be found buried. And all we'd be likely to dig up there would be an old jam-tin. The apochryphal element in African cartography was something we had had experience of.

"All I can say," Gysbert van Tonder observed at this stage, "is that I don't know so much about a lost city. But it seems to me there's going to be more than one lost expedition. Depending on how far the expeditions are going into the desert beyond Kang-Kang."

Several of us looked surprised when Gysbert van Tonder said that. Surprised and also impressed. We knew that in his time Gysbert van Tonder had penetrated pretty deeply into the Kalahari, bartering beads and brass wire for cattle. That was, of course, before the Natives in those parts found that they didn't need those things, any more, since they could buy their clothes ready-made at the Indian store at Ramoutsa. Nevertheless, we had not imagined that he had gone as far into the desert as all that.

"But is there -" Jurie Steyn enquired after a pause, "is there really a place by that name, though?"

Gysbert van Tonder smiled.

"On the map, yes" he said, "it is. On the map in my youngest son's school atlas you can read that name for yourself there, big as anything. And in the middle of the Kalahari. Well, there's something one of those expeditions can go and look for. And maybe that is their lost city. At least, it's lost enough. Because you certainly won't be able to tell it from any other spot in the Kalahari that you're standing in the middle of, watching a couple of families of Bushmen disappearing over the horizon from."

So Jurie Steyn said, yes, he reckoned that if it was a lost city that an expedition was after, why, then he reckoned that just about any part of the Kalahari would do for that. Because when the expedition came back from the Kalahari without having found anything, it would prove to the whole world just how lost that city actually was, Jurie Steyn reckoned. If that was what an expedition into the Kalahari was for, then that expedition just couldn't go wrong. In fact, the less that an expedition like that found, then, the better. Because it would show that the city had been lost without as much as a trace, even, Jurie Steyn added.

"It's a queer thing, though," the schoolmaster said, "when you come to think of it, that for so many hundreds of years, when the interior of South Africa was still unexplored, there should have been a legend of a Golden City. And people were so convinced of the existence of this city that they went searching for it. They were so sure that there was that city of gold that they even marked it on their maps. And what seems so extraordinary to me is that one day the Golden City actually would arise, and not too far away, either, from where the old geographers had centuries before indicated on their maps. It was as though they were all prophesying the rise of Johannesburg. And at most they were only a few hundred miles out."

That men should have been able to mark on a map, centuries beforehand, a city that was not there yet. That to him was one of the mysteries of Africa, the schoolmaster declared.

Thereupon Oupa Bekker said that if it was a thing like that that the schoolmaster thought wonderful, then the schoolmaster had a lot to learn, still.

"After all, with South Africa so big," Oupa Bekker said, "they were bound to go and build cities in it, somewhere. That stands to reason. And so, for a person to go and put a mark on a map and to say that someday there is going to be a city there, or thereabouts - well, what would have been wonderful was if it *didn't* work out, some time. And to say that it's surprising how that man made that mark on the map centuries ago, even. Well, I think that only shows how bad he was at it. If Johannesburg got started soon after he had prophesied it, then there might have been something in it, then. But it seems to me that the man who made that map wasn't only a few hundred miles out, as Meneer Vermaak says, but that he was also a few hundred years out. What's more, he also got the name wrong. Unless you also think that that name - what's it, again -"

"Monomotapa," young Vermaak announced.

"- isn't far out from sounding like Johannesburg," Oupa Bekker said.

It made him think of his grand-uncle Toons, all this, Oupa Bekker said. Now, there was something that really did come as a surprise to us. The general feeling we had about Oupa Bekker was a feeling of immense antiquity, of green and immemorial age. In the lost olden-time cities that our talk was about we could, without thinking twice, accord to Oupa Bekker the rights of a venerable citizenship. And in that crumbled town we could conceive of Oupa Bekker as walking about in the evening, among cobwebbed monuments. He seemed to belong with the battered though timeless antique.

It was foolish, of course, to have ideas like that. But that was the impression, in point of appearance and personality, that Oupa Bekker did make on us.

And so when Oupa Bekker spoke of himself as having had a grand-uncle, it just about took our breath away.

"You were saying about your grand-uncle?" Jurie Steyn, who was the first to recover, remarked. From the tone in his voice, you could see that Jurie Steyn pictured Oupa Bekker's grand-uncle as a lost city in himself, with weeds clambering over his ruined walls.

"My grand-uncle Toons," Oupa Bekker continued, unaware of the stir he had caused, "also had the habit, when he first trekked into the Transvaal, that was all just open veld, then, of stopping every so often and looking around him and saying that one day a great city would arise right there where he was standing, where it was now just empty veld. On his way up, when he trekked into the Northern Transvaal, he stopped to say it at where there is today Potchefstroom, and also at where there is today Johannesburg and Pretoria. In that way you could say that he was just as good as the man that did that map. And I suppose he was, too. That is, if you don't count all those hundreds of other places where my grand-uncle Toons also stopped to say the same thing, and where there is today still just open veld."

It was Jurie Steyn who brought the conversation back to where we had started from.

"Those expeditions going to search for the lost city," he asked of At Naudé, "have they set out yet? And do you know if they are likely to pass this way, at all? Because, if it's last letters they want to send home, and so on, then my post office is as good as any. I mean, their last letters have got a good chance of getting to where they are addressed to. I don't say the expeditions have got the same chance of getting to the lost city. But instead of taking all that trouble, why don't they just drop a letter in the post to the lost city - writing to the mayor, say? Then they'll at least know if the lost city is there or not."

But At Naudé said that from what he had heard over the wireless the expeditions were on the point of leaving, or had already left, Johannesburg. And as for what Jurie Steyn had said about writing letters - well, he had the feeling that more than one letter that he had himself posted had ended up there, in that lost city.

"Johannesburg?" Oupa Bekker queried, talking as though he was emerging from a dream. "Well, I've been in Johannesburg only a few times. Like with the Show, say. And I've passed through there on the way to Cape Town. And I've always tried to pull down the curtains of the compartment I was in when we went through Johannesburg. And I have thought of the Good Book, then.

"And I have thought that if ever there was a lost city, it was Johannesburg, I have thought. *And how lost,* I have thought ... The expedition doesn't need to leave Johannesburg, if it's a lost city it wants."

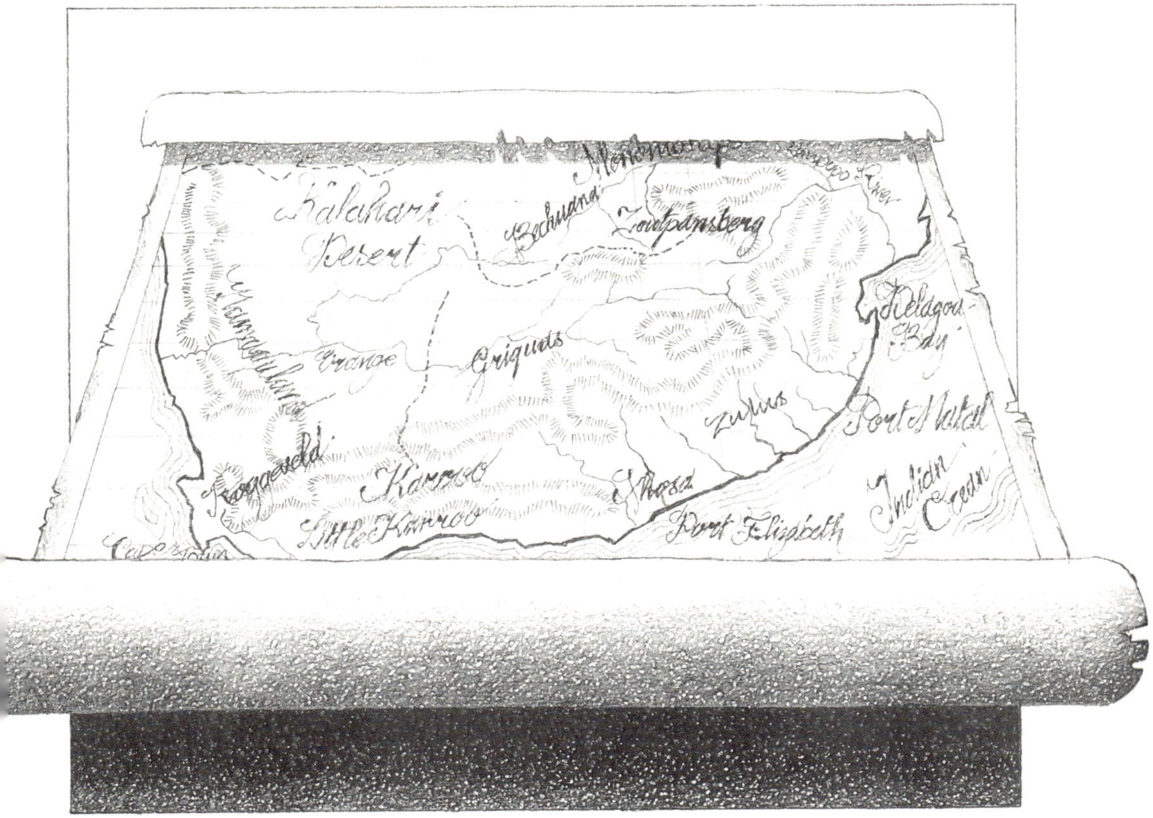

BEKKERSDAL CENTENARY

We were talking about the centenary celebrations at Bekkersdal. They were doing it in real style, we said, and it gave us a deep sense of pride, in this part of the Marico, to think that our town, that we had regarded as just *being* there, kind of, should have so impressive and stirring a history, and what was more, a future resplendent with opportunity and promise.

"Well, I had never thought of Bekkersdal in quite that way before," Chris Welman said, "but when I went in week before last to have this tooth pulled out" – he inserted a couple of toil-discoloured fingers in his mouth to disclose the cavity – "I did notice a few of these centenary things they were talking about."

Chris Welman made some further remarks, but there was a certain lack of precision in his articulation through his holding his mouth open that way while he was talking.

After Jurie Steyn had said that with Chris Welman having his mouth so wide it was like there was a draught in his post office that he hadn't noticed before, and after young Vermaak, the schoolmaster, had explained about how he had been trembling, all the time, in fear that one of Chris Welman's fingers might slip into a part of his mouth where the teeth were still all in, and so get bitten off – in his classical studies at University he had read about a boxer who, having stopped one from a Greek boxing-glove, was spitting out teeth, the schoolmaster said, and he did not feel happy at the thought of somebody spitting out fingers on the floor of Jurie Steyn's voorkamer - after all that, Chris Welman said that he had a good mind not to go on talking any more about his impressions of the Bekkersdal 100th year celebrations, seeing how unappreciative we were.

And as for the Greek boxing-gloves that the schoolmaster had mentioned as what he had learnt about in the classics, Chris Welman said, well, they didn't seem, by the sound of it, to be much different from the brass boxing-gloves that members of the Jeppe gang just wore over the knuckles of the right hand.

And he did not think that the Jeppe gang were students of the classics so that you would notice it, much, Chris Welman said.

Thereupon At Naudé remarked that Chris Welman having a tooth out in Bekkersdal wasn't really of historical importance. It wasn't of much significance one way or the other, he reckoned. Especially today, with the newspapers and the wireless having a lot to say about Bekkersdal's centenary.

"If it had been a Voortrekker leader that had a tooth pulled out there a hundred years ago, it would have been different, perhaps," At Naudé continued. "If it had been the Voortrekker leader Andries Loggenberg, say, and it had been the time of the trouble between the Hervormde church and the Doppers, say – well, that would have been something.

"With Andries Loggenberg having his face all bandaged up, I mean, through the way they had of pulling out a back tooth a hundred years ago, well, he just wouldn't have been able to get onto an ox-wagon, then, and make a two-hour speech straight out of the Bible about what a blot on this part of the Dwarsberge the Cape Groote Kerk was.

"All he would be able to do, with his face all swathed in cloth like that, just his eyes and a piece of beard sticking out, would be to join a little in the hymn-singing afterwards perhaps, singing a few of the easier bass notes, that would still sound all right coming from behind the folds of dressing."

All the same, At Naudé informed us, we would be surprised to know what progress had been made in Bekkersdal in recent years. We would not perhaps observe it so much ourselves, he said, just going there to buy things, or to take produce to the market or to drop in for a talk with the bank manager to find out could we draw a little against next year's substantial cheques from the creamery that we were sure to get.

Indeed, it was actually in the course of a friendly exchange of views in that manner with the bank manager - the inkpot as likely as not upsetting on his desk from the way you were banging it to show him how amicable you felt towards him - that you might be inclined to feel that Bekkersdal had a considerable amount of leeway to make up, At Naudé said.

A ten-minute conversation with the bank manager could, At Naudé proceeded, leave you quite flabbergasted at the thought that Bekkersdal was only a hundred years old. The cobwebbed absence of forward-thinking, At Naudé said, the inability to keep pace with modern development that you encountered in that office with the leather-upholstered easy chairs that the doorman conducted you into when you had an up-to-date idea for the bank to be able to benefit itself by, was really astounding, seeing that the bank had to pay out nothing more than, immediately, a few hundred pounds in cash.

"'You've got *Founded in 1875* on the front of the bank, Mr Coetsee,' I said to the bank manager last time," At Naudé informed us, "and I said to him, 'I see the *one* is so worn, you can hardly read it any more, through the years of wind and rain. And I think, well, you should just let it weather like that, Mr Coetsee. Because, from the ideas going on in here, it wouldn't be far wrong for this bank to *have* in front *Founded in 875.*'"

We felt that At Naudé was using rather a lot of words to tell us that he didn't get an overdraft. Well, we had more than one of us had that same difficulty. But we weren't so expansive about it. We merely said, in a few well-chosen words – short words – just what we thought of Mr Coetsee. And we said it, always, when Mr Coetsee wasn't there.

"But in other ways," At Naudé went on, when he saw that he wasn't getting any sympathy from us, "the town of Bekkersdal is advancing with rapid strides. There has been a lot over the wireless and in the newspapers about it. The newspapers have had mostly photographs and the wireless has had mostly what the Town Clerk says. Take population now.

"Well, I read the increase in population in the newspapers and I heard it over the wireless. Did you know that there has been an increase in the White population of Bekkersdal during the last ten years of over 18 per cent? No, I didn't, either, but there has. And there has also been an increase in the Native population. But the biggest increase of all – and the Town Clerk talking over the wireless coughed a bit uncomfortably when he said it – was in the Indian population.

"And then, what do you think is Bekkersdal's income? No, I don't know the exact figures, either. But it's big, I tell you. It's big, not only for a municipality the size of Bekkersdal, but it's big also for a municipality a lot bigger. That's how everything that's going on in Bekkersdal is, it's big."

Because At Naudé was not able to quote exact figures, Chris Welman could revert to his eye-witness account of his recent visit to Bekkersdal that happened to coincide with some of the less exuberant features of the town's preparations for its centenary festival.

"I couldn't enjoy anything very much, of course," Chris Welman said, "on account of my tooth, I mean, even after it was pulled; it was just as sore, almost, as if it was still in. Except that, when it was still in, I didn't have to look every 20 yards or so for a likely place, not exactly in the street and not exactly on the sidewalk either, where I could spit – seeing that my tooth went on bleeding all day.

"Well, anyway, that was one thing I found out about a town, then. How hard it is, in a town, to find a place to spit. I mean, when you're on a farm, and you've got a few thousand morgen, none of it under irrigation, you can then just spit anywhere. And it needn't be because you've had a tooth out, either. Or because of the plug of chewing tobacco that you've got in your mouth. Or because of something you've just thought of.

"The thing is that on a farm you can just spit anywhere, and for no reason, and without thinking about it again. If you're taking a walk along the edge of your mealie-land, for instance, and there's been no rain, and you see what's coming up, on your mealie-land, and more particularly what isn't coming up – and you happen to remember that you sowed there – why, there's no place at all, then, on the edge of your mealie-land, that you aren't allowed to come to a stop and stand and spit. And you can't do that just anywhere you like to in a town.

"But what I did come across quite a lot of in Bekkersdal was how enthusiastic everybody was about the progress the place was making. Like one man said to me how his daughter had been picked to dance in the Volkspele part of the hundred-year birthday celebrations of Bekkersdal. 'I don't mean she's *dancing*, actually,' he said to me. 'My wife and I would never allow that, of course. All my daughter does is she moves in Voortrekker costume in time to the Boere-orkes music – and you simply can't keep your feet still, when it's Boere-orkes music – and she is partnered by a young man also in Voortrekker costume, and she springs, too, naturally, when it comes to that portion of the Boere-orkes music, and the young man in Voortrekker costume springs, too, when it comes there, because he would look silly if he didn't just then, spring, but of course, I would never allow my daughter to *dance*.' They're holding the Volkspele on that piece of vacant ground where the next jam factory is going to be. How's that for progress, hey?"

Except for the schoolmaster, who said that it sounded a bit sticky – the jam factory part of it, he meant – we agreed that Bekkersdal was indeed making an impressive sounding advance.

"And that old building with the thick walls and the small window-panes and the gable," Chris Welman went on, "that we called the Old

Drosdy, standing right there in the middle of the main street – it must have been one of the first buildings they put up in Bekkersdal: I mean, it was just about stinking with age, what with those cracked tambotie-wood ceiling beams and those ridiculous iron gates that they say came from ... oh, I just can't remember now, but they were so heavy, you could hardly push them open - well, the Old Drosdy is gone, now.

"You've got no idea how different the main street looks. A man with a camera who came to photograph the Old Drosdy cried when he saw that it wasn't there any more. But they told him that he didn't have to worry, because that was where the new bioscope was going up that would have electric signs at night that you could see as far as Sephton's Nek. And he could come and photograph the new bioscope in a few months' time, they said to the man with the camera who was looking around him in a lost way, crying."

Right in our time, too, we said, and never mind about the centenary celebrations, there had been a lot of progress made in Bekkersdal. Look at the year they chopped down all those oak-trees, we said, that lined the road going to the north. At least five miles of old oak-trees they must have chopped down, we said. And, well, how was that for advance? Didn't that show that Bekkersdal was really getting somewhere? On the map, wasn't Bekkersdal getting somewhere, we asked.

When people hinted, sometimes, that we weren't keeping pace with the oncoming floodtide of civilization here in the Marico, well, there were a few things we could draw their attention to, all right. We spoke at considerable length, then, and Chris Welman was able to acquaint us with some of the details, that he had heard in the town, of the size of the sideshows that were going to be erected by the merry-go-round people who had contracted to help with the centenary celebrations.

"Is there going to be a merry-go-round?" Oupa Bekker inquired, his eyes lighting up. "Why didn't you say so before? Bekkersdal was named after my grandfather. But I didn't even think of going to the hundred-year birthday. I never thought they would have a merry-go-round, too. They're doing it grand, hey? The first merry-go-round I saw was when I was a child, and we had to go all the way to Zeerust. But you say they're really going to bring the merry-go-round to Bekkersdal? The horses going round, and brass music, and silver paper stars?"

"More than anything else, silver paper stars," Chris Welman said.

Oupa Bekker was genuinely excited.

"My! My!" he said, and again, "My! My! To think that after all these years such a thing should happen to Bekkersdal. We're all going, of course, aren't we? Bekkersdal's hundredth year's birthday. What Chris Welman says is as good as a centenary, just about. And brass music and silver paper stars."

We all said yes, of course we would go. The only person that seemed a bit out of it was the schoolmaster.

And because what he said was what he had learnt at University, the schoolmaster's words did not make sense to us, overmuch.

"The Drosdy," young Vermaak said, "gone. It's like the front teeth knocked out of Bekkersdal's main street. It's as though I've had my own front teeth knocked out by a caestus. It's like I'm myself spitting out teeth."

"Silver paper stars," Oupa Bekker said, who hadn't heard what the schoolmaster was saying, and wasn't interested, anyway.

Peter Badcock

YOUNG MAN IN LOVE

Gysbert van Tonder told us, in Jurie Steyn's voorkamer, that afternoon, that Johnny Coen would be along later. He had seen Johnny Coen, Gysbert said, by the mealie-lands, and Johnny Coen was busy scraping some of the worst turf-soil off his veldskoens with a pocket-knife that had only the short blade left. Johnny Coen was also making use of various wisps of yellow grass, performing wiping movements along the side of his face. Well, we all knew that if, in the middle of the ploughing season, a man took all that trouble with his personal appearance, it must be that he was thinking of going visiting.

"Of course, it doesn't necessarily mean that he's coming *here*," At Naudé observed. "I mean, if he was busy to make himself *so* smart, well, it might perhaps mean that he was working up the courage to go and see *her*. You know what I mean – Johnny Coen taking all the trouble to get the turf-soil off his veldskoens *and* to get the turf-soil off his face.

"If he was coming just here to see us, well, he wouldn't care how much black turf there was on his face. All he would be concerned about was that he didn't leave a lot of thick mud where he walked, here, in the post office, where Jurie Steyn's wife would complain about it."

Oupa Bekker shook his head.

"We know that Johnny Coen hasn't been around to the post office here since he heard that Pauline Gerber was coming back from finishing school," Oupa Bekker said. "And I think we can understand why. We know the kind of talk that there was about Johnny Coen and Pauline Gerber before Pauline suddenly decided to go that ladies' school in the Cape, after all. If you remember, we said that Johnny Coen couldn't have been much of a young man if Pauline Gerber thought that going to a ladies' academy would be more exciting. Of course, we never said any of those things in Johnny Coen's presence –"

Thereupon Chris Welman remarked that since Pauline Gerber's return from the ladies' school in the Cape we hadn't seen much of Johnny Coen's presence.

It was almost as though Johnny Coen wasn't so much shy about seeing Pauline Gerber again, as that he was shy about seeing *us*. There was a thing now, Chris Welman remarked.

Oupa Bekker banged his tambotie walking-stick on the floor, making small holes in the floor and sending up yellow dust. For the first time we realized that he was getting annoyed.

"You won't listen to me," Oupa Bekker said. "You'll never let me finish what I was going to say. Always, you just let me get so far. Then somebody says something foolish, and so I can't get to the important thing. Now, what I want to say is that At Naudé is quite right. And Johnny Coen is coming here. He's coming here this afternoon because he wants to know what *we* think. A young man in love is like that. He wants to know what we've got to say. And all the time he will be laughing to himself, secretly, about the things we're saying. A young man in love is like that, also. And his titivating himself, with the short blade of a pocket-knife and a handful of dry grass – well, you've got no idea how vain a young man in love is.

"And he's not making himself all stylish for the girl's sake but for his own sake. It's himself that he thinks is so wonderful. He knows less than anybody what she is like, the girl he is in love with. And it's only the best kind of pig's fat he'll mix with soot to shine his bought boots with. Because he's in love with the girl, he thinks he's something. Oh, yes, Johnny Coen will come around here this afternoon, all right. And what I want to say –"

At this point, Oupa Bekker was interrupted once more. But because it was Jurie Steyn who broke in upon his dissertation, Oupa Bekker yielded with good grace. The post office we were sitting in was, after all, Jurie Steyn's own voorkamer. There was something of the spirit of old-world courtesy in the manner of Oupa Bekker's surrender.

"— you, then, Jurie Steyn," Oupa Bekker said. "You talk."

Several of us looked in the direction of the kitchen. We were relieved to see that the door was closed. That meant that Jurie Steyn's wife did not hear the low expression Oupa Bekker had used.

"What I would like to say," Jurie Steyn said, "is that I had the honour to drive Juffrou Pauline Gerber to her home in my mule-cart, the day she arrived here at my post office, getting off from the Government lorry and all –"

"What do you mean by 'and all'?" Gysbert van Tonder demanded.

Jurie Steyn looked around him with an air of surprise.

"But you were all here," Jurie Steyn declared. "*All* of you were here. Maybe that's what I mean by *and all*. I am sure I don't know. But you did see Pauline Gerber. You each one of you saw her. When she alighted here that day from the Zeerust lorry, on her return from the Cape finishing school. You saw the way she walked around here in my voorkamer, picking her heels up high – and I don't blame her. And her chin up in the air. And as pretty as you like. You all saw how pretty she was, now, didn't you? And the way she smelt. Did you smell her? You must have. It was too lovely. It just shows you the kind of perfume you can get in the Cape.

"And I am sure that if a church elder smelt her – even if he was an Enkel Gereformeerde Church elder from the furthest part of the Waterberge, I am sure that that Waterberg elder would have known that Pauline Gerber had class – just from smelling her, I mean. I am sure that that scent that Pauline bought at the Cape must have cost at least seven shillings and sixpence a bottle. Look at my wife, now, for instance. Well, I once bought my wife a bottle of perfume at the Indian store at Ramoutsa. And what I say is, you can *smell* the difference between my wife and – and Pauline Gerber."

Chris Welman, who had not spoken much so far, hastened to remark that there were other ways, too, in which you could tell the difference.

It was an innuendo that, fortunately enough, escaped general attention.

For it was Johnny Coen himself that came in at the front door of the post office at that moment. In one way, it was the Johnny Coen that we had always known. And yet, also, it wasn't him. In some subtle fashion Johnny Coen had changed. After greeting us, he went and found a place for himself on a riempies chair, sitting very upright.

He seemed from his manner to be almost unaware of our presence as he whittled a matchstick to a fine point and commenced scraping out the grime from under one of his fingernails.

Gysbert van Tonder, who always liked getting straight down to things, was the first to talk.

"Nice bit of rain you've been having out your way, Johnny," Gysbert van Tonder remarked. "Dams should be pretty full, I'd imagine."

"Oh, yes, indeed," Johnny Coen answered.

"Plenty of water in the spruit, too, I should think," Gysbert continued.

"Yes, that is very true," Johnny Coen replied.

"New grass must be coming along all right in the vlakte where you burnt," Gysbert van Tonder went on.

"Yes, very nicely," Johnny agreed.

Gysbert van Tonder grew impatient.

"What's the matter with you, man – can't you talk?" Gysbert demanded. "You know all right what I am trying to say. Have you seen her at all since she's been back?"

"I saw her yesterday," Johnny Coen said, "on the road near their house. I had to go quite a long distance out of my way to be *passing* there, at the time."

Gysbert van Tonder made a swift calculation.

"Matter of just under eleven miles out of your way, counting in the short cut through the withaaks," he announced. "Did she have much to say?"

Johnny Coen shook his head.

"Please don't ask me," he almost implored of Gysbert, "because I really can't remember. We did speak, I know. But after she had gone there was nothing we said that I could recall. It was all so different, after we had met, and we had spoken there by the road, and she had gone on back home again. It was all so different after she had gone. I wish I *could* remember what we said. What I said must have all sounded very foolish to her, I am sure."

Gysbert van Tonder was not going to allow Johnny Coen to get by so easily.

"Well, how did she look?" Gysbert asked.

"That was what I also tried to remember, afterwards," Johnny Coen declared. "How she looked. What she did. All that. But I just couldn't remember. After she had gone it was all just like it had been a dream, and there was nothing that I could remember for sure. She was picking yellow flowers there by the side of the road, she was, to stick in her hair. Or she was carrying a sack of firewood over her back for the kitchen fire, she was. And it would have been just the same *thing*, the way I felt. But I don't know. All I was able afterwards –"

"That was what I was trying to explain to them, Johnny," Oupa Bekker interjected, "but they never let me finish anything I start to say. They always –"

"Afterwards," Johnny Coen repeated, "after she had gone, that is, there was a kind of sweetness in the air. It was almost hanging in the air, sort of. Once I even thought that it might be a kind of scent, like what some women put on their clothes when they go to Nagmaal.

But, of course, I knew that it couldn't be that. I mean, I knew Pauline wouldn't wear scent, I mean. She's not that kind."

"What I wanted to say earlier on, when you all interrupted me," Oupa Bekker declared, then, with an air of triumph, "is that a young man in love is like that."

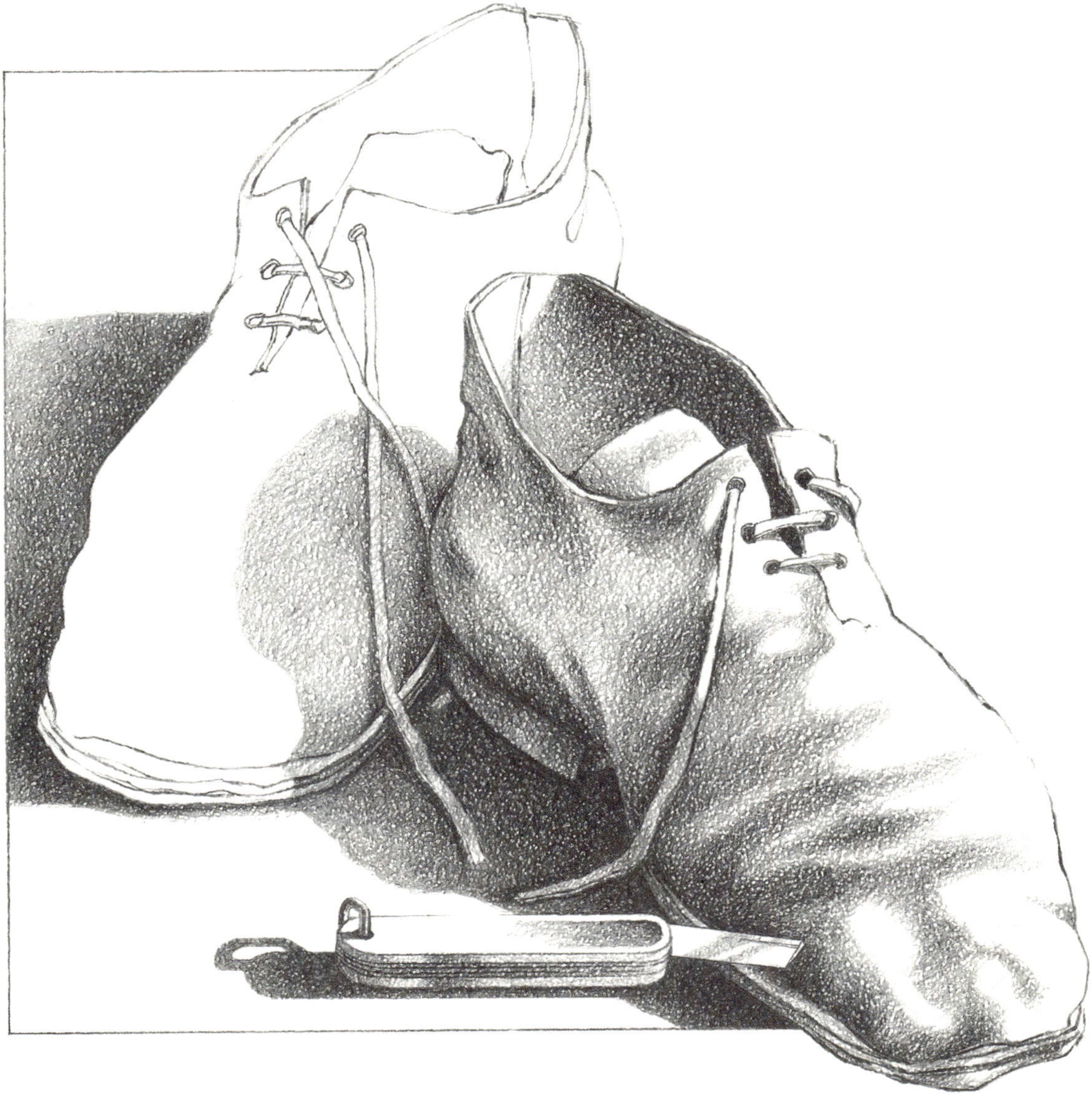

GO-SLOW STRIKE

When At Naudé, who reads the newspapers, came into the post office he was wearing a wide grin.

"Ha, ha," he said to Jurie Steyn, who was leaning forward with his elbows on the counter. "Don't tell me, Jurie. I know why you're standing like that. You're on a go-slow strike. Ha, ha."

Jurie Steyn gazed at At Naudé uncomprehendingly.

"The newspapers say that it's not an official go-slow strike," At Naudé went on, laughing some more, "but of course, you've joined it, haven't you, Jurie? We all know you started before the others. Years before, I should say. I mean, ever since this post office was opened here ..."

"Go-slow strike?" Jurie Steyn enquired blankly. "First I've heard of it. What do they want a thing like that in the post office for? Especially when I'm having all this trouble already with the new mealie-planter."

In a few words At Naudé acquainted Jurie Steyn with the latest news, which had to do with the go-slow strike that the post office employees were staging.

Jurie Steyn was indignant. "Well, if that's what the Postmaster General wants me to start doing now, on top of everything else," Jurie Steyn said, "then I say he can keep his job. Let the Postmaster General come over here and look at my new mealie-planter with the green paint on it. If he still wants a go-slow strike after that I'll tell him he can go and sit down outside and have it on his own. My wife can take him out coffee."

Thereupon At Naudé explained to Jurie Steyn that a go-slow strike was not an additional duty imposed on a Bushveld postmaster by the Postmaster General. Indeed, as far as he knew, the Postmaster General was not even in favour of the go-slow strike that the post office employees were taking part in. For that matter, he doubted if the Minister of Posts and Telegraphs himself was terrifically keen on it, At Naudé said.

Before Jurie Steyn could take it all in, however, Gysbert van Tonder was saying that he had also bought one of those new mealie-planters. In consequence, we all started talking animatedly, several of us at the same time.

More than one farmer from the far side of the Dwarsberge had purchased one of those new mealie-planters after having had it demonstrated in front of the hardware store, the demonstration consisting of the shop assistant filling the seed hopper with mealies and the farmer pulling the mealie-planter up and down on the stoep so that he could see how it worked, the mealies falling out just the right distance from each other with the way the wheels turned; and the farmer enjoying himself.

"Up and down, up and down I went on Policansky's stoep," Gysbert van Tonder said. "I promised David Policansky that I would be careful and not knock any of the new green paint off his mealie-planter. But he said just go ahead. Just make myself at home, he said. He would send somebody along later on to sweep up the mealies I had sown on his stoep, he said. I was not to worry at all.

"Well, I went on until about midday, and by that time I was perspiring quite a lot, because that mealie-planter gets quite heavy to pull, after a while, and the stoep of the hardware store was inches deep in mealies, the way I had been sowing them.

"And then, when it was about midday, to judge by the sun, a whistle blew somewhere – at the sawmill, I think – and Policansky came out of his store and said he thought I could knock off now for lunch. Everybody was knocking off for lunch now, Policansky said."

Chris Welman was able to confirm Gysbert van Tonder's remarks in a considerable measure.

"I just about laughed my head off, too," Chris Welman said, "on Policansky's stoep. How that mealie-planter could drop seeds at any distance you wanted – because you can adjust it, too, you know."

So we all said, yes, we knew you could adjust a mealie-planter. That was when the trouble started. If it didn't start even before then, At Naudé commented, sombrely.

"That's just the point," Chris Welman continued. "The mealie-planter doesn't seem to work so well on the lands, behind a plough, going over kweekgras sods and pieces of turned-up anthill, as it does on the smooth stoep of Policansky's hardware store. It doesn't work nearly so well, I mean. With its new green paint and all, what does a mealie-planter do, as likely as not?"

Meanwhile, Jurie Steyn had put a further question to At Naudé.

"Are you sure you read it right, At?" Jurie asked. "What it said in the newspapers, that is? Did it say all that about the go-slow strike? You know, you have been wrong once or twice ..."

"Once," At Naudé admitted. "I know you're thinking of the time when I came and told you about the money for the Kunswedstryd that got stolen, that I had read about in the Bekkersdal newspaper. But then it came out afterwards that it was a mistake the printer had made in the newspaper."

Several of us spoke up for At Naudé, then. Because we remembered the circumstances. And so it wasn't At Naudé's fault at all for having given us incorrect information. It was just what he had read, about the Kunswedstryd funds getting embezzled. But Dominee Welthagen wrote to the newspaper about it, and what Dominee Welthagen wrote was so strong, we said that even a lawyer couldn't have done it better. And he got an answer right away from the editor. And the editor was very nice about it, the way he explained that it was all a mistake made by the printer. We all said afterwards that the editor of the newspaper couldn't have acted any more handsomely than he did, how he put all the blame on the printer.

And we said that it would be a good idea if, before he just wrote a thing, a printer went and made sure of his facts first.

And what made the whole thing still more peculiar was that there actually *wasn't* any money for the Kunswedstryd, that year.

"Yes, that mealie-planter, green paint and all, wasn't nearly as clever at the bottom end of my turf-lands," Gysbert van Tonder said. "I'll go so far as to say that for that kind of soil the old-fashioned way of getting a Mtosa to walk behind the plough and stick each seed-mealie in with his finger is even better. Yes, I really think that when it comes to the stickier sort of black turf, then a mealie-planter is less educated than a Mtosa."

We felt that was a sweeping statement. Gysbert van Tonder sensed our thoughts.

"I know it doesn't *sound* right what I've just said," Gysbert continued, "but I'm only talking about turf-soil, mind. I know that a mealie-planter with its shining wheels *looks* much more clever than a Mtosa just arrived for work in the morning from his hut. And I won't say that a mealie-planter hasn't perhaps got more human feelings, also, than a Mtosa. I'm not arguing about that, see?"

What Gysbert van Tonder insisted on, however, was that on turf-soil you had to hand it to a Mtosa for education.

"What's more, a Mtosa doesn't need to paint himself all green," Gysbert van Tonder added, as though that clinched the case. "All a Mtosa puts on himself, at a Ndlolo dance, say, is perhaps a little white and blue."

"But does it mean I've got to work slower, right here in my voorkamer?" Jurie Steyn asked of At Naudé while the rest of the conversation was going on.

"Yes, that's the idea," At Naudé replied. "You've got to work only half as fast. It's for more pay."

Jurie Steyn's eye gleamed.

"More pay, hey?" he repeated. "Well, there's a thing for you, now. You'd imagine you'd get less pay for working only half as fast, wouldn't you? But I suppose it all goes to show. You've got to know these things."

At Naudé nodded.

"Yes, it's no good being ignorant, like what Gysbert van Tonder says that mealie-planter is – more ignorant than a Mtosa even, Jurie," At Naudé acknowledged. "You've got to know what's going on. The newspapers I got this morning says just why those unofficial leaders of the post office workers decided to take this kind of action."

Jurie Steyn said that was a good one, too, if you liked.

"Calling it *action*," Jurie Steyn said. "When what they mean is *less* action. When they meant that I've got to do just half as much action, here in my voorkamer, that is. They should call it *un*-action, rather, I'm thinking."

Gysbert van Tonder's voice sounded very loud, all of a sudden.

"– a whole piece with no mealies at all," Gysbert van Tonder was saying. "And then a short stretch with every single seed in the hopper planted into it. And planted in such a way that you can't get the mealies out again, unless you go down on your hands and knees and scrape."

Thereupon Chris Welman said that they should have a machine for doing that, also.

"A machine for scraping out the seeds that have been sown in the wrong place," Chris Welman said. "The mealie un-planter you could call it, I suppose. That would be a funny thing, now, wouldn't it? Useful though."

But Jurie Steyn said that it was no more funny than what At Naudé had just told him, it was, indeed, similar.

Then, when the lorry-driver's assistant came in with the mail-bags, Jurie Steyn attended to him with an air of studied leisureliness. And Jurie Steyn opened only one mail-bag.

"The rest of your letters, kêrels," he said, indicating the second mail-bag, which he had placed under the counter, "I'll let you have to-morrow. I get more pay if I do it like that."

Nor did the latest intelligence, as supplied by the lorry-driver's assistant – to the effect that the go-slow strike had been called off – make any impression on Jurie Steyn. Half-speed and more pay was quite good enough for him, he said. He asked for nothing better. He could keep it up longer even than the Minister of Posts and Telegraphs could, Jurie Steyn reckoned.

MONUMENT TO A HERO

We all said afterwards, talking about it in Jurie Steyn's voorkamer, that the unveiling of the monument erected to the memory of Hartman van Beek had been a most impressive ceremony. We felt privileged to have been present at a great and unforgettable occasion, we said, talking like some of the speakers at the unveiling.

"What I think was the best was Dominee Welthagen's address," Chris Welman started to say, when Jurie Steyn interrupted him.

"What about the Volksraad member's words?" Jurie asked. "There was something for you, now. How the Volksraad member said that at last and after many years we were honouring the debt we owed the memory of Hartman van Beek, rearing a pillar of plain granite –"

"That was like Hartman van Beek's own life had been, strong and plain," Chris Welman interjected. "But Dominee Welthagen said that also."

So Jurie Steyn said that maybe Dominee Welthagen *had* used those words. He wouldn't argue. But his point was that the Volksraad member had also said it. What was more, the Volksraad member had said it louder.

"Dominee Welthagen also declared," Gysbert van Tonder said, for the first time taking part in the conversation, "that it was an inspiration to have said nothing more about Hartman van Beek but just to have carved his name and surname on the plain foot of the rough-hewn piece of granite. Hartman van Beek's life had been like that, too – rough."

But Jurie Steyn asked if we didn't remember that the Volksraad member had said that same thing as well.

"Why, the Volksraad member said distinctly," Jurie Steyn explained, "that he was sure that Hartman van Beek would have preferred to have just that piece of undressed stone, rather than a bronze statue of him riding a horse. Or a sculptured statue of himself standing up and holding in his hand a – well, the Volksraad member didn't seem to know exactly what Hartman van Beek might be holding in his hand. A sword, likely. Or perhaps one of those long pieces of rolled-up paper with 'Traktaat' written on them. I don't know. The Volksraad member didn't say, either."

"Dominee Welthagen," Gysbert van Tonder went on, "said that Hartman van Beek would have liked that piece of raw stone better even than a sitting-down statue of himself, seeing that he was himself so unpolished. He didn't care much for brass or something else that I couldn't quite catch. I didn't care much for it myself. It sounded too foreign."

"*Monumentum aere perennius,*" the schoolmaster pronounced. "It's Latin."

Johnny Coen observed, then, that he was pleased that what the dominee had spoken was Latin. He admitted that he had not been able to follow those words himself, exactly, either. But he had thought at the time, from the way the dominee uttered it, that it was another way of saying how ill-bred and unsmooth Hartman van Beek was, generally.

Johnny Coen said, straight out, that that was something he hadn't liked at the unveiling ceremony, the way each speaker just tried to dig up new words to say how coarse and plain-spoken Hartman van Beek had been.

"Foul-mouthed, too, I thought one of the speakers was going to say about him," Johnny Coen added, "but that speaker just seemed to stop himself in time."

He could not sincerely feel, Johnny Coen went on, that an unveiling ceremony was the right occasion to pick for calling a person names. There was a time and place for everything, he said, and if Hartman van Beek was indeed some sort of an ugly customer, they shouldn't have brought it all up *then.*

"What was more," Johnny Coen said, "every time a speaker made a particularly dirty remark about Hartman van Beek, everybody cheered. When somebody described him as an unlettered son of the soil, there was wild applause."

The conversation took a happier turn, however, when Gysbert van Tonder mentioned the horse commando that had circled the monument at sunset, Oupa Bekker riding in front.

Yes, that was something very fine, we all agreed. And what we would not forget easily, either, was the young men in Voortrekker dress firing a volley into the air as the sun was going down.

There was not the same unanimity of feeling, however, about the President Tableau, that was put on after it had got properly dark. For one thing, we had had to wait too long round that platform that had bucksails raised on it to look like a veld-tent, with flaps that two Mchopis, standing one on each side of it, had to draw apart by pulling on ropes.

For another thing, we felt that they could have got some more suitable person to act the role of the President. Not that the one that took the part wasn't *good*, we said.

After all, it wasn't every day that we got somebody so prominent on the Afrikaans stage to come and present a tableau in the Groot Marico. We were honoured, of course, and we also felt that it was a great honour that was being conferred on Hartman van Beek, he being so unrefined and all. But there were some of the more conservative farmers present who felt that it would have been better if somebody else had been chosen, even if it was somebody that maybe couldn't act so well.

Then it had taken some time to get the motor car lamps fixed in such a way as to throw a searchlight beam on the place where the opening would come in the veld-tent when, at a given signal, the Mchopis pulled on the ropes.

Members of the audience had started getting impatient.

"Maak klaar, kêrels," some of them had said, "Ons moet ry."

It was already well past milking time when the car headlights were switched on and a beam of light got trained onto the platform.

Through some slight error in the manipulation of the lamps, however, the light beam missed the flaps of the veld-tent and instead illuminated, very vividly, the protuberant rump of a Mchopi, who was at that moment engaged in the act of picking up a cigarette-end.

Before the error was rectified there were audible, around the platform, sundry sniggers of so homespun a character that they might almost have emanated from Hartman van Beek himself.

Nevertheless, we all agreed that what followed immediately afterwards was *good*.

When the bucksails in front of the veld-tent were pulled aside, there stood revealed in the full beam of the headlights, a frock-coated figure, broad-shouldered and robust, and wearing a top hat and a presidential sash and side-whiskers. In the silence that followed, the frock-coated figure boomed out, in a deep voice, the well-known words of the President's last message.

Well, as we acknowledged freely afterwards, she was *good*. In this role, we said, Anna Wessels-Wessels was as good as in anything she had done since the play *Dronk op Haar Bruilof*. But there was something about it that wasn't just quite right, somehow. And it wasn't just because she had left a hair-slide sticking out at the side of her top hat.

We were still talking about this – Gysbert van Tonder claiming that he had seen her powder-puff sticking out of the upper of one boot – when young Vermaak, the schoolmaster, suddenly asked a question.

"But who is this Hartman van Beek that the monument was raised to?" he asked. "I mean ... I mean ... I know something about his character from what the speakers at the unveiling said. But who is he? Or who was he? Or what was he?"

We looked at the schoolmaster in surprise.

Jurie Steyn was the first to speak.

"You don't know ...?" Jurie Steyn began. "You haven't heard ...?"

"No," young Vermaak said, bluntly, "I haven't."

Thereupon Chris Welman spoke.

"You," Chris Welman said, his tone sounding grieved. "You, a schoolmaster and all and you really don't know who Hartman van Beek was?

"But you were there – didn't you hear what all those speakers said? I mean, even if you hadn't heard of Bartman – I mean, Hartman van Beek before, you should have learnt then. And here you're supposed to be teaching children in a classroom."

The schoolmaster bridled.

"It's because I'm a schoolteacher," he said, "that I want to know what to teach my pupils. But at the unveiling ceremony not one of the speakers said anything about what Hartman van Beek *did*, to get that monument erected to him. All they talked was the usual son-of-the-veld clap-trap that gets talked when any monument is raised in the Transvaal."

Jurie Steyn shook his head. Several of us followed his example. We shook our heads, also. We wanted to make it quite clear to the schoolmaster that we were shocked at his ignorance.

"But there was the horse commando," Jurie Steyn said in astonishment. "And there was that volley that the young Voortrekker men fired. You *heard* that, didn't you? Next thing you'll be saying is that there wasn't that tableau, even. Maybe you even think, now, that there *isn't* that monument there?"

This time it was the schoolmaster's turn to shake his head. He waited quite a while before he spoke.

"You know what," he said. "I don't think any of those speakers at the ceremony knew anything about Hartman van Beek, either.

"And why has that monument got only his name on it, and not the date of his birth and his death – if he is dead, that is? And that was why the Volksraad member didn't know, if they made a statue of him, what Hartman van Beek should be holding in his hand – if it is an olive branch he should be holding, or a bottle of dop. Or a pump-thing for spraying cockroaches with."

Thereupon Johnny Coen said that the schoolmaster should be ashamed of himself for talking like that about a hero. It was bad enough, some of the remarks the speakers at the unveiling had passed about Hartman van Beek, Johnny Coen said.

But the schoolmaster said that was the last thing he would dream of doing. All he wanted was some information about the man we had honoured by erecting a memorial to him in our midst. And nobody seemed to know anything about him.

"I mean, who was Hartman van Beek?" the schoolmaster asked again. "Was he a leader or a statesman? Was he a missionary or a great hunter or a great fighting man? Or did he save a lot of people's lives, like Wolraad Woltemade? Or was he maybe just even a writer? What *was* he?"

We said that *that* of course, we didn't know. And did it matter, really, we asked the schoolmaster. We realized, also, that it was useless trying to argue with him.

If it wasn't enough that there were the speeches and the volleys and the horse commando *and* the tableau, then there was just nothing, we reflected, that would satisfy young Vermaak.

THE BUDGET

We were sitting in Jurie Steyn's voorkamer at Drogevlei, waiting for the Government lorry from Bekkersdal, that brought us letters and empty milk-cans. Jurie Steyn's voorkamer had served as the Drogevlei post office for some years, and Jurie Steyn was postmaster. His complaint was that the post office didn't pay. It didn't pay him he said, to be called away from his lands every time somebody came in for a penny stamp. What was more, Gysbert van Tonder could walk right into his voorkamer whenever he liked, and without knocking. Gysbert was Jurie Steyn's neighbour, and Jurie had naturally not been on friendly terms with him since the time Gysbert van Tonder got a justice of the peace and a land surveyor and a policeman riding a *skimmel* horse to explain to Jurie Steyn on what side of the vlei the boundary fence ran.

What gave Jurie Steyn some measure of satisfaction, he said, was the fact that his post office couldn't be paying the Government either.

"Maybe it will pay better now," At Naudé said. "Now that you can charge more for stamps, I mean."

At Naudé had a wireless, and was therefore always first with the news. Moreover, At Naudé made that remark with a slight sneer.

Now, Jurie Steyn is funny in this way. He doesn't mind what he himself says about his post office. But he doesn't care much for the ill-informed kind of comment that he sometimes gets from people who don't know how exacting a postmaster's duties are. I can still remember some of the things Jurie Steyn said to a stranger who dropped in one day for a half-crown postal order, when Jurie had been busy with the cream separator. The stranger spoke of the buttermilk smudges on the postal order, which made the ink run in a blue splotch when he tried to fill it in. It was then that Jurie Steyn asked the stranger if he thought Marico buttermilk wasn't good enough for

Peter Badcock

him, and what he thought he would get for half a crown. Jurie Steyn also started coming from behind the counter, so that he could explain better to the stranger what a man could get in the Bushveld for considerably less than half a crown. Unfortunately, the stranger couldn't wait to hear. He said that he had left his engine running when he came into the post office.

From that it would appear that he was not such a complete stranger to the ways of the Groot Marico.

With regard to At Naudé's remark now, however, we could see that Jurie Steyn would have preferred to have let it pass. He took out a thick book with black covers and started ticking off lists with a pencil in an important sort of a way. But all the time we could sense the bitterness against At Naudé that was welling up inside him. When the pencil-point broke, Jurie Steyn couldn't stand it any more.

"Anyway, At," he said, "even twopence a half-ounce is cheaper than getting a Mchopi runner to carry a letter in a long stick with a cleft in the end. But, of course, you wouldn't understand about things like progress."

Jurie Steyn shouldn't have said that. Immediately three or four of us wanted to start talking at the same time.

"Cheaper, maybe," Johnny Coen said, "but not better, or quicker – or – or – *cleaner*." Johnny Coen almost choked with laughter. He thought he was being very clever.

Meanwhile, Chris Welman was trying to tell a story we had heard from him often before about a letter that was posted at Christmastime in Volksrust and arrived at its destination, Magoeba's Kloof, twenty-eight years later, and on Dingaan's Day.

"If a Native runner took twenty-eight years to get from Volksrust to Magoeba's Kloof," Chris Welman said, "we would have known that he didn't run much. He must at least have stopped once or twice at huts along the way for kafir-beer."

Meanwhile, Oupa Sarel Bekker, who was one of the oldest inhabitants of the Marico and had known Bekkersdal before it was even a properly measured out farm, started taking part in the conversation. But because Oupa Bekker was slightly deaf, and a bit queer in the head through advancing years, he thought we were saying that Jurie Steyn had been running along the made road, carrying a letter in a cleft stick. Accordingly, Oupa Bekker warned Jurie Steyn to be careful of mambas. The kloof was full of brown mambas at that time of year, Oupa Bekker said.

"All the same, in the days of the Republics you would not get a White man doing a thing like that," Oupa Bekker went on, shaking his head. "Not even in the Republic of Goosen. And not even after the Republic of Goosen's Minister of Finance had lost all the State revenues in an unfortunate game of poker that he had been invited to take part in at the Mafeking Hotel. And there was quite a big surplus, too, that year, which the Minister of Finance kept tucked away in an inside pocket right through the poker game, and which he could still remember having on him when he went into the bar. Although he could never remember what happened to that surplus afterwards. The Minister of Finance never went back to Goosen, of course. He stayed on in Mafeking. When I saw him again he was offering to help carry people's luggage from the Zeederberg coach station to the hotel."

Oupa Bekker was getting ready to say a lot more when Jurie Steyn interrupted him, demanding to know what all that had got to do with his post office.

"I said that even when things were very bad in the old days, you would still never see a White postmaster running in the sun with a letter in a cleft stick," Oupa Bekker explained, adding, "like a Mchopi."

Jurie Steyn's wife did not want any unpleasantness. So she came and sat on the riempies bench next to Oupa Bekker and made it clear to him, in a friendly sort of way, what the discussion was all about.

"You see, Oupa," Jurie Steyn's wife said finally, after a pause for breath, "that's just what we have been saying. We've been *saying* that in the old days, before they had proper post offices, people used to send letters with Mchopi runners."

"But that's what I've been saying also," Oupa Bekker persisted. "I say, why doesn't Jurie rather go in his mule-cart?"

Jurie Steyn's wife gave it up after that. Especially when Jurie Steyn walked over to where Oupa Bekker was sitting.

"You know, Oupa," Jurie said, talking very quietly, "you have been an ouderling for many years, and we all respect you in the Groot Marico. We also respect your grey hairs. But you must not lose that respect through – through talking about things that you don't understand."

Oupa Bekker tightened his grip on his tambotie-wood walking-stick.

"Now if you had spoken to me like that in the Republican days Jurie

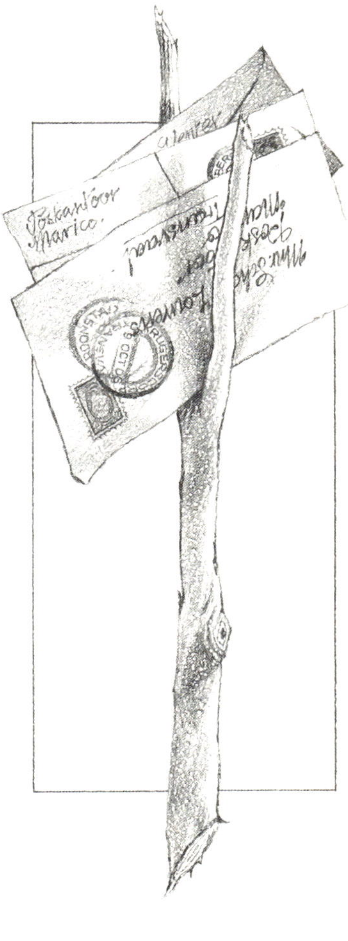

Steyn," the old man said, in a cracked voice, "in the Republic of Stellaland, for instance –"

"You and your Republics, Oupa," Jurie Steyn said, giving up the argument and turning his back to the counter. "Goosen, Stellaland, Lydenburg – I suppose you were also in the Orighstad Republic?"

Oupa Bekker sat up very stiffly on the riempies bench, then.

"In the Orighstad Republic," he declared, and in his eyes there gleamed for a moment a light as from a great past, "in the Republic of Orighstad I had the honour to be the Minister of Finance."

"Honour," Jurie Steyn repeated, sarcastically, but yet not speaking loud enough for Oupa Bekker to hear. "I wonder how *he* lost the money in the State's *skatkis*. Playing snakes and ladders, I suppose."

All the same, there were those of us who were much interested in Oupa Bekker's statement. Johnny Coen moved his chair closer to Oupa Bekker, then. Even though Orighstad had been only a small Republic, and hadn't lasted very long, still there was something about the sound of the words "Minister of Finance" that could not but awaken in us a sense of awe.

"I hope you deposited the State revenues in the Reserve Bank, in a proper manner," At Naudé said, winking at us, but impressed all the same.

"There was no Reserve Bank in those days," Oupa Bekker said, "or any other kind of banks either, in the Republic of Orighstad. No, I just kept the national treasury in a stocking under my mattress. It was the safest place, of course."

Johnny Coen put the next question.

"What was the most difficult part of being Finance Minister, Oupa?" he asked. "I suppose it was to make the budget balance?"

"Money was the hardest thing," Oupa Bekker said, sighing.

"It still is," Chris Welman interjected. "You don't need to have been a Finance Minister, either, to know that."

"But, of course, it wasn't as bad as today," Oupa Bekker went on. "Being Minister of Finance, I mean. For instance we didn't need to worry about finding money for education, because there just wasn't any, of course."

Jurie Steyn coughed in a significant kind of way, then, but Oupa Bekker ignored him.

"I don't think," he went on, "that we would have stood for education in the Orighstad Republic. We knew we were better off without it. And then there was no need to spend money on railways and harbours, because there weren't any, either. Or hospitals. We lived a healthy life in those days, except maybe for lions. And if you died from a lion, there wasn't much of you left over that could be *taken* to a hospital. Of course, we had to spend a good bit of money on defence, in those days. Gunpowder and lead, and oil to make the springs of our old sanna's work more smoothly. You see, we were expecting trouble anyday from Paul Kruger and the Doppers. But it was hard for me to know how to work out a popular budget, especially as there were only seventeen income-tax payers in the whole of the Republic. I thought of imposing a tax on the President's state coach, even. I found that that suggestion was very popular with the income-tax paying group. But you have no idea how much it annoyed the President.

"I imposed all sorts of taxes afterwards, which nobody would have to pay. These taxes didn't bring in much in the way of money, of course. But they were very popular, all the same. And I can still remember how popular my budget was, the year I put a very heavy tax on opium. I had heard somewhere about an opium tax. Naturally, of course, I did not expect this tax to bring in a penny. But I knew how glad the burghers of the Orighstad Republic would be, each one of them, to think that there was a tax that they escaped."

Oupa Bekker was still talking about the measures he introduced to counteract inflation in the early days of the Republic of Orighstad, when the lorry from Bekkersdal arrived in a cloud of dust. The next few minutes were taken up with a hurried sorting of letters and packages, all of which proceeded to the background noises of clanking milk-cans. Oupa Bekker left when the lorry arrived, since he was expecting neither correspondence nor a milk-can. The lorry-driver and his assistant seated themselves on the riempies bench which the old man had vacated. Jurie Steyn's wife brought them in coffee.

"You know," Jurie Steyn said to Chris Welman, in between putting sealing-wax on a letter he was getting ready for the mail-bag. "I often wonder what is going to happen to Oupa Bekker – such an old man and all, and still such a liar. All that Finance Minister rubbish of his. How they ever appointed him an ouderling in the church, I don't know. For one thing, I mean, he couldn't even have been *born*, at the time of the Orighstad Republic." Jurie reflected for a few moments. "Or could he?"

"I don't know," Chris Welman answered truthfully.

A little later the lorry-driver and his assistant departed. We heard them putting water in the radiator. Some time afterwards we heard them starting up the engine, noisily, the driver swearing quite a lot to himself.

It was when the lorry had already started to move off that Jurie Steyn remembered about the registered letter on which he had put the seals. He grabbed up the letter and was over the counter in a single bound.

Chris Welman followed him to the door. He watched Jurie Steyn for a considerable distance, streaking along in the sun behind the lorry and shouting and waving the letter in front of him, and jumping over thorn-bushes.

"Just like a Mchopi runner," Chris Welman said.

MARICO MAN

We were talking about the fossil remains discovered in a gulley of the Malopo by Dr Von Below, the noted palaeontologist. Dr Von Below claimed that what he had found were the remains of the First Man. And it was going to do us on this side of the Dwarsberge a lot of good, we said, especially as Dr Von Below had paid us the compliment of giving his discovery the name of the Marico Man.

The distinguished professor had already given a talk over the wireless about the Marico Man that At Naudé had listened in to. And the schoolmaster, young Vermaak, had read an article on the Marico Man in a scientific magazine to which he subscribed.

"The professor made his find using just the simplest tools you can think of," At Naudé informed us. "Just a simple digging-stick and a plain hand-axe."

"Sounds like the professor is a bit of a Stone Age relic himself," the schoolmaster observed, "using that kind of tools." Nobody laughed.

The important thing, the schoolmaster added, when his joke hadn't gone over, was that as a result of this discovery the Marico Man would now take his place alongside of the Piltdown Man and the Neanderthal Man all over the world in scientific circles where the question as to who was the First Man on earth was being discussed. It was an inspiring thought that the Groot Marico was the ancestral home of the human race.

"That here in the Dwarsberge the First Man, millions of years ago, lower than any savage, started painfully on his upward progress," the schoolmaster said.

But Jurie Steyn said that, speaking for himself, he wasn't too keen on that "lower than any savage" part. Especially as the professor had decided to call his discovery the Marico Man, Jurie Steyn said, with a quick wink at Chris Welman that the schoolmaster did not intercept.

"Yes, that's true," Chris Welman said, coughing and also shutting and opening his left eye too quick for the schoolmaster to see. "I must say I don't fancy it, either – calling an ignorant creature like that the Marico Man. It's that sort of thing that gives us Marico farmers a bad name."

And we didn't want any worse name than what we already had, Chris Welman reckoned.

"And look now what it says about the professor finding the Marico Man's remains in a ditch," Jurie Steyn continued, almost spluttering at the thought of the way that he and Chris Welman were pulling young Vermaak's leg. "Right away people will start getting to think we're so low here that when a person dies his relatives don't give him a proper Christian burial but they just go and throw him away in the first ditch they see. Next thing they'll say is that the Marico Man was found buried with a clay pot next to him. And beads."

By this time Gysbert van Tonder had also tumbled to what was going on. If it was a bit of fun at the schoolmaster's expense, he didn't mind joining in himself.

Frowning on the suggestion of Bushman obsequies in relation to the Marico Man, Gysbert van Tonder declared that he would "rather just lie in the veld and get eaten up by wild animals than to be buried with the Bushman religion. For one thing, what won't my children think of me, I mean, when we meet in the next world and it comes out that I was buried according to the Bushman religion? Or take the Pastor of the Apostolic Church, now, that I told to his face how un-Christian his Nagmaal service was that I looked in at through the window of his church and saw.

"I can just imagine how tight the Pastor will draw his mouth when he comes across me in the hereafter, me having been buried under a half moon and with an ostrich egg painted blue. I'd feel that I was walking with nothing more than a stert-riem on, in the hereafter."

Not able to keep his face as straight as the Apostolic Church Pastor's Gysbert van Tonder burst out laughing. And so he pretended that he was just laughing at the incongruity of the thought of himself wearing a Bushman's wildcat-skin loin-cloth. "Isn't that a scream," he asked, "the thought of me wearing a stert-riem in the *hiernamaals*?" When nobody answered, Gysbert van Tonder's face fell.

It seemed a bad afternoon for jokes. The only people who appeared to be enjoying themselves were Jurie Steyn and Chris Welman.

They kept it up quite a while, saying silly things about how much discredit the Marico Man was going to bring on the inhabitants of the

Dwarsberge area, and doing their best to sound earnest.

"People all over the world will think we don't even know enough to have an ouderling saying words at the graveside," Jurie Steyn was announcing.

"But what's all this talk of funerals and the rest?" the schoolmaster interrupted, looking perplexed. "It's not as though the Marico Man died just the other day, after a long and painful illness that he bore with a patience that was an example to the whole of the Dwarsberge. He's got nothing to do with anybody living here now. So I can't understand your talking about him almost as though you're feeling sentimental about him. After all, it's millions of years ago since the Marico Man was on the earth."

It was when Jurie Steyn, choking over his words, started to say that that was what made it all the more sad, that young Vermaak realized what Jurie Steyn and Chris Welman had been up to.

The schoolmaster thought deeply for a few minutes.

"Anyway, it's like this," he said, eventually. "We know that it can do us a lot of good, in these parts, to have the Marico Man. He's going to make our district world famous. In radio talks and newspapers, in lectures and theses and textbooks, wherever the Neanderthal Man and the Piltdown Man get mentioned, the Marico Man will have to be spoken of, also. Now, that's something, isn't it? Quite a bit of an achievement for a South African, don't you think?"

Young Vermaak recognized, however, that a certain element of jealousy crept into these things. Even the world of science was not altogether immune from that regrettable spirit of partisanship which, in the Education Department, for instance, could lead to a man who had only a Third Class Teacher's Certificate getting appointed to an A-post over the head of somebody who had excellent academic qualifications, failing only in blackboard work.

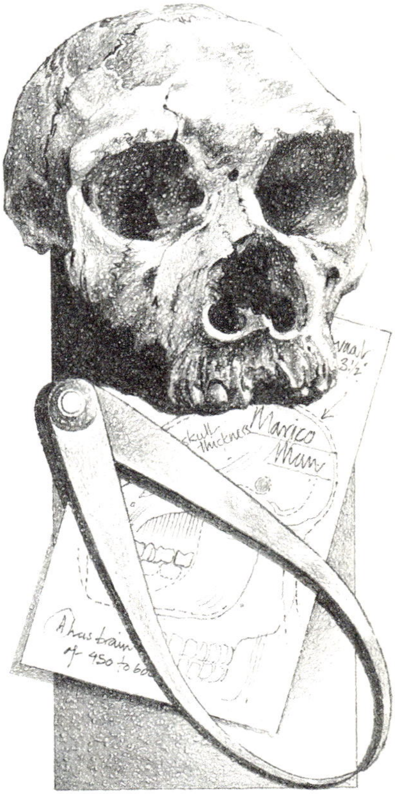

"And I still say," young Vermaak declared – speaking, as it were, in parentheses – "that, give me a piece of chalk that *writes* and a blackboard easel that doesn't fall over backwards the moment you touch it - the Department examiner hopping about directly afterwards, holding his one foot - then I still say I'm as good at blackboard work as the next man."

We felt that it would have been in better taste, on young Vermaak's part, if he had abstained from drawing aside the veil that had, until then, screened from public gaze the circumstances attendant on his having got low marks in one of the subjects he took for his teacher's diploma.

"I am only trying to explain," he continued – closing, in a somewhat self-conscious fashion, the parentheses – "that in the scientific world there will as likely as not be prejudice against the Marico Man. And just because he's so *good*, that is, they'll have spite against him. And so they won't sometimes mention his name when they ought to – like when they're mentioning the Neanderthal Man's name, say, or the Piltdown Man's name.

"He's great, I'm telling you - the Marico Man is. As a claimant for being the First Man, why, the Marico Man has got the Piltdown Man licked hollow. And as for the Neanderthal Man – I really believe that next to the Marico Man the Neanderthal Man hasn't got a leg to stand on, leave alone two legs *and* two hands to stand on, which I believe is how the Marico Man actually stood, if the truth were only known. That is how good I think the Marico Man is.

"And so you can quite understand that there would be scientists that would be jealous of the Marico man, and they would talk slightingly of him.

"They don't like to have to accept it that their Neanderthal Man went up like a rocket but came down like a stick, the moment the Marico Man arrived on the scene - arriving on the scene walking on all-fours, even, and with his mouth hanging sort of half-open in surprise.

"There are going to be scientists that will hesitate to let on, in fashionable places, that they have even heard of the Marico Man. And all just because they think he's a bit too crude. Everybody naturally expects the First Man to have been somewhat rough. But when he's just out-and-out offensive, like it looks as though the Marico Man must have been, well, you can understand that quite a lot of scientists are going to be pretty haughty in their treatment of him. Especially when they've got the future of their pet, the Neanderthal Man, to think of. Or their other pet, the Piltdown Man. *His* career. Next think they know, the Piltdown Man will be out of a job. He'll be on the sidewalk, cadging sixpences for drink."

Needless to say, the way the schoolmaster put it then made it all look different. If there was going to be prejudice against the Marico Man, merely because he came from this side of the Dwarsberge, well, we wouldn't stand for it, that was all.

"I'd like to know what right they've got to despise the Marico Man," Jurie Steyn said, "just as long as he did the best he could, while he was alive. That's what I say. Just so's they can crack up one of those – what are they, again?"

"The Neanderthal Man?" the schoolmaster asked. "The Piltdown Man?"

"Yes," Jurie Steyn said, "those. A couple of foreigners – immigrants – that a Marico-born man has got to stand cheek from, when he's just as good."

The point, the schoolmaster said, about the Marico Man, was not only that he did his best, but that he achieved far more than any of his closest rivals in the competition for being acclaimed the First Man. From the shape of his skull, you could see that the Marico Man had all the opposition beaten to a frazzle in respect of weakness of brain-pan.

The Marico Man was so much slower witted than the Piltdown Man that it was pitiful. Pitiful for the Piltdown Man's chances of getting recognized as having been the First Man, that was. Nobody, no matter how primitive, had any chance of being accorded senior classification as a human being, when all the time there was the Marico Man lurking in the background. *Skulking* in the background would probably be a more accurate way of expressing it.

It was a solemn thought, the schoolmaster said, to contemplate the Marico Man as we knew him - the Marico Man supporting himself in an upright position with the help of his knuckles, his eyebrows lifted high and his jaw protruding several inches more than the Neanderthal Man's jaw. The Marico Man in that particular posture, looking at a planet. It made you think, the schoolmaster said.

Gysbert van Tonder was the first to tumble to it that in all this long thing he was saying the schoolmaster was just being sarcastic – on account of his leg having been pulled earlier on.

"But I still say," Gysbert van Tonder declared, doggedly. "With all this nonsense that has been talked, I still say that if the Dr Von Below knows what is good for him, he'll keep away from this part of the Dwarsberge. We won't think twice of running him out of the place. Running him *and* his precious Marico Man out of the place. And seeing which of them goes quicker. What I can't get over is the cheek of this scientist – digging up a handful of bones and calling it the Marico Man. And talking about him walking almost four-footed; and having a weak brain-pan; and a jaw like a gorilla; and –"

"It's a closely reasoned treatise," the schoolmaster said. "I've read it."

"About the only insulting thing," Gysbert van Tonder observed, "that this scientist doesn't say about the Marico Man is that the Marico Man is also cross-eyed and left-handed."

This was one of those days when Oupa Bekker was somewhat more deaf than usual. He had heard and followed only part of our conversation.

"The first man in the Marico?" Oupa Bekker asked. "You mean, the first Marico White man? Well, that's Louw Combrink ... Louw Toutjies, we used to call him in the old days. He used to walk sort of bent forward ... Hey? What's that? ... No, not his beard. It's the way his jaw stuck out ... Louw Toutjies? ... Of course, he's still alive. He's living in the mountains just other side Derdepoort ... Scientist? Well, I'd like to see what Louw Toutjies does to a scientist that's been telling people he's dead. I'd like to *see* it, that's all."

GHOST TROUBLE

They were having ghost trouble again in the Spelonksdrift area, Chris Welman said to us when we were sitting in Jurie Steyn's post office. The worst kind of ghost trouble Chris Welman added.

We could guess what that meant.

Everybody knew, of course, that Spelonksdrift was swarming with ghosts, any time after midnight. The ghosts came out of the caves in the Dwarsberge nearby. During the day it was quite all right. Then even the most difficult spectres would go and lie down in the hollowed-out places at the foot of the koppie and try and get some rest. But after dark they would make their way to the drift, dragging chains and carrying on generally. That much we all knew. I mean, there was not even a Mtosa cattle-herd so ignorant as willingly to venture near the drift after nightfall.

When it comes to having to do with ghosts, a Mtosa can be almost as educated as a White man.

Again, with regard to ghosts, we could still remember the time when the new schoolteacher, Charlie Rossouw, who was fresh from college, taught the standard V class, in the history lesson, about the Great Trek. He was talking about the Voortrekker leader, Lodewyk Loggenberg, and about the route his party took, and about the Dagboek that Lodewyk Loggenberg kept. The young schoolteacher said that he did not want his class to think of history as just names of persons that they had to remember, but that the Voortrekkers belonged to their own nation, and were people like their own fathers, say, or – if that was too unpleasant a thought – perhaps like their uncles.

Then, drawing on the blackboard with a piece of chalk, Charlie Rossouw explained to the class that Lodewyk Loggenberg had passed through the Groot Marico with his wagons. "Perhaps the trek passed right in front of where this schoolhouse is today," the teacher said.

"Maybe Lodewyk Loggenberg's long line of wagons, with *voorryers* and *agterryers* and with the Statebybel in the *bok* and with copper moulds from which to make candles six at a time after you had fixed the wick in the middle, properly (I mean, you know the difference now between a form candle and a water candle: we did that last week) – maybe those Voortrekkers passed along right here, and the tracks that their wagon wheels made over the veld were the beginning of what we today call the Government road. Think of that. I wonder what Lodewyk Loggenberg wrote in his Dagboek when he went along this way towards Spelonksdrift? What he thought of this part of the country, I mean. That grand old Patriarch. Does anybody here know what a Patriarch is?"

Practically every child in that standard V class put up his or her hand, then. No, they did not know what a Patriarch was. But they did know what Lodewyk Loggenberg wrote in his Dagboek about Spelonksdrift. And they told the schoolmaster. And the schoolmaster, because he was young and fresh from college, laughed in a lighthearted manner at the answers the pupils gave him. It was all the same answer, really. And it was only after Faans Grobler, who was chairman of our school committee, had spoken earnestly to Charlie Rossouw about how serious a thing it was to laugh at a standard V pupil when he gave the right answer, that Charlie Rossouw went to Zeerust on a push-bicycle over a week-end. Charlie Rossouw spent several hours in the public library at Zeerust. When he came back he was a changed man.

After that, he put in even more time than he had done in the Zeerust library in explaining to standard V – which was the top class – that he had not known, until then, that that particular passage about the haunted character of Spelonksdrift appeared in Lodewyk Loggenberg's Dagboek. He had never been taught that at University, Charlie Rossouw said. But it was clear enough now, of course. He had read it in print. It gave him an insight into Lodewyk Loggenberg's mind that he did not have before, he acknowledged. But then, while he was at the teachers' college, he was not able to go into all those details about South African history. He had to study subjects like blackboard work and cardboard modelling and the theory of education and the depth of the Indian Ocean and the Scholastic Philosophers, including Archbishop Anselm and Thomas Aquinas and Peter Lombard and Duns Scotus. And there was also Albertus Magnus, Charlie Rossouw said. So he should not be blamed for not knowing *everything* that Lodewyk Loggenberg wrote in his Dagboek. He had been so busy, night after night, trying to make out what Duns Scotus was trying to get at. But now that he had himself gone into the world a bit, the schoolmaster said, it seemed to him that there was quite a lot in common between Duns Scotus and Lodewyk Loggenberg. In his opinion, they would both of them have got pretty high marks for cardboard modelling.

Francina Smit, who was in standard V, and who was good at arithmetic, said afterward that Charlie Rossouw made that remark with what she could only describe as a sneer.

All the same, Charlie Rossouw said to his class, even though it was true that Lodewyk Loggenberg *had* written those things about Spelonksdrift in his Dagboek, it would be best if the class kept quiet about it when the inspector came. He was sure that the school inspector would misunderstand an answer like that. He did not believe that the inspector knew Lodewyk Loggenberg's Dagboek very well. He even went so far as to doubt whether the school inspector knew much about Thomas Aquinas.

A little later, when Charlie Rossouw was sacked from the Education Department, we in the Groot Marico were pleased about it. There was just something about Charlie Rossouw that made us feel he was getting too big for his boots. The next thing he would be telling his class was that the earth turns round the sun. Whereas you've only got to lie in the tamboekie-grass on Abjaterskop towards evening and *watch*, and you'll see for yourself that it isn't so. All those astronomers and people like that – where would they be if they once lay on Abjaterskop in the setting sun, and shredded a plug of roll-tobacco with a pocketknife, in the setting sun, and looked about them, and thought a little?

Anyway, even though we who were sitting in Jurie Steyn's voorkamer, that also served as the Dwarsberg post office, were not astronomers, or anywhere near, we were nevertheless much impressed by Chris Welman's statement that they were having ghost trouble at Spelonksdrift. When it came to seeing a ghost you didn't need to be an astronomer and to have a telescope: a ghost was something that you could actually see best just with the naked eye.

Now, if the spirits of the dead were content to haunt only the drift after nightfall, then no harm could come to any human being. No human being was ever *there* after nightfall. It was when a pale apparition took to the road, and wandered through the poort to have a look round, that unfortunate incidents occurred.

If you were travelling along the Government road at night and you saw a person walking – or riding on horseback, even – and you saw the moon shining through that person, then you would know, of course, that you had met a ghost. If there was no moon, then you would see the stars shining through the ghost. Or you might even see a withaak tree or a piece of road showing through the ghost.

Gysbert van Tonder once encountered an elderly ghost, riding a mule, right in the middle of the poort. And Gysbert van Tonder held long converse with the ghost, whom he took to be an elderly farmer that had come back from a dance at Nietverdiend – coming back so late because he was elderly. It was when Gysbert van Tonder recognized the mule that the elderly farmer was sitting on as old Koffiebek, that had belonged to his grandfather and that had died many years before of grass-belly, that Gysbert van Tonder grew to have doubts. What made him suspicious, Gysbert van Tonder said, was that he had never in his life seen Koffiebek standing so still, with a man sitting on his back, talking. During the whole conversation Koffiebek did not once try to bite a chunk out of his rider's leg. In the same moment Gysbert van Tonder realized that it was because there wasn't much of his rider for Koffiebek to bite.

"What made it all so queer," Gysbert van Tonder said, "was that I had been talking to the elderly farmer on the mule about a new comet that there was in the sky, then. And I had asked him if he thought it meant the end of the world, and he said he hoped not, because there were several things that he wanted to do still. And it didn't strike me that, all the time we were talking about the comet, the old farmer was sitting between me and the comet, and I was seeing the comet through the middle of his left lung. I could see his right lung, too, the way it swelled out when he breathed."

It was getting late, not only in Jurie Steyn's post office, but everywhere in the Marico, and the lorry from Bekkersdal had not yet arrived with our letters and milk-cans. They must be having trouble along the road, we said to each other.

And because of the line of conversation that Chris Welman had started, we were glad when Jurie Steyn, on his return from the milking-shed, lit the paraffin-lamp in the voorkamer before it was properly dark.

Oupa Bekker had been very quiet, most of the evening. Several times he had looked out into the gathering dusk, shaking his head at it. But after Jurie Steyn had lit the oil-lamp, Oupa Bekker cheered up a good deal. Then he started telling us about the time when *he* encountered a ghost near Spelonksdrift, in the old days.

"I had lost my way in the dark," Oupa Bekker declared, "and so I thought that that stretch of water was just an ordinary crossing over the Malopo River. I had no idea that it was Spelonksdrift. So I pulled up at the edge of the stream to let my horse drink. Mind you, I should have known that it was Spelonksdrift just through my horse not having been at all thirsty. Indeed, afterwards it struck me that I had never before seen a horse with so little taste for water. All he did was to look slowly about him and shiver."

At Naudé asked Jurie Steyn's wife to turn the paraffin-lamp up a bit higher, just about then. He said he was thinking of the lorry-driver. The lorry-driver would be able to see the light in Jurie Steyn's voorkamer from a long way off, if the lamp was turned up properly, At Naudé explained. It was queer how several of us, at that moment, started feeling concern for the lorry-driver. We all seemed to remember, at once, that he was a married man with five children. Jurie Steyn's wife did not have to turn much on the screw to make the lamp burn brighter. We men did it all for her. But then, of course, we Groot Marico men are chivalrous that way.

In the meantime, Oupa Bekker had been drooling on in his old-man way of talking, with the result that when we were back in our seats again we found that we had missed the in-between part of his story. All we heard was the end part. We heard about his dispute with the ghost, that had ended in the ghost letting him have it across the chops with the back of his hand.

"So I went next day to see Dr Angus Stuart," Oupa Bekker continued. "In those days he was the only doctor between here and Rysmierbult. I didn't tell him anything about what had happened at Spelonksdrift. I just showed him my face, with those red marks on it ... And do you know what? After he had had a good look at those marks through a magnifying glass, the doctor said that they could have been caused only by a ghost hitting me over the jaw with the back of a blue-flame hand."

That story started Johnny Coen off telling us about the time he was walking through the poort, one night, with Dawie Ferreira, who had once been a policeman at Newclare. And while he and Dawie Ferreira were walking through the poort, a Bechuana through whom they could see the Milky Way shining came up to them. In addition to having the Milky Way visible through his spine, the Bechuana was also carrying his head under his arm. But Dawie Ferreira, because he was a former policeman, knew how to deal with that Bechuana, Johnny Coen said. He promptly asked him where his pass was for being on a public road at that time of night. You couldn't see the Bechuana for dust after that, Johnny Coen said. In fact, the dust that the Bechuana with his head under his arm raised on the Government road of the Marico seemed to become part of, and to reach beyond, the Milky Way that shone through his milt and was also a road.

The lorry from Bekkersdal arrived very late. The driver looked perturbed.

"We had big-end trouble at Spelonksdrift," the lorry-driver said, "and an old farmer riding a mule came up and gave me a lot of sauce. He acted as though he was a ghost, or something. As though I'd take notice of that sort of nonsense. I saw through him, all right. Then he sloshed me one across the jaw. When I tried to land him one back he was gone."

The lorry-driver had marks on his cheek that could have been caused by a backhander from an elderly farmer riding a mule.

Peter Badcock

COFFIN IN THE LOFT

"There's nothing to be *afraid* of in a ghost," Jurie Steyn said, "so I don't know why there should be all this fuss now – people saying they won't travel by the Abjaterskop road at night."

So Gysbert van Tonder said that he had never heard of any ghost ever doing a human being harm. "Real harm, that is," he made haste to supplement his statement.

That made Chris Welman feel that he would like to go even further. There were actually instances of ghosts being helpful to human beings, Chris Welman said. Like a ghost pointing out to a party of treasure-hunters where to dig.

Ghosts were also known to have assisted in the maintenance of law and order, putting the police onto the right track when they were investigating a crime.

"Yes, and I'd like to know where the police would *be*, if it wasn't for ghosts telling them what to do," Gysbert van Tonder declared. "And not only ghosts, but a man's own neighbour, too, sometimes. A neighbour that he trusts, what's more."

So Jurie Steyn said that Gysbert van Tonder was just being silly, now. If Gysbert van Tonder thought that it was he, Jurie Steyn, that had told Sergeant Rademeyer about those long-horned cattle in the camp by the kloof, then it was the biggest mistake Gysbert van Tonder had made in his life.

"In any case, you've got nothing to complain about," Jurie Steyn ended up. "You got them out of the way in time. All except the red heifer with the white markings on the left foreleg."

"You seem to know a lot about it," Gysbert van Tonder said, sounding suspicious again. "Anyway, the markings are on the right foreleg. You can go and tell that to your friend Sergeant Rademeyer. You can also tell him that how I got the animals away in time was because I knew he was coming. I heard it from a ghost."

It took a little while, after that, for the conversation to resume a placid tenor and by that time Oupa Bekker was telling a long story about a coffin in a loft.

The ghost that stayed in that coffin was, of course, as harmless as anything, Oupa Bekker said. It would just lift up the lid at midnight and descend from the loft, using the outside stairs and not making much noise, and it would then just haunt the neighbourhood a bit, returning to its coffin well before sunrise and then letting down the lid again – and so quietly that you could hardly hear it. That ghost wouldn't hurt a fly, Oupa Bekker added.

Thereupon Johnny Coen interrupted Oupa Bekker to remark that, while we all knew that a ghost was harmless, at the same time we were none of us anxious to encounter a ghost, if we could help it.

"I mean, no matter how quiet a ghost acts, or how friendly he is, even," Johnny Coen said, "if he comes on you from behind, suddenly, and you're alone in the bush, and it's a particularly dark night, say – well, you'd rather *not* have that ghost around.

"No matter what Oupa Bekker says about how harmless such a ghost is, or about how helpful, even. I think it makes it even worse if such a ghost tries to be helpful. I don't say I'd get frightened –"

So we all said, no, of course we wouldn't get frightened, either. It wasn't a question of fear, we said. Not that we mightn't run a little, naturally, if we were on foot, or urge the horse on, slightly, if we were on horseback.

But it wasn't fear, or anything like that, we said. It just stood to reason that it was a disagreeable experience to meet a ghost alone in the veld at night. After all, it was human nature to feel like that.

Thereupon Chris Welman mentioned something he had seen just outside the Bekkersdal graveyard one night.

"It's a lonely sort of graveyard," Chris Welman explained, "and so just out of human nature I didn't worry to pick my hat up when it fell off."

Then At Naudé told us about the height of the barbed-wire fence that he had cleared at one leap near Nietverdiend, in the dark, on account of human nature and arising out of what he saw.

Before Oupa Bekker could get back to his coffin-in-the-loft story, At Naudé asked what was the strength of the report about the Abjaterskop road being haunted.

Everybody seemed to be talking about it. Not that that sort of thing made any difference to him, At Naudé said. He didn't care if the Abjaterskop road *was* haunted, seeing that he hardly ever went that way – and certainly never at night.

"Well, it seems that it was some of Gysbert van Tonder's Bechuanas who first said they saw a ghost there," Chris Welman said. "Isn't that right, Gysbert?"

"They *and* others," Gysbert van Tonder replied.

"The ghost is supposed to haunt the part of the road near the broken-down walls of the old farmhouse, that we call the murasie," Chris Welman proceeded. "That's right, hey, Gysbert?"

"That part *and* other parts," Gysbert van Tonder announced. "But mostly near the murasie."

There was something decidedly creepy in the way Gysbert van Tonder spoke, so that it came in the nature of a relief to us when Oupa Bekker returned to his coffin-ghost tale.

"What made it all seem so queer," Oupa Bekker said, "was that it was an *unused* coffin that the ghost stayed in. The coffin had been in the loft of that farmhouse for as long as almost anybody could remember."

Johnny Coen asked why they didn't go up and open the coffin and look. Oupa Bekker gazed steadily at Johnny Coen for some moments.

"Would you have liked to have gone and looked?" Oupa Bekker asked him. "In the old days, that is?"

Johnny Coen acknowledged that he wouldn't have liked it. Either in the old days or today, he said. Certainly, on his own he would not have cared to go. It would be different, perhaps, going in the company of a few people he could rely on. Say about seven or eight people.

Oupa Bekker nodded. "That's what happened in the end," Oupa Bekker said. "The farmer got a good Malay ghost-catcher up from the Cape. And when the Malay opened the coffin in the presence of the whole family, there were the mouldering bones of a human skeleton inside."

The Malay was able to tell them, also, Oupa Bekker said, that that was the kind of ghost that could never be laid. Ordinary kinds of ghosts he could catch in a bottle of sea-water that he had brought up with him for that purpose from the Cape, but the ghost in the coffin would go on haunting the place until the end of the world, becoming worse the older he got.

The police were called in, Oupa Bekker said, and they were satisfied that it was murder. A more horrible murder even than ordinary, they said, because they couldn't find any clues. And the mystery was never solved, even though the ghost gave the police what help it could.

"And the Malay was proven right," Oupa Bekker concluded. "Even after his skeleton was given decent Christian burial, the ghost kept on haunting the house. The family trekked away, afterwards, and nobody else would live in the place, which is today a ruin. That ghost is still there, and, as the Malay prophesied, with the years he gets worse."

Gysbert van Tonder yawned.

"Ah, well, I've got to be going," he said, "Maybe it would be different if I met that ghost alone in the veld at night. But on an afternoon like this – ah, well."

He walked out of the voorkamer still yawning.

"You know," Jurie Steyn said, after Gysbert van Tonder had left, "Gysbert van Tonder seemed a bit mysterious about that ghost on the Abjaterskop road, didn't he?"

We agreed that it was so.

"Well, I can see it's something he's made up – that the road is haunted," Jurie Steyn continued. "Because, from what Sergeant Rademeyer told me, that was just the trouble he had, following Gysbert and the herd of cattle, that night. It was along the Abjaterskop road, and when they came to the part near the murasie, Rademeyer's police-boys said that they had heard that the place was haunted and they wouldn't go any further. That was how Gysbert van Tonder got away. Through having spread that ghost story."

After we had said, well, how's that for cunning, Jurie Steyn acquainted us with this further insight into the police sergeant's point of view:

"Well, I could, I expect, have gone on and followed him on my own," Sergeant Rademeyer had said. "I mean, I'm not afraid of ghosts. That would be absurd. But I could see it looked funny there, by that murasie, with those dark shadows amongst the trees. And the wind makes an awful sound about there, too. And I've got a wife and four children to think of. It's not that I was afraid –"

No, it was just human nature, we said, when Jurie Steyn repeated that part of the sergeant's statement to us.

But Oupa Bekker said that Gysbert van Tonder would find out his mistake, yet. And then Gysbert van Tonder would turn grey just in one night, Oupa Bekker said.

"Because the Abjaterskop road *is* haunted," Oupa Bekker said. "And by the worst kind of ghost that there is, too, now. The murasie there is the ruins of the old farmhouse with the loft. And what that ghost must be like today, I would much rather just not think."

CIRCUMSTANTIAL EVIDENCE

One story we heard was that Pauline Gerber's eldest brother, Dons, spoke to young Vermaak, the schoolmaster, on the platform at Zeerust station. According to this story, the schoolmaster was just getting ready to board the train, and Dons Gerber had a single-barrelled shotgun in the bend of his arm when he spoke to the schoolmaster.

According to the second story we heard, young Vermaak was sitting in the classroom, after school, correcting excercise books, and it was Pauline Gerber's youngest brother, Floris, who addressed him, Floris oiling the mechanism of a Mott-Mauser at the time.

It was difficult to know what to believe, exactly. Each story was so well authenticated. The circumstances relating to Dons and the railway platform embraced the language that the the train-guard used when he had to stop the train, after having blown the whistle, so that the schoolmaster could get his suitcases out of the compartment again.

"It's how a ticket examiner spoke to me, once," Gysbert van Tonder observed, "when I was travelling on a mail-train to De Aar. I may say that I didn't have a ticket at the time that the ticket examiner addressed me."

If they weren't exactly *alike*, Gysbert van Tonder added, the ticket examiner's words still bore a family resemblance to the expressions employed by the Zeerust train-guard in advising the schoolmaster to make up his mind.

Thereupon At Naudé was also able to recall a less happy travel experience of his own, that had to do with his ejecting an empty half-jack of brandy from a train window at Rysmierbult. He never knew where that empty half-jack *got* the ganger, exactly, At Naudé said, but he could still remember how the ganger who happened to be on the line at the time complained about if for the full twenty minutes that the train halted at Rysmierbult.

"By the time-table, the train should have stopped there only ten minutes," At Naudé proceeded, "but I think that why there was that long wait that day was because the engine-driver got a respect for the ganger's language, after listening to it for a bit, and so he felt he wanted to give him a bit of a show. I won't say that the ganger didn't take full advantage of the extra ten minutes that the engine-driver allowed him, either. All the same, I still wonder, today, where that bottle did hit the ganger."

On the other hand, the other story, which had to do with Pauline Gerber's youngest brother, Floris, seemed to be quite as well-appointed in respect of circumstantial detail.

For the railway platform's strident bustle you had only to substitute the scholarly calm of the Drogedal schoolroom with its thatched roof and whitewashed walls, the pupils, their textbooks cast aside, having long since departed, on foot or by school donkey-cart.

The only sounds in that peaceful classroom, with the day drawing to its close, would be the even scratchings of the schoolmaster's red-ink pen in double-ruled exercise books supplied by the Transvaal Education Department.

At intervals, the schoolmaster's pen would *slash*, somewhat, and there would be a measure of unsteadiness about the schoolmaster's breathing. But those were matters readily to be understood. Mistakes in composition and sums. But, I mean, infamous mistakes.

And then, very suddenly, there would obtrude the click-clock sound of the bolt mechanism of a Mauser being operated. It was a situation not wanting in drama. After all, we all know why a Mauser has got to be oiled so often. Its magazine system lacks the smoothness of the Lee Enfield.

You can't fire an old Mott-Mauser as fast as a Lee Enfield, maybe. But over 800 yards aimed at a person running, it's more accurate.

Nevertheless, Jurie Steyn said that it seemed rather a silly thing for Pauline Gerber's youngest brother, Floris, to have done – going along oiling his gun there in the classroom.

"Why couldn't he have done all that at home?" Jurie Steyn wanted to know. "He must have been a bit soft in the head, if you ask me. Perhaps he still is."

But Chris Welman said he did not think that Jurie Steyn was well-advised in making that particular kind of remark. Not where Pauline Gerber's youngest brother was concerned, Chris Welman said. Or her eldest brother, either. Or even any of her in-between brothers.

Perhaps it would have been best if Jurie Steyn had merely said that Pauline Gerber's youngest brother had been a bit playful, walking into the classroom with a gun *and* an oil-can, and if Jurie Steyn had then just left it at that. Perhaps that was all Jurie Steyn *wanted* to imply, Chris Welman suggested, his voice sounding very gentle, all at once.

Jurie Steyn bridled.

"If you think I'm scared of the Gerbers, old Koos Gerber or any one of his sons, or the whole lot of them together, even," Jurie Steyn announced, "then you don't know me, that's all. A lot of loud-mouthed braggarts, that's all they are. Bullies, too, if you ask me. Cowards, that's what."

But Gysbert van Tonder reminded Jurie Steyn that on the railway platform Pauline Gerber's eldest brother, Dons, had said hardly a word. It was the train-guard that did all the talking. It was the train-guard that you could say was perhaps loud-mouthed, Gysbert van Tonder said. Telling young Vermaak to hustle with his traps, and what to do with his umbrella.

Similarly, in the classroom of the Drogedal school, Chris Welman interjected, Pauline Gerber's youngest brother, Floris, had said nothing at all.

"As far as we *know*, Floris Gerber didn't talk," Chris Welman said. "Of course, I don't suppose he had any need to talk, exactly. Working on the bolt of the Mott-Mauser was taking up all his attention, I suppose, and if he spoke he might have spilt some of the oil over the school-books."

It was clear, however, that Chris Welman had got Jurie Steyn going. Maybe even Chris Welman himself, when he had in a spirit of Bushveld perversity hinted to Jurie Steyn not to speak out of his turn where the men of the Gerber family were involved – maybe even Chris Welman had not counted on so complete a success for his stratagem.

"The more I think of this whole business," Jurie Steyn declared, "the more my heart warms to young Vermaak. The way that young schoolteacher has been treated here, in the Groot Marico, just because he's a stranger. All I can say is that it's unchristian."

There was something for you, now.

It took our breath away. We tried to remember over how long a while Jurie Steyn had regularly gone out of his way to make the schoolmaster feel small. And just because, as we all knew, Jurie Steyn's wife had a soft spot for the schoolmaster.

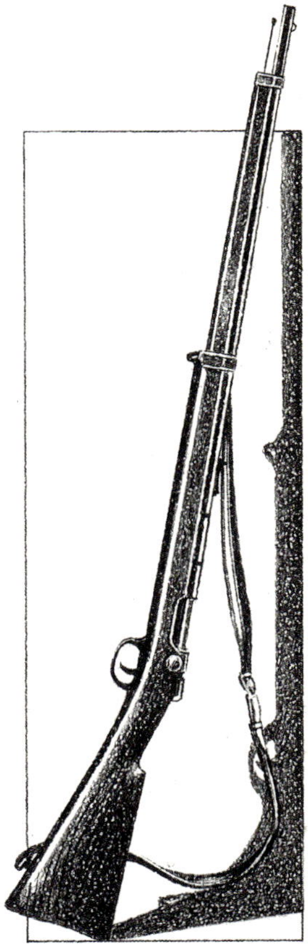

And yet a few simple words spoken by Chris Welman (Chris Welman having done nothing more than to impugn Jurie Steyn's physical fortitude when faced by the Gerber brothers) could have the effect of changing Jurie Steyn's outlook in a single moment.

Here was Jurie Steyn actually declaring, for all of us to hear, that he was siding with the schoolmaster. That gave you some idea as to how scared Jurie Steyn must be of the Gerber brothers, all right. His next remark bore it out even more clearly.

"I only wish I had Dons Gerber and Floris Gerber right here in front of me now," Jurie Steyn announced, sticking out his chest. "I'd let them know where they got off, all right. But, of course, they never come round here. They pretend it's because Post Office Welgevonden is nearer, for them. But I know that's not the only reason.

"I know it's because the postmaster at Welgevonden is too soft. He allows himself to be put upon, by bullies."

We felt that, after those remarks of Jurie Steyn's, there was very little that we ourselves could say. We had no more to say than what Dons Gerber had had to say on the Zeerust railway platform. We could express our thoughts in less words than what Floris Gerber had employed in the classroom at Drogedal.

That was when Johnny Coen started taking a hand in the conversation.

"Doesn't it strike you, at all," Johnny Coen asked, "that it can't both be true, these two different stories about how the schoolmaster came in the end to ask Pauline Gerber to marry him? Don't you think it's possible that perhaps both those stories are lies, I mean."

We were shocked to hear Johnny Coen using language like that.

Naturally enough, we were quite willing to make many sorts of allowances for Johnny Coen. For one thing, we knew perfectly well how Johnny Coen had been feeling about Pauline Gerber. We realized, also, that he had entertained those sentiments about Pauline Gerber long before she had ever set eyes on young Vermaak, the schoolmaster.

But we also knew that Pauline Gerber had been to finishing school, in the meanwhile, and so it was only reasonable that things should no longer have been the same between Pauline Gerber and Johnny Coen, after she came back to the Marico. For, if she did feel the same way about Johnny Coen, it would mean that all the money her father had spent on her at finishing school at the Cape had been wasted.

Johnny Coen appeared to sense the constraint in Jurie Steyn's voorkamer then, following on the statement he had just made.

"I don't mean to say that you're all of you just a lot of ... liars," Johnny Coen said, giving utterance to a couple of words that the train-guard had also found useful on Zeerust station. "I don't mean that at all."

So Gysbert van Tonder said to Johnny Coen that we were grateful to him for that, he was sure.

"It's not that," Johnny Coen persisted, half-ashamed of himself for having put it so impolitely. "But what I mean is, if young Vermaak was on the Zeerust railway station, with Dons Gerber with him, then who was sitting in the classroom marking copy-books in red ink, when Floris Gerber was there?"

"I mean, they couldn't both of those things be true, could they, now? The next thing you'd be saying is that it was Floris Gerber sitting at the table marking the standard V spelling mistakes in red ink. That would be a muck-up, *wouldn't* it?"

The thought of that provoked Johnny Coen to laughter. We smiled indulgently. Only Oupa Bekker seemed to think that Johnny Coen did have something there. He himself didn't believe either of these stories about how young Vermaak came to ask Pauline Gerber for her hand, Oupa Bekker said.

"Jolliest passengers we've had in a good while," the lorry-driver's assistant remarked, walking into the voorkamer with the mail-bags. "Laughing all the way up from Bekkersdal."

So Chris Welman said that he supposed it was more of those Native convicts that were coming to work at Derdepoort.

"But what they've got to laugh about I don't know," Chris Welman continued. "And yet that's what I always think, when I see those Native convicts sitting in the lorry in their striped jerseys – laughing their heads off about something. And the warder with them looking so miserable, you feel you want to go and ask can't you do something for him."

"No, not convicts, this time," the lorry-driver's assistant said. "Only Pauline Gerber and her brothers, Dons and Floris and – I forget the names of the other two –"

"Out there in the lorry?" Jurie Steyn enquired, looking not too comfortable suddenly.

"No, they got off at Welgevonden," the lorry-driver said. "And, of course, young Vermaak was with them, too. You know, he's engaged to Pauline. They went to Bekkersdal to celebrate."

The lorry-driver looked surprised at the question Gysbert van Tonder put to him.

"How did the schoolmaster propose to Pauline Gerber?" the lorry-driver repeated. "Well, what do we all do? He rode over to the farm, one afternoon, and asked her father, of course. And Oom Koos Gerber shook him by the hand and said he wanted a young man to help look after the farm - as though he didn't have enough already, with all those sons he's got. But why did you ask?"

Thereupon Gysbert van Tonder said, no, it was nothing. It was just something Jurie Steyn had been mentioning, Gysbert van Tonder said.

HOME TOWN

Oupa Bekker told us about how he had once gone back – very many years later – to revisit a village where he had lived as a child. Jurie Steyn asked him how many years, but he did not answer. He pretended to be too deaf to hear Jurie Steyn's question.

That was a peculiarity of Oupa Bekker's. He not infrequently, by implication, made claims to great age. But he never allowed himself to be pinned down into stating how old he actually was in terms of years. It seemed that he wanted to give himself a certain measure of room for manoeuvering in, on that score.

Nor did Oupa Bekker acquaint us with the name of the little place that he went back to have a look at after an interval of many years. But that did not matter. Since, for each of us, they were the remembered scenes of our own childhood, that Oupa Bekker spoke about.

"Of course, there was a railway station, now, which there of course hadn't been before," Oupa Bekker said.

"Yes, and tarred streets and a filling station with petrol pumps," Chris Welman said.

"And a fish and chips shop and a milk bar with high stools," Gysbert van Tonder said.

"And where there had been an old garden wall of red bricks with honeysuckle growing over it –" Jurie Steyn began.

"No, not honeysuckle," Chris Welman interrupted him, "but a creeper with those broad leaves and blue flowers. I forget what it's called now."

"And the wall isn't red brick," Gysbert van Tonder said, "but a whitewashed earth wall."

They were in general agreement, however, that whatever building had been erected on the site of that old garden wall must be something pretty awful, anyway.

Oupa Bekker took our remarks in bad part.

"Who's telling this – me or the lot of you?" he asked.

Then he went on to say that from the station there was a bit of a rise before you got to the village itself.

"And so you decided to walk," Jurie Steyn said, "so you could enjoy each moment of it, recalling how you had run over the veld there as a carefree boy."

"Yes," Oupa Bekker snapped. "That's what I did do. I did walk. But the way you're carrying on I'm sorry now I didn't take a taxi, instead."

That shut Jurie Steyn up for a while. And so Oupa Bekker told us how, having deposited his suitcase in the railway cloakroom, he set off along that road, which was tarred now (as Chris Welman had *said* it would be), and there was a soft wind blowing that was always there, on the rise, when in the village in the hollow the air was very still.

And Oupa Bekker said that he thought what a strange thing it was, that after all those years, the same wind should still be there. You think of the wind as something that blows and is gone, Oupa Bekker said. And yet after so many long years there, on the rise, there that wind still was, and not changed in any way.

So Chris Welman said that was how it always was. When you revisited a place after a long interval, the first impression you always got was that it hadn't changed. The first building you would see, as likely as not, would be the church. And the church steeple would look just like it did when you were a child, except not so tall, any more. Only afterwards you found out how much the place had really altered.

"And when you were a child the steeple even then needed paint on it," Gysbert van Tonder observed.

"What I *noticed*," Oupa Bekker proceeded, getting bitter at the interruptions, "what I noticed, as I walked up the rise, was that rise was not as high as it had seemed when I was a boy. Only, when I was a boy I could get up over it easier. Maybe it was the fault of the tarred road. But when Chris Welman says that the church steeple did not look so tall any more, then he's quite wrong. Because the church steeple looked *taller*, when I got there. And the church looked three times bigger than it used to be. And it seemed to be standing right at the other end of the kerkplein from where it had stood in the old days.

And why it all looked like that to me was because the church *had* been rebuilt on the other end of the plein. And it *was* three times bigger."

That should have put Chris Welman in his place. But it didn't. Instead, a twinkle came into his eye.

"Where was the bar, Oupa Bekker?" he asked. "I hope you found that, all right. I mean, they didn't go and shift the saloon bar, too, did they, where you couldn't find it?"

Oupa Bekker said he was coming to that.

First he had walked about the kerkplein a good while, searching for the site of the old church.

And then he came across a row of stones that were half-buried in the long grass, and that he knew were the foundations of the old church. He went and sat on a stone, Oupa Bekker said, and a –

"And a host of childhood memories came back to you," Jurie Steyn said.

Then Oupa Bekker got really huffy.

"Look here," Oupa Bekker said. "I only hope that the same thing happens to you, all of you, as what happened to me. I only hope that one day, when you take it into your minds to go and visit your childhood homes again, you'll also find everything as changed as what I found it, that's all. Then you won't see anything to laugh at, in it.

"And I only hope you also feel as lonely as what I felt, when I turned away from the kerkplein and walked down the main street of the village, and everywhere I saw only strange faces and strange buildings, and there was nobody I could say to – and there was nobody who was interested, even – that that was my home town. But, of course, it wasn't the place, any more, that I had spent my childhood in. Not the way they had changed it, it wasn't."

Chris Welman started feeling sorry for Oupa Bekker then.

"Was it really as altered as all that, Oupa?" he asked.

"Altered?" Oupa Bekker repeated. "Take the hotel, now. It used to be a wood and iron building with a long verandah. Now it was a double-storey brick building. And where there had been a hitching-post in front of that we children used to swing on, there was now one of those upright iron box things that have to do with electricity. Electricity – why, in the old days we had hardly even paraffin-lamps."

It all sounded quite sad. But then, as Gysbert van Tonder remarked, there had to be such a thing as progress. We couldn't expect the world just to stand still for Oupa Bekker's sake, or for any one of our sakes, for that matter, either.

"I went to look for the place that we children used to call the river," Oupa Bekker went on, "and that we used to fish in, and that people used to lead water into their gardens from, and that had a bridge over it."

Well, we knew what was coming, of course. And we almost wished that Oupa Bekker wouldn't go to the length of telling us about it. Because they would have put pipes there, of course. And the stream would have been covered up. And where the bridge had been there would now be the new power-station. Or the glue factory.

We would rather not think what there was on the site of the garden wall that Jurie Steyn and Chris Welman and Gysbert van Tonder had spoken about earlier.

The piece of garden wall that every person who spent his childhood in a village remembers. A red-brick and honeysuckle wall, or a white-washed wall wildly rich with convolvulus.

"After I had had dinner in the hotel," Oupa Bekker proceeded – and without his having to say so, we gathered that he did not eat much: his voice told us all that – "I went to the bioscope. I had been there earlier in the day, and it had said that there would be an afternoon show.

"It was a picture about cowboys and Indians, or about cowboys and something. Or it might not even have been cowboys. I'm not sure. Seeing that the talking was all in English, I couldn't understand very much of it.

"But there was a coach in the picture, like the Zeederberg coaches they used to have here in the old days, before they had trains, much. And there was a fat man in the picture with a black *manel* who had other fat men under him. And he looked important, like a raadslid that they had in that village when I was a boy. And that fat-man-with-the-*manel*'s job seemed to be to work out for the other fat men what was the best way to rob that Zeederberg coach, every time.

"And after a while, sitting in that bioscope, I began to get quite happy again, and I didn't mind so much that my home town had changed. Because the places they had there, on the picture, where all those things were going on, was just like my village had been when I was a boy. And there was the same sort of riding on horses, that I remembered well. And the hotel in the picture had the same kind of verandah. And although I didn't actually *see* any children swinging on the hitching-post, they might have been, but the picture just didn't show it. Anyway, I knew it was the same hitching-post. I mean, I would know it anywhere.

"And I was pleased to see the bridge, too. It was exactly the same bridge that we had over our stream, in the old days. And there was a young fellow who wasn't as fat as the fat-man-in-the-*manel*'s men, and who seemed to be on the opposite side from what they were on, and got in their way, every time. And the young fellow stood on that very bridge that I remembered from my childhood. He stood on the bridge with a lovely girl in his arms. And if you had looked under the bridge I am sure there would have been the same pieces of tree-trunk washed up under the side of it.

"And afterwards, when there was shooting in the hotel, it was exactly the same paraffin-lamps and candles they had there that used to be in the village hotel in the old days, before they had made it into two storeys."

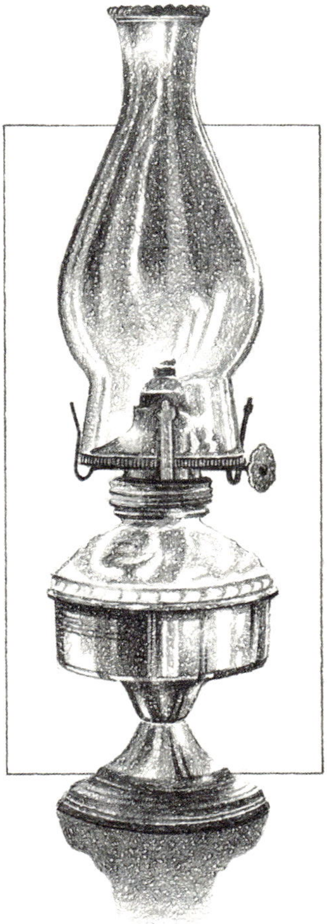

Afterwards, Oupa Bekker said, when it came to the end of the picture, and that lovely girl got married to the young fellow who wasn't as fat as the man-in-the-*manel*'s men were fat, he felt happier than he had done for a considerable while – happier than he had felt at any time since he got off the train, that morning, and saw that the road over the rise was tarred.

"Because the church they got married in was the old church just as I had known it," Oupa Bekker said. "It was like the church used to be, before they made it three times bigger and moved it to the other end of the plein."

And when he went back to the station in the evening, Oupa Bekker said, descending the rise with the light wind that he knew so well blowing about him, it was with much satisfaction that he realized how, through all those years, his home town had not changed.

"But that bioscope itself," Jurie Steyn said. "That must be quite a new thing, I should imagine. They certainly couldn't have had a bioscope in that village when you were a boy."

"No," Oupa Bekker said. "Where they built that bioscope there was, before that, when I was a boy, a stretch of garden wall with creeper over it."

JIM FISH

He was an African from a kraal in the Waterberg, and he had not been in Johannesburg very long. His name was Mletshwa Kusane. That was his name in the kraal in the Waterberg. In Johannesburg he was known as Jim Fish. That name stood on his pass, too.

In those days a Black man didn't mind what sort of "working name" he adopted. He had not come to Johannesburg to stay, anyway. At least that was what he hoped. And while he stayed in the city, saving up money as fast as he could to take back to the farm with him, he didn't particularly care what name his employer chose to bestow on him, provided that his employer handed over his wages with due regularity on pay-day.

Jim Fish had found work in a baker's shop in a part of the town known as the Mai-Mai. He lived in a shack behind the bakery, the proprietor of which in this way received back as rent a not inconsiderable part of his employees' emoluments. Since his employees were also his tenants, the owner of the bakehouse did not have to employ a rent-collector. Afterwards, when Johannesburg took on more of the external characteristics of a city, the owner of the bakery was to find that this arrangement did not pay him quite so well, any more.

For the city council began introducing all sorts of finicky by-laws relating to hygiene. In no time they brought in a regulation making it illegal for the owner of a bakery to accommodate his Black servants on the bakery premises. The result was that, at a time when business wasn't too good, the owner of the bakery found himself with a municipal health inspector on his pay-roll. Afterwards it was two health inspectors. And they came round every month for their rake-off, like clockwork. Because of this increase in his overheads the bakery proprietor had been reluctantly compelled to cancel an advertisement that he had been running in a religious magazine for a long time.

Peter Backcock
4
CONFECTIONARY
5

It was purely a goodwill advertisement, bread being a staple commodity that didn't require advertising. But on the following Sunday the baker – who was also a sidesman – had to listen to a sermon on the evils of avarice. He knew the parson meant him, of course. Because he had cancelled the advertisement that for years had been the church magazine's mainstay. But there were moments, in the course of the sermon, when the baker could not, in his sinful mind, help associating words like "cupidity", "selfishness" and "money-grubbing" with those two municipal health inspectors.

Jim Fish's main work at the bakery consisted of helping his Black colleagues – there were quite a number of them – to carry in the sacks of meal and to clean the mixers of yesterday's dough. (The mixers *were* cleaned, quite often, in spite of what quite a number of bread-consuming citizens might have thought, going by the taste.) He had also to carry the pans to the oven, and to help stoke the fires, and to help pull out the baked loaves with long wooden scoops. Because Jim Fish was Black, that was about as far as his duties went. The White men on the night-shift were there in a supervisory capacity.

There had been one or two nights, however, when Jim Fish and his black-skinned colleagues had, through the machinery breaking down, to perform certain additional duties, that brought them into somewhat more intimate contact with the ancient rites of bread-baking.

On those occasions that particular bakery's proud boast that its products were, from start to finish, untouched by human hand, was only literally correct, in the sense that it excluded human feet. Strict adherents of the school of thought that places the Coloured races outside of the pale of humanity as such would in this situation find themselves in something of a dilemma. For it would not be human hands *or* feet, but just the feet of Blacks that kneaded the dough, in long wooden troughs, at those times when the electric power at the bakery failed.

The White supervisors would be in a state of nerves, all right, on a night when there was mechanical trouble. They would be all strung-up – hysterical and panicky, almost, like ballet-dancers.

"Hey, you, go and wash that coal off your feet before you get into that — trough," the night foreman would shout at a Black. And at another one the foreman would shout, "Hey, you black sausage – don't you sweat so much, right into the kneading trough and all!"

For it is a characteristic of any person whose ancestors have lived in Africa for any length of time that he *does* sweat a lot. Whether he's a Black man, or a White Afrikaans-speaking Boer or a White English-speaking jingo from Natal, if his forbears have resided in Africa for a couple of generations, he sweats at the least provocation. Readers of Herodotus will recall that that great historian and geographer said the same thing about the Nubians of his time.

Because he was a simple soul, Jim Fish was, taken all in all, happy in his work. If he were asked by an American newspaper correspondent, or by an earnest enquirer delegated to the task by a UNO committee (the UNO being in those days as much of an anachronism as nylons), Jim Fish would probably have confessed that he was deserving of one shilling and sixpence extra on a night when the bread-making machinery did not function as it should. The one shilling and sixpence would be to cover all that extra work he had in treading, Jim Fish would explain, marking time, left right, left right, to explain. And also to recompense him for all that trouble he took in cleaning himself, washing his legs and feet and toes in hot water. No, not when he got *into* the kneading trough. He never worried much about *that*, Jim Fish would declare, truthfully. It was when he had to get the sticky white dough off him afterwards. There was a job for you, now.

The real trouble about his job at the bakery, Jim Fish, alias Mletshwa Kusane, would confide to the correspondent of an American newspaper, was the fact that it was nearly all-night work. He didn't mind the pay so much. That was all right. Even after he had paid his rent and he had bought mealie-meal and goat's meat and such odds and ends of clothing as he needed, he was still able to save quite a bit, each month. This was a lot more than most White wage or salary-earners were able to do, incidentally. All that happened to White people who worked for a boss was that they got deeper into debt, every month. Jim Fish would admit that he was saving, here in the city of Johannesburg. But he needed every penny he could scrape together. All the money he saved in Johannesburg had to go in lobola, when he got back to the kraal.

Late one night Mletshwa Kusane, alias Jim Fish, came away from the bakery with a deep sense of inner satisfaction. He felt he was somebody, and no mistake. For the mixing machine had broken down again. And this time he had been set to tread the dough in a confectionary trough. Not the dough for plebeian quartern-loaves and twist-loaves and standard brown loaves. But he walked up and down, left right, left right, in a trough that had chilled eggs, even, mixed with the flour and water and yeast. Left right, left right, he was kneading, with his feet – brown on top and pinkish between the toes – the dough for slab cake and cream cakes and (with a few sultanas thrown in) for wedding cakes. The night foreman had noticed that, last time there was trouble with the merchandised equipment, Jim Fish had seemed to sweat somewhat less than the other Blacks. And that was how Mletshwa got promoted to the confectionary trough. What the night foreman didn't notice was the effect that this unexpected promotion had on Mletshwa. Because he had been picked out for the unique honour of treading the dough in the confectionary trough, Mletshwa suddenly started thinking that he was a king. A great king, he thought he was. And he started chanting in the Tswana tongue a song that he had made up about himself, in the same way that any primitive African makes up a song about himself when he finds that, by chance, he is standing first in a line of pick-and-shovel labourers digging a ditch; or, if it's a gang of railway labourers, moving a piece of track, and he happens to be walking in front.

And so that night, having been selected to tread the dough in the confectionary trough because he sweated less than the other Blacks, Mletshwa really let himself go. He felt no end proud of himself.

"Who is he, who is he, who is he?" Mletshwa chanted, going left right, left right, in double-quick time:

"Who is he chosen by the Great White Man
To walk fast in the fine meal with the broken eggs in it?
Who is he but Mletshwa? –
Who is he but Mletshwa Kusane whose kraal is by the Molopo?

"Who is he, the Mighty Trampling Elephant, elephant among
elephants,
He, with his feet washed clean in carbolic soap?
Who is the mighty Elephant with his feet washed clean
With the thick white bubbles coming out of
The red carbolic soap – the White Man's red carbolic soap?
Who is he but Mletshwa Kusane whose kraal is by the Molopo?

"Who is he that treads heavier than the rhinoceros –
The rhinoceros with his feet washed in the water from the White
Man's faucet?
Who is he that treads with his feet washed cleaner than the White
Man's feet?
Treading out white flour and yellow, stinking eggs and yeast
That is the beautiful food of the White Man?
Who is he but Mletshwa –
Who is he but Mletshwa Kusane whose kraal is by the Molopo?"

Inspired to unwonted exertions by his singing, Mletshwa was making a first-class job of treading that dough. When the night foreman looked again, Mletshwa was leaping up and down in the tub. One hand was raised up to the level of his shoulder, balancing an imaginary assegai. His other arm supported an equally imaginary raw-hide shield. What were not fictitious were the pieces of dough clinging to his working pants and his shirt and even to one side of his neck. The night foreman was not a little surprised to see a Black man performing a Zulu war-dance in a kneading trough at that time of the night. Especially when those white splashes of dough could have passed as war-paint.

"None of that, Jim Fish," the night foreman called out – impressed, in spite of himself. "Get on with your work."

One of the other Blacks guffawed. But it *was* his work, this Black man thought. In prancing up and down like that, in the dough, Mletshwa was only doing his *work*. And here was the boss angry with Mletshwa about it. Surely, the ways of the White man were strange.

It was only a little later that the night foreman noticed what other effect the violent exercise had had on Jim Fish: he was sweating like a dozen men; the sweat was pouring off Mletshwa as though from a shower bath.

This time the night foreman swore.

"Get out of that tub, you —!" he shouted. "That's for cake for White people to eat, you —! Look at all the sweat running off your — backside into White people's cake!"

Mletshwa's was a temperament that was easily cowed. In a moment the sound of the night foreman's voice had changed him from a bloodthirsty warrior to a timid Bushveld thing trying to escape from a trampling rhinoceros among rhinoceroses. In a split second he was out of the tub and halfway across the bakery floor towards his kya in the backyard.

He had to return to the tub, however. The night foreman saw to that. The night foreman also saw to it that Mletshwa scraped all the dough off his feet and other parts of his person, and stuck it back where it belonged.

"Trying to make off with half the confectionary dough sticking to him," the night foreman said to the mechanic who was working at the motor, working to get it started again. Then the night foreman addressed Mletshwa once more.

"*Cha-cha*!" he shouted. "*Inindaba wena* want to steal wet meal, huh? Come on, put it all back. That lump between your toes, too. It's for the cake for White people to eat. You *meningi* skelm you!"

THE MISSIONARY

That kafir carving hanging on the wall of my voorkamer? (Oom Schalk Lourens said.) It's been there many years. It was found in the loft of the pastorie at Ramoutsa after the death of the Dutch Reformed missionary there, Reverend Keet. Of course, he was a sick man before he came here. Therefore, there may be nothing unusual in the circumstances of his death. Anyway, I'll tell you all I know about it. You can then judge for yourself.

To look at, that wooden figure is just one of those things that a kafir wood-carver cuts out of soft wood, like *'mdubu* or *mesetla*. But because I knew him quite well, I can still see a rough sort of resemblance to Reverend Keet in that carving, even though it is now discoloured with age and the white ants have eaten away parts of it. I first saw this figure in the study of the pastorie at Ramoutsa when I went to call on Reverend Keet. And when, after his death, the carving was found in the loft of the pastorie, I brought it here. I kept it in memory of a man who had strange ideas about what he was pleased to call "Darkest Africa".

Reverend Keet had not been at Ramoutsa very long. Before that he had worked at a mission station in the Cape. But, as he told us, ever since he had paid a visit to the Marico district, some years before, he had wanted to come to the Northern Transvaal. He said he had obtained, in the bushveld along the Malopo River, a feeling that here was the real Africa.

On his previous visit here Reverend Keet had stayed long enough to meet Elsiba Grobler, the daughter of Thys Grobler of Drogedal. Afterwards he sent for Elsiba to come down to the Cape to be his bride.

And so we thought that the missionary had remembered with affection the scenes that were the setting for his courtship. And that that was why he came back here. So you can imagine how disappointed we

Peter Bardcock

were when Reverend Keet said there was a spirit of evil in these parts that he believed it was his mission to overcome. We who had lived in the Marico for the greater part of our lives wondered much as to what it was that was going on in his soul. Reverend Keet had a thin neck and a fat stomach and an unhealthy colour. So we thought that perhaps his illness was responsible for his state of mind.

Nevertheless, I found it interesting to listen to him, just because he had such peculiar ways. And so I called on him quite regularly when I passed the mission station on my way back from the Indian store at Ramoutsa.

Reverend Keet and I used to sit in his study, where the curtains were half drawn, as they were in the whole pastorie. I supposed it was to keep out the bright sunshine that Darkest Africa is so full of. I told him that I thought he would feel better if he got out among the trees and the grass oftener.

"Yesterday a kafir child hurt his leg falling out of a withaak tree," Reverend Keet said. "And the parents didn't bring the child here so that Elsiba or I could bandage him up. Instead, they said there was a devil in the withaak. And so they got the witch-doctor to fasten a piece of crocodile skin to the child's leg, to drive away the devil."

So I said that that just showed you how ignorant a kafir was. They should have fastened the crocodile skin to the withaak, instead, like the old people used to do. "The devil isn't in the kafir child but in the withaak," I said. "Though, goodness knows, the average kafir child has got enough devils in his skin!" I added that a length of leopard entrail tied to the trunk was best for driving a devil out of a maroela.

Reverend Keet did not answer. He just shook his head and looked at me in a pitying sort of a way, so that I felt sorry I had spoken.

To change the subject I pointed to a kafir wood-carving standing on a table in a corner of the study. The same wood-carving you see today hanging on the wall of my voorkamer.

"Here's now something that we want to encourage," Reverend Keet said. "Through the teaching of craft we can perhaps bring enlightenment to these parts. The kafirs here seem to have a natural talent for wood-carving. I have asked Willem Terreblanche to write to the Education Department for a textbook on the subject. It will be another craft that we can teach to the children at the school." Willem Terreblanche was the assistant teacher at the mission station. "Anyway, it will be more useful than the things to make that were explained in the last textbook we got," Reverend Keet went on, half to himself. Then it was as though an idea struck him. "Oh, by the way," he asked, "would you perhaps like, say, a few dozen paper serviettes with green tassels to take home with you? They are free."

I declined his offer in some haste.

Reverend Keet started talking about that carving again.

"You wouldn't think it was meant for me, now, would you?" he asked. And because I am always polite, that way, I said no, certainly not. "I mean, just look at the top of the body," he said. "It's like a sack of potatoes. Does the top part of *my* body look like a sack of potatoes?" And once again I said no, oh, no.

Reverend Keet laughed, then – rather loudly, I thought – at the idea of that wood-carver's ignorance. I laughed quite loudly, also, to make it clear that I, too, thought that that kafir wood-carver was very uneducated.

"All the same, for a raw kafir who has had no training," the missionary continued, "it's not bad. But take that self-satisfied sort of smile, now, that he put on my face. It only came out that way because the kafir who made the carving lacks the disciplined skill to carve my features as they really are."

I thought, well, maybe that Bechuana didn't have much of what Reverend Keet called disciplined skill. But I did think he had a pretty shrewd idea how to carve a wooden figure of Rev. Keet.

"If a kafir had the impudence to make a likeness like that of me, with such big ears and all," I said to Reverend Keet, "I would kick him in the ribs. I would kick him for being so ignorant, I mean." I went on to say that the figure was carved out of *mesetla* and that the kafirs used the wood of that tree in their magic rituals for making black spells with.

"Because they are so ignorant," I again added quickly. For I could see that Reverend Keet was going to shake his head once more, at the thought of a White man having fallen so low as to believe in heathen superstitions.

It was then that Elsiba brought us in our coffee. Although she was now the missionary's wife, I still thought of her as Elsiba, a Bushveld girl whom I had seen grow up.

"You've still got that thing there," Elsiba said to her husband after she had greeted me. "I won't have you making a fool of yourself. Every visitor to the pastorie who sees this carving goes away laughing at you."

"They laugh at the kafir who made it, Elsiba, because of his lack of disciplined skill," Reverend Keet said, drawing himself up in his chair.

"Anyway, I am taking it out of here," Elsiba answered.

I had since then often thought of that scene. Of the way Elsiba Keet walked from the room, with the carving standing upright on the tray she had carried the coffee-cups on. Because of its big feet the wooden figure did not fall over when Elsiba flounced out with the tray. And in its stiff, wooden bearing the figure seemed to be expressing the same sorrow at the kafir wood-carver's lack of training that Reverend Keet himself felt.

I remained in the study a long time. And all the while the missionary talked of the spirit of evil that hung over the Marico like a heavy blanket. It was something brooding and oppressive, he said, and it did something to the souls of men. He asked me whether I hadn't noticed it myself.

So I told him that I had. I said that he had taken the very words out of my mouth. And I proceeded to tell him about the time Jurie Bekker had impounded some of my mules that he claimed had strayed into his mealie-lands.

"You should have seen Jurie Bekker the morning that he drove off my mules along the Government road," I said. "An evil blanket hung over him, all right. You could almost see it. A striped kafir blanket."

I also told the missionary about the sinful way in which Niklaas Prinsloo had filled in those drought compensation forms for losses which he had never suffered, even. And about the time Gert Haasbroek sold me what he said was a pedigree Afrikaner bull, and that was just an anima he had smuggled through from the Protectorate, one night, with a whole herd of other beasts, and that died afterwards of grass-belly.

I said that the whole of the Marico district was just bristling with evil, and I could give him many more examples, if he would care to listen.

But Reverend Keet said that that was not what he meant. He said he was talking of the unnatural influence that hovered over this part of the country. He had felt those things particularly at the swamps by the Malopo, he said, with the green bubbles coming up out of the mud and with those trees that were like shapes oppressing your mind when it is fevered. But it was like that everywhere in the Bushveld, he said. With the sun pouring down as though there was a high black wind, somewhere. And he felt a chill in all his bones, he said, and it was something unearthly.

It was interesting for me to hear Reverend Keet talk like that. I had heard the same sort of things before from strangers. I wanted to tell him what he could take for it. But because the remedy I knew of included part of a crocodile's tooth ground fine and soaked in vinegar I felt that Reverend Keet might form a still lower opinion of me.

"Even here in this study, where I am sitting talking to you," he added, "I can sense a baleful influence. It is some form of – of something skulking, somehow." I knew, of course, that Reverend Keet was not referring in an underhand way to my presence there in his study. He was too religious to do a thing like that. Nevertheless, I felt uncomfortable. Shortly afterwards I left.

On my way back in the mule-cart I passed the mission school. And I thought then that it was funny that Elsiba was so concerned that a kafir should not make a fool of her husband with a wood-carving of him. Because she did not seem to mind making a fool of him in another way. From the mule-cart I saw Elsiba and Willem Terreblanche in the doorway of the schoolroom. And from the way they were holding hands I concluded that they were not discussing the making of paper serviettes with green tassels.

Still, as it turned out, it never came to any scandal in the district. For Willem Terreblanche left some time later to take up a teaching post in the Free State. And after Reverend Keet's death Elsiba allowed a respectable interval to elapse before she went to the Free State to marry Willem Terreblanche.

Some distance beyond the mission school I came across the Ramoutsa witch-doctor that Reverend Keet had spoken about. The witch-doctor was busy digging up roots on the veld for medicine. I reined in the mules and the witch-doctor came up to me. He had on a pair of brown leggings and carried an umbrella. Around his neck he wore a few feet of light-green tree-snake that didn't look as though it had been dead very long. I could see that the witch-doctor was particular about how he dressed when he went out.

I spoke to him in Sechuana about Reverend Keet. I told him that Reverend Keet said the Marico was a bad place. I also told him that the missionary did not believe in the cure of fastening a piece of crocodile skin to the leg of a child who had fallen out of a withaak tree. And I said that he did not seem to think, either, that if you fastened crocodile skin to the withaak it would drive the devil out of it.

The witch-doctor stood thinking for some while. And when he spoke again it seemed to me that in his answer there was a measure of wisdom.

"The best thing," he said, "would be to fasten a piece of crocodile skin onto the baas missionary."

Then the witch-doctor told me of a question that the Reverend Keet had asked him, and that surprised me a great deal.

Nevertheless, I have often since then thought of how almost inspired Reverend Keet was when he said that there was evil going on around him, right here in the Marico. In his very home – he could have said. With the curtains half drawn and all. Only, of course, I don't suppose he meant it that way.

Yet I have also wondered if, in the way that he did mean it – when he spoke of those darker things that he claimed were at work in Africa – I wonder if there, too, Reverend Keet was as wide off the mark as one might lightly suppose. And it seemed to me that the witch-doctor might have been speaking the truth when he told me that the missionary had asked him certain strange questions. That thought occurred to me after Reverend Keet's death and Elsiba's departure. In fact, it was when the new missionary took over the pastorie at Ramoutsa and this wood-carving was found in the loft. But as I have said, Reverend Keet was a sick man before he came here. So his death might have had nothing to do with all this.

Yet, before I hung up the carving where you see it now, I first took the trouble to pluck off the lock of Reverend Keet's hair that had been glued to it. And I also pulled out the nails that Elsiba must have driven into the head and heart.

TOYS IN THE SHOP WINDOW

"You ought to see David Policansky's store," the lorry-driver's assistant said. "My, but it does look lovely. All done up for Christmas. It's worth going all the way to Bekkersdal just to see it. And the toys in the window – you've got no idea. There's a mirror with a little ship on it and cotton wool over it for clouds, and little trees at the side of it, so the mirror looks just like it's water. And there's a toy Chinaman that goes up and down on a ladder with baskets over his shoulder on a stick when you wind him up –"

Jurie Steyn interrupted the lorry-driver's assistant to say that he was sure to go and drive all those miles and miles to Bekkersdal, just to go and look at the toys in Policansky's window. Catch *him* going all that way to stare at a wound-up Chinaman going up and down on a ladder with baskets, Jurie Steyn said.

Thereupon, speaking earnestly to him because this was no time for foolishness, Gysbert van Tonder said to the lorry-driver's assistant that he hoped he hadn't been talking about those same toys at every Bushveld farmhouse and post office that the lorry had stopped at on the way north from Bekkersdal. Because if he *had*, why, the children would make their parents' lives impossible between now and Christmas. He himself had several children that were still of school-going age, Gysbert van Tonder said. And so he knew.

The lorry-driver's assistant looked embarrassed.

"Well, I did talk a little," he admitted. "But I didn't say too much, I don't think. Except maybe at Post-bag Laatgevonden. Yes, now I come to think of it, I did, perhaps, say one or two things I shouldn't have, at Post-bag Laatgevonden. You see, the driver had trouble with a sparking plug, there, and so in between handing the driver a spanner or a file, maybe, I *might* have said a few things more than just about the ship and the Chinaman.

"Yes, now I come to think of it, I did, at Post-bag Laatgevonden, make some mention of the train that goes underneath tunnels and then waits at a siding for the signal to go up before it goes rushing on again through the vlakte, past railwaymen cottages and windmills and Mtosa huts, and then it gets switched onto another line – but I'm sorry, kêrels.

"Yes, I'm really sorry. I know, now, that I talked too much there. But Laatgevonden was the only place where I mentioned the train. At the other Post-bags where we stopped we didn't stop long enough – having just to hand over the mail-bag and unload the milk-cans – and so I didn't say anything at those places about the train. You see, that train in Policansky's window goes such a long distance, round and round and round, and taking up water supplies, too, at one spot, that you can't talk about it unless you've got a long *time* to talk – as I did have at Post-bag Laatgevonden, where the lorry-driver was trying to fix a sparking plug, and shouting that I was handing him the wrong tools as often as not."

In making that remark, the lorry-driver's assistant grinned.

"All the same," he added, "you've got no idea what that train is like. It's so real that you almost expect to see a gang of platelayers running away and the passengers throwing empty bottles at them out of the windows."

We could see from this that there must have been a good deal of realism about the clockwork railway in Policansky's store. We could also see in what way the lorry-driver's assistant and his friends amused themselves, whenever they went on a train ride from Ottoshoop.

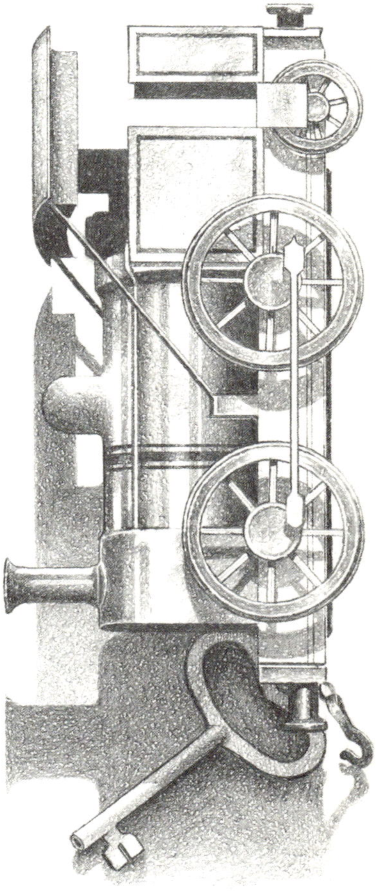

Meanwhile Johnny Coen, who had once worked on the South African Railways, was asking the lorry-driver's assistant if the toy train in Policansky's window was one of the new kind of toy train, such as he had heard about. Did it have bogie wheels? he asked. And did it have a miniature injector steam-pipe? But when he asked if it also had miniature superheater flue-tubes, the lorry-driver's assistant said that was something that Johnny Coen should perhaps rather go and ask David Policansky. He himself only thought that it looked like a train. And it looked a lot like a train, to him, the lorry-driver's assistant said. But maybe there were parts missing. He wouldn't be able to tell. It *went* all right, though, he added.

The lorry-driver's assistant was in the middle of telling us about something else that Policansky was arranging to have in the toy department of his store, for Christmas, when the lorry-driver called through the door and asked did the assistant think they could waste all day at a third-rate Dwarsberge post office where the coffee they got was nearly all roast kremetart root.

By the time Jurie Steyn had walked round from behind his counter to the front door, the lorry was already driving off, so that most of the long and suitable reply that Jurie Steyn gave was lost on the driver.

Before that, with his foot on the clutch, the lorry-driver had been able to explain that his main grievance wasn't the coffee, which he was not by law compelled to drink. But he did have to handle Jurie Steyn's mail-bag, the lorry-driver said. And although he was pressing down the accelerator at the time, we could still hear what it was that the lorry-driver took exception to about Jurie Steyn's mail-bag.

By the time Jurie Steyn had finished talking to the driver the lorry was already halfway through the poort.

"What do you think of that for cheek?" Jurie Steyn asked of us, on his way back to the counter. "He's just a paid servant of the Government, and he talks to me like I'm a Mtosa. I mean, he's no different from me, that lorry-driver isn't. I mean, I am after all the postmaster for this part of the Dwarsberge. I also get paid to serve the public. And that lorry-driver talks to me just like I talk to any Mtosa that comes in here to buy stamps."

We felt it was a pity that this unhappy note should have crept into what had until then been quite a pleasant summer afternoon's talk. What made it all the more regrettable, we felt, was that it was only another few weeks to Christmas. The way Jurie Steyn and the lorry-driver spoke to each other didn't fit in with the friendly spirit of Christmas, we felt. Nor did it fit in, either, with the even more friendly spirit that there should be at the New Year.

"And did you hear what he said about my mail-bag?" Jurie Steyn demanded, indignantly. We confessed that we had. Indeed, we would have to have been more deaf yet than Oupa Bekker if we had missed any of the lorry-driver's remarks about the mail-bag. Even though the engine of his lorry was running at the time, we could hear every word he said, the driver spoke so clearly. And what made what he said even more distinct was that kind of hurt tone in his voice. When a lorry-driver talks like he's injured, why, you can hear him from a long way off.

"What he said about my fowls," Jurie Steyn burst out. "That's what I can't get over. When he spoke about the mail-bag that my fowls had ... had been on."

Well, Jurie Steyn was expressing it more politely than the lorry-driver had done, we thought.

"And that he said afterwards that he had to handle that mail-bag," Jurie Steyn continued.

Several of us spluttered, then, remembering the *way* in which the lorry-driver had said it.

"And that he declared they were a lot of speckled, mongrel, dispirited Hottentot hoenders," Jurie Steyn finished up, "with sickly hanging-down combs. Well, that *got* me all right. There isn't a hen or a rooster on my farm that isn't a pure-bred Buff Orpington. Look at that hen pecking there, next to At Naudé's foot, now. Could you *call* it a speckled –"

Words failed Jurie Steyn, and he stopped talking.

Nevertheless, we all felt that it was unfortunate that Jurie Steyn should have had that misunderstanding with the lorry-driver. Because what the lorry-driver's assistant had told us about the toy train in Policansky's window, at Bekkersdal, was something quite interesting. And we would have liked to talk about it some more. We felt that, in spite of Bekkersdal being so many miles away, it might perhaps be worthwhile to take our children to go and have a look at that shop window, all the same. It would be instructive for the children, we felt. But as a result of what had happened since, we weren't quite in the mood for that any more.

It was only Gysbert van Tonder who did not seem to have his feelings completely quenched.

"When that young lorry-driver's assistant spoke about the toy train in Policansky's window," Gysbert van Tonder remarked, "well, you know how it is, a toy train, with tunnels and all. I thought right away how my children would enjoy it. I even thought of driving over to Bekkersdal in my mule-cart next week, taking Oupa Bekker with me. And then we could come back and tell my children all about it, I thought. We could also tell the children all about that Chinaman that climbs up and down a ladder with baskets. We could get Policansky to wind up that Chinaman several times, I thought, so that we could explain exactly to the children how it works.

"But I haven't got quite that feeling for it, any more, if you know how it is. So my children will have to go without. And it would have been such fun for them, having me and Oupa Bekker telling them all about what makes that train work. What does make it work, I wonder? It might help them with their exams, to know."

But it was then that Chris Welman remembered what the lorry-driver's assistant was saying just before the lorry-driver shouted to him to get going. And it was as though that cloud that had come over us had never been.

For David Policansky had said that he was going to get a Father Christmas at his store again, this year. He said he had to have a Father Christmas. The toy trade was no good without a Father Christmas with a red cap and overcoat and white whiskers shaking hands with the children in the toy department, Policansky said. And we laughed and said that we would have thought that the toy trade was no good with a Father Christmas. And we also said that we hoped, for his own sake, that this year Policansky wouldn't get old Doors Perske to be Father Christmas again, the same as he did last year.

We went on discussing last year's Father Christmas at Policansky's store for quite a long time.

As far as looks went, Doors Perske should have made a very good Santa Claus. He was fat and he had a red face. The circumstance of his face being on some occasions more red than on others would as likely as not escape the innocent observation of childhood.

But where Doors Perske went wrong was in his being essentially an odd-job man. For years he had contrived to exist in the small town of Bekkersdal by getting a contract to erect a sty, or to chop wood, or to dig a well. And that was how he had learnt to sub.

And so, when he was Santa Claus in Policansky's store, Doors Perske would every so often go and get a small advance against his pay from the bookkeeper. After a bit, the sight of Santa Claus entering the local public bar for a quick one no longer excited comment. The bartender no longer thought it funny to ask if he'd come down the chimney. No scoffing customer asked any more could he go and hold his reindeer.

In Policansky's store, too, everything was, at first, all right. If, in shaking hands with Doors Perske, a small child detected his beery breath, the small child would not think much of it. Since he had a father – or, maybe, a stepfather – of his own, the small child would not see anything incongruous in Father Christmas having had a few.

One day Doors Perske's wife had come charging into the toy department, swearing at Father Christmas and loudly accusing him of subbing on his wages, on the sly. And Doors Perske had called his wife an old — and had ungraciously clouted her one on the ear before bundling her out of the store. But even that incident did not have a disillusioning effect on the mind of David Policansky's juvenile clientele.

For the altercation had taken place at a counter where there were prams and dolls' houses and little crockery sets, and the children thronging that part of the shop were familiar with domestic scenes of the sort they had just witnessed. All they thought was that Father Christmas had just had a fight with Mother Christmas.

But it was the day before Christmas Eve that Doors Perske got the sack. He had just come back from the bar, again. And the first thing he had to do was to stumble over the shilling dips. Then, to save himself, he grabbed at an assortment of glassware stacked halfway up to the ceiling. This was foolish – as he realized next moment. The glassware offered him no sort of purchase at all. All that happened was that the whole shop shook when it fell. The next thing that went was the counter with the toy soldiers. And there didn't seem anything very martial in the way the little leaden soldiers – no longer in their neat toy rows – were scattered around, lying in heaps and with pieces broken off them: it looked too much like the real thing. Grim it looked.

When Policansky came rushing in, it was to find Doors Perske sitting in the wash-tub, with a teddy bear in his arm. His red cap had come off and his Father Christmas beard was halfway round his neck. And from the position of his beard the children in the shop knew that he wasn't Father Christmas, but just a dressed-up drunk.

"I couldn't get a proper grip on those glasses," Doors Perske explained. "That's how I fell."

Policansky got a proper grip on Santa Claus, all right. And he ran him out of his shop and when he got to the pavement, he kicked Father Christmas, and told him not to come back again.

"Go on, there *isn't* any Father Christmas," Doors Perske jeered, suddenly recovering himself, when he got to the corner. "It's just a lie that you make up for kids."

David Policansky's face twisted into a half-smile.

"I wish I could believe you," he said, surveying the wreckage of his shop through the door. "I wish I could believe there *wasn't* a Father Christmas."

Peter Badcock

ROMAUNT OF THE SMUGGLER'S DAUGHTER

Long ago, there was more money (Oom Schalk Lourens said, wistfully) to be made out of cattle-smuggling than there is in these times. The Government knows that, of course. But the Government thinks that why we Marico farmers don't bring such large herds of native cattle across the Bechuanaland border any more, on moonless nights, is because the mounted police are more efficient than they used to be.

That isn't the reason, of course.

You still get as good a sort of night as ever – a night when there is only the light of the stars shining on the barbed-wire that separates the Transvaal from the Protectorate. But why my wire-cutters are rusting in the buitekamer from disuse, is not because the border is better patrolled than it was in the old days. For it is not the mounted police, with their polished boots and clicking spurs, but the barefoot Bechuana kafirs that have grown more cunning.

We all said that it was the fault of the mission-school at Ramoutsa, of course. Afterwards, when more schools were opened, deeper into the Protectorate, we gave those schools a share of the blame as well ... Naturally, it wasn't a thing that happened suddenly. Only, we found, as the years went by, that the kafirs in the Bechuanaland Protectorate wanted more and more for their cattle. And later on they would traffic with us only when we paid them in hard cash; they frowned on the idea of barter.

I can still remember the look of grieved wonderment on Jurie Prinsloo's face when he told us about his encounter with the Bapedi chief near Malopolole. Jurie came across the Bapedi chief in front of his hut. And the Bapedi chief was not squatting on an animal skin spread on the ground; instead, he was sitting on a real chair, and looking quite comfortable sitting on it, too.

"Here's a nice, useful roll of copper wire for you," Jurie Prinsloo said to the Bapedi chief, who was lazily scratching the back of his instep against the lower cross-piece of the chair. "You can give me an ox for it. That red ox, there, with the long horns and the loose dewlap will be all right. They don't know any better about an ox on the Johannesburg market."

"But what can I do with the copper wire?" the Bapedi chief asked. "I have not got a telephone."

This was a real problem for Jurie Prinsloo, of course. For many years he had been trading rolls of copper wire for kafir cattle; and it had never occurred to him to think out what the kafirs used the wire for.

"Well," Jurie Prinsloo said, weakly, "you can make it into a ring to put through your nose, and you can also – "

But even as Jurie Prinsloo spoke, he realized that the old times had passed away forever.

And we all said, yes, it was those missionaries, with the schools they were opening up all over the place, who were ruining the kafirs. As if the kafirs weren't uncivilized enough in the first place, we said. And now the missionaries had to come along and educate them on top of it.

Anyway, the superior sort of smile that came across the left side of the chief's face, at the suggestion that he should wear a copper ring in his nose, made Jurie Prinsloo feel that he had to educate the Bapedi chief some more. What was left of the chair, after Jurie Prinsloo had finished educating the Bapedi chief, was produced in the magistrate's court at Gaberones, where Jurie Prinsloo was fined ten pounds for assault with intent to do grievous bodily harm. In those days you could buy quite a few head of cattle for ten pounds.

And, in spite of his schooling, the Bapedi chief remained as ignorant as ever. For, during the rest of the time that he remained head of the tribe, he would not allow a white man to enter his *stat* again.

But, as I have said, it was different, long ago. Then the Bechuana kafirs would still take an interest in their appearance, and they would be glad to exchange their cattle for brass and beads and old whale-bone corsets and tins of axle-grease (to make the skin on their chests shine) and cheap watches. They would even come and help us drive the cattle across the line, just for the excitement of it, and to show off their new finery, in the way of umbrellas and top hats and pieces of pink underwear, at the kraals through which we passed.

Easily the most enterprising cattle-smuggler in the Marico bushveld at the time of which I am talking was Gerrit Oosthuizen. He had a farm right next to the Protectorate border. So that the barbed-wire that he cut at night, when he brought over a herd of cattle, was also the fence of his own farm. Within a few years Gerrit Oosthuizen had made so much money out of smuggled cattle that he was able to introduce a large number of improvements on his farm, including a new type of concrete cattle-dip with iron steps, and a piano for which he had a special kind of stand built into the floor of his voorkamer, so as to keep the white ants away.

Gerrit Oosthuizen's daughter, Jemima, who was then sixteen years of age and very pretty, with dark hair and a red mouth and a soft shadow at the side of her throat, started learning to play the piano. Farmers and their wives from many miles away came to visit Gerrit Oosthuizen. They came to look at the piano-stand, which had been specially designed by a Pretoria engineer, and had an aluminium tank underneath that you kept filled with water, so that it was impossible for the white ants to effect much damage – if you wiped them off from the underneath part of the piano with a paraffin rag every morning.

The visitors would come to the farm, and they would drink coffee in the voorkamer, and they would listen to Jemima Oosthuizen playing a long piece out of a music-book with one finger, and they would nod their heads solemnly, at the end of it, when Jemima sat very still, with her dark hair falling forward over her eyes, and they would say, well, if that Pretoria engineer thought that, in the long run, the white ants would not be able to find a way of beating his aluminium invention, and of eating up all of the inside of the piano, then he didn't know the Marico white ant, that's all.

We who were visitors to the Oosthuizen farm spoke almost with pride of the cleverness of the white ant. We felt, somehow, that the white ants belonged to the Marico Bushveld, just like we did, and we didn't like the idea of a Pretoria engineer, who was an Uitlander, almost, thinking that with his invention – which consisted just of bits of shiny tin – he would be able to outwit the cunning of a Marico white ant.

Through his conducting his cattle-smuggling operations on so large and successful a scale, Gerrit Oosthuizen soon got rich. He was respected – and even envied – throughout the Marico. They say that when the Volksraad member came to Gerrit Oosthuizen's farm, and he saw around him so many unmistakable signs of great wealth, including green window-blinds that rolled up by themselves when you jerked the sash-cord – they say that even the Volksraad member was very much impressed, and that he seemed to be deep in thought for a long time. It almost seemed as though he was wondering whether, in having taken up politics, he had chosen the right career, after all.

If that was how the Volksraad member really did feel about the matter, then it must have been a sad thing for him, when the debates in the Raadzaal at Pretoria dragged far into the night, and he had to remain seated on his back bench, without having much heart in the proceedings, since he would be dreaming all the time of a herd of red cattle being driven towards a fence in the starlight. And when the Chairman of the Committee called another member to order, it might almost have sounded to this Volksraad member as though it was a voice coming out of the shadows of the maroelas and demanding, suddenly, "Who goes there?"

To this question – which he had heard more than once, of course, during the years in which he had smuggled cattle – Gerrit Oosthuizen nearly always had the right answer. It was always more difficult for Gerrit Oosthuizen if it was a youthful sounding voice shouting out that challenge. Because it usually meant, then, that the uniformed man on horseback, half-hidden in the shadow of a withaak, was a young recruit, anxious to get promotion. Gerrit Oosthuizen could not handle him in the same way as he could an elderly mounted police sergeant, who was a married man with a number of children and who had learnt, through long years of service, a deeper kind of wisdom about life on this old earth.

It was, each time, through mistaken zeal on the part of a young recruit – who nearly always got a transfer, shortly afterwards – that Gerrit Oosthuizen had to stand his trial in the Zeerust court-house. He was several times acquitted. On a few occasions he was fined quite heavily. Once he was sentenced to six months' imprisonment without the option of a fine. Consequently, while Gerrit Oosthuizen was known to entertain a warm regard for almost any middle-aged mounted policeman with a fat stomach, he invariably displayed a certain measure of impatience towards a raw recruit. It was said that on more than one occasion, in the past, Gerrit Oosthuizen had given expression to this impatience by discharging a couple of Mauser bullets – aimed high – into the shadows from which an adolescent voice had spoken out of turn.

Needless to say, all these stories that went the rounds of the Marico about Gerrit Oosthuizen only added to his popularity with the farmers. Even when the predikant shook his head, on being informed of Gerrit Oosthuizen's latest escapade, you could see that he regarded it as being but little more than a rather risky sort of prank, and that, if anything, he admired Gerrit Oosthuizen, the Marico's champion cattle-smuggler, for the careless way in which he defied the law. Whatever he did, Gerrit Oosthuizen always seemed to act in the right way. And it seems to me that, if he adheres to such a kind of rule, the man who goes against the law gets as much respect from the people around him as does the law-giver. More, even.

"The law stops on the south side of the Dwarsberge," Gerrit Oosthuizen said to a couple of his neighbours, in a sudden burst of pride on the day that the piano arrived and was placed on top of the patent aluminium stand. "And north of the Dwarsberge I am the law."

But soon after that Gerrit Oosthuizen did something that the Marico farmers did not understand, and that they did not forgive him for so easily. Just at that time when his daughter, Jemima, was most attractive, and was beginning to play herself in on the piano, using two fingers of each hand – and when quite a number of the young men of the district were beginning to pay court to her – Gerrit Oosthuizen sent her away to the seminary for young ladies that had just been opened in Zeerust.

We expressed our surprise to Gerrit Oosthuizen in various ways. After all, we all liked Jemima, and it didn't seem right that an attractive Bushveld girl should be sent away like that to get spoilt. She would come back with city affectations and foreign ways. She would no longer be able to make a good, simple wife for an honest Boer lad. It was, of course, the young men who expressed this view with the greatest measure of indignation – even those who were not so particularly honest, either, perhaps.

But Gerrit Oosthuizen said, no, he believed in his daughter having the best opportunities. There were all sorts of arts and graces of life that she would learn at the finishing school, he said. Among the Marico's young men, however, were some who thought that there was very little that any young ladies' seminary would be able to teach Jemima that she did not already know.

We lost confidence in Gerrit Oosthuizen after that, of course. And when next we got up a deputation to the Government to protest about the money being spent on native education – because there were already signs of a falling-off in the cattle-trade with the Bechuanas – then we did not elect Gerrit Oosthuizen as a delegate. We felt that his ideas on education, generally, were becoming unsound.

It is true, however, that, during the time that Jemima was at the seminary, Gerrit Oosthuizen did once or twice express doubts about his wisdom in having sent her there.

"Jemima writes to say that she is reading a lot of poetry," Gerrit Oosthuizen said to me, once. "I wonder if that isn't perhaps, sort of ... you know ..."

I agreed with Gerrit that it seemed as if his daughter was embarking on something dangerous. But she was still very young, I added. She might yet grow out of that sort of foolishness. I said that when the right young man for her came along she would close that book of poetry quick enough, without even bothering to mark the place that she had got up to. Nevertheless, I was glad to think that Gerrit Oosthuizen was not so happy, any more, about his daughter's higher education.

"Still, she gets very good reports from her teachers," Gerrit Oosthuizen said, but without any real enthusiasm. "Especially from her poetry teacher."

Meanwhile, the cattle-smuggling business was going from bad to worse, and by the time Jemima returned from her stay at the seminary, Gerrit Oosthuizen had his hands full with his personal affairs. He had made a few singularly unsuccessful cattle-smuggling trips into the Protectorate. By that time the kafirs had got so educated that one squint-eyed Mtosa even tried to fall back on barter – but the other way around. He wanted Gerrit Oosthuizen to trade his mules and cart for a piece of glass that the Mtosa claimed was a Namaqualand diamond. And, on top of everything else, when Gerrit Oosthuizen did on a few occasions get back into the Transvaal with a likely herd of cattle, it was with Daniel Malan, a new recruit to the border patrol, hot on his trail.

It was under these circumstances that Jemima Oosthuizen returned to the bushveld farm from the young ladies' seminary in Zeerust. Just to look at her, it seemed that the time she had spent at the finishing school had not changed her very much. If anything, she was even prettier than she had been before she left. Her lips were still curved and red. There was still that soft shadow at the side of her throat. Only, it seemed to me that in her dark eyes there was now a dreamy look that wouldn't fit in too readily with the everyday life of a bushveld farm.

And I was right. And it didn't take the young fellows of the neighbourhood very long to find out, either, that Jemima Oosthuizen had, indeed, changed. It saddened them to realize that they could do very little about it.

Jemima Oosthuizen was, as always, friendly to each young man who called. But it was easy for these young men to detect that it was a general sort of friendliness – which she felt for them all equally and alike. She would read poetry to them, reading and explaining to them passages out of the many books of verse that she had brought back with her. And while they were very ready to be thrilled – even when they knew that it was a foolish waste of time – yet they felt that there was no way in which they could make any progress with her. No matter what any young man might feel about her, Jemima's feelings for him remained impersonal.

"What's wrong with me?" Andries Steyn asked of a number of other young men, once. "She can go on reading that poetry to me as long as she likes. I don't mind. I don't understand anything about it, in any case. But the moment I start holding her hand, I know that she isn't thinking of me at all. It's like she wants me to come to her out of one of those books."

"Yes, like that fellow by the dam, looking all pale and upset about something," Fritz Pretorius interrupted him. "Yes, I know all that nonsense. And there am I sitting on the rusbank next to her, wearing my best clothes and my veldskoens rubbed smooth with sheep's fat. And she doesn't seem to see me, at all. I don't mind her explaining all about that stuff she reads. I like the sound of her voice. But she doesn't make me feel that I am even a human being to her."

They went on to say that perhaps Jemima didn't want a man who was a human being. Maybe she wanted a lover who reminded her of one of those young men in the poetry books. A young man who wore shining armour. Or jet-black armour. Or even rusty armour. They had all kinds in the different poems that Jemima Oosthuizen explained to her suitors. But where did a young man of the Marico Bushveld come in, in all that?

Lovers came and went. Jemima was never long without a suitor. But she never favoured one above the other – never warming noticeably to anyone. Whatever the qualities were that she sought in a lover – going by the romantic heroes that she read about in old poetry – Jemima never found a Marico lover who fitted in with the things that she read about.

Yes, Gerrit Oosthuizen certainly had a lot of trouble. We even began to feel slightly sorry for him. Here was his daughter who, at a marriageable age, was driving all the young men away from her because of some fantastic ideas that they had put into her head at the finishing school. Then there were the kafirs in the Protectorate, who were daily getting more difficult to deal with. And then, finally, there was that new police recruit who was putting in all his time trying to trap Gerrit.

And those who sympathized with Gerrit Oosthuizen also thought it right to blame his daughter on the score of ingratitude. After all, it had cost her father a good deal of money to see Jemima through the finishing school. He had sent her to the young ladies' seminary at Zeerust in order that she should gain refinement and culture: instead, she had come back talking poetry. Others, again, said that it was her father's lawlessness – which was also, after a fashion, romantic – that had come out in Jemima in that way.

It was on an afternoon when a horseman came riding from over the veld up to her front gate, that Jemima saw the young man that she had read about in olden poems. And she recognized him instantly as her lover. She did not take great note of what he looked like. Nor did she even observe, at first glance, that he was wearing a uniform. All that Jemima Oosthuizen saw very clearly was that, when he came riding up to her from the highway, he was seated on a white horse.

And when she had gone hastily into her bedroom – and had come out again, wearing a pink frock – Jemima hardly understood, at first, the meaning of the young policeman's words when she heard him say, to her father, that he had a warrant for his arrest.

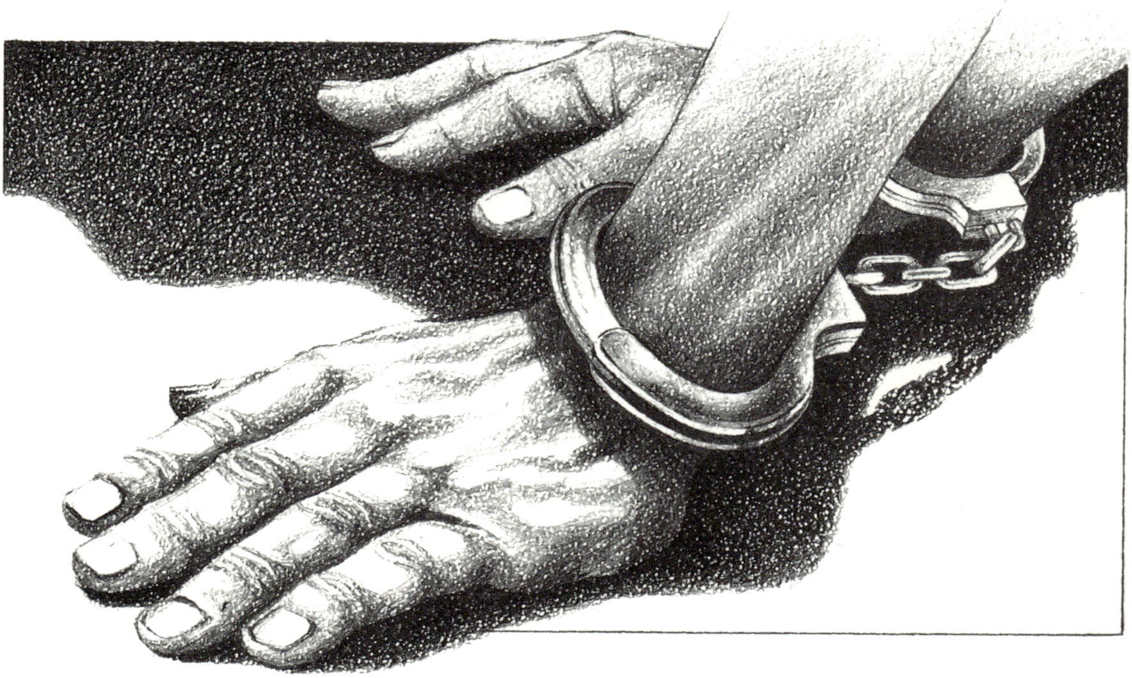

COLD STONE JUG

In 1926 Herman Charles Bosman was condemned to death after a catastrophic incident in which his stepbrother was killed. On the judge's recommendation, however, a reprieve was granted and at the age of twenty-one Bosman went to serve a four-year term of imprisonment with hard labour. Cold Stone Jug *is the unique chronicle of his prison experiences, and the following extracts have been taken from the novel.*

PREAMBLE

"Murder," I answered.

There were about a dozen prisoners in the cells at Marshall Square. It was getting on towards the late afternoon of a Sunday that we had spent locked up in a cell that was three-quarters underground and that had barred apertures opening onto the pavement at the corner of McLaren and Marshall Streets, Johannesburg. I had been arrested about fifteen or sixteen hours before.

Those first hours in the cells at Marshall Square, serving as the overture to a long period of imprisonment in the Swartklei Great Prison, were the most miserable I have ever known. By standing on a bench you could get near enough to the barred opening to catch an occasional glimpse of the underneath part of the shoe-leather of passing pedestrians, who, on that dreary Sunday afternoon, consisted almost entirely of natives. The motley collection of prisoners inside the cell took turns in getting onto the bench and trying to attract the attention of the passers-by. Now and again a native would stop. A lengthy discussion would follow. Occasionally (this constituting a triumphant termination to the interview), a piece of lighted cigarette-end would be dropped in through that little hole in the wall against the pavement. This was over twenty years ago. But it is still like that. You can go and look there.

For the rest of the time the dozen inmates of the cell carried on a desultory conversation, a lot of it having to do with what appeared to be highly unbecoming activities on the part of plain-clothes members of the police force, who seemed to spend all their waking hours in working up spurious cases against law-abiding citizens. Then, when it was getting towards late afternoon, one of the prisoners, a dapper little fellow who had done most of the talking and who seemed to exercise some sort of leadership in the cell, felt that it was time we all got sort of cosy together, and started taking more of a personal interest in one another's affairs.

"I'm in for a liquor-selling, myself," he announced to a man standing next to him, "What they pinch you for?"

"Stealing a wheel-barrow from the P.W.D.," was the reply, "Not that I done it, mind you. But that's the charge."

"And what are you in for?" the cell-boss demanded of the next man.

"Drunk and disorderly and indecent exposure," came the answer.

"And what's your charge?"

"Forgery. And if I drop this time I'll get seven years."

And so this dapper little fellow who was doing the questioning worked his way through the whole lot until it came to my turn.

"Say, what are you pinched for?" he asked, eyeing me narrowly.

"Murder," I said. And in my tone there was no discourtesy.
And I did not glower much. I only added, "And I'm not feeling too good."

"Struth!" my interrogater remarked. And his jaw dropped. And that bunch of prisoners in the cell, the whole dozen of them, moved right across to the other side, to the corner that was furthest away from me.

CHAPTER ONE

1

It was a Sunday on which the Dutch Reformed Church was honouring the mothers of the country.

And for the mothers' day service in the Swartklei Prison chapel the predikant had brought along a large number of paper labels, coloured respectively green and purple. The labels were passed round. This was something new and exciting. It made all us convicts attending the Dutch Reformed service in the prison chapel feel important people, somehow. If your mother was still alive you were expected to fix a green strip of paper onto the lapel of your brown corduroy jacket. If your mother was dead you fastened a purple strip. No pins were provided, but the backs of these strips of coloured paper were gummed. So we stuck the labels on with spit. And we sat there, on the wooden benches, straight up and very proud, feeling not only that we were doing homage to our mothers, but that we were participating in a ceremony that was on that day being observed in the magical world known as "outside".

"They are having mothers' day outside, also," one convict would say to another.

People in churches outside, men as well as women (the entrancing sound of the word "women"!) were wearing little labels like these on their breasts. We were just like *outside* for those minutes during which the service in the prison chapel lasted. And we relished that period to the full, basking in the pride of being, for a while, like people who were free to roam the streets. Able to do the same things that men and women who were not in prison were doing. Sharing in *their* emotions. Feeling about things the way *they* felt.

The predikant spoke in a very moving way about our mothers, and about us, also, about those of us whose mothers were still alive and who accordingly were privileged to wear green labels, and about those of us who had unfortunately lost our mothers, and so wore purple labels in sorrowful remembrance. (The predikant pointedly made no reference to those convicts in his congregation who, through ignorance or misguided zeal, had stuck whole rows of labels, purple and green mixed up just anyhow, onto their jackets, like they were military ribbons.) The result was, what with the hymn-singing and all, that the convicts got worked up to such a pitch of emotionalism that even the most hardened blue-coats (habitual criminals) broke down and sobbed. Men who had spent many years in prison and had grown grey behind bars, looking at the pathetic strips of coloured paper stuck onto their lapels with spit, dissolved into tears.

When the service ended and we tramped down the iron stairs back to the cells (encountering the Methodists, who were coming up the stairs as we were going down), a blue-coat in front of me, his face still tearful after the sermon, inadvertently collided with a convict tramping up to attend the Methodist service.

"As jy my weer stamp sal ek jou donder," the blue-coat said, but his tone was kindly. The thought of the way he had been breaking his mother's heart through the years had softened him. His language, through long habit, held low menace. But his tone was unexpectedly mild.

2

As the law used to be (and still is, I believe), after a man has committed the same offence a number of times - twice, I think, in some cases, and about twenty-seven times in others - the judge in passing sentence warns the culprit that if he again appears before a court of law and is convicted he will be declared an habitual criminal. That means that the word "Indeterminate Sentence" gets inscribed on his ticket. His release from prison is then a matter that rests with the Board of Visitors, who come to the Swartklei Great Prison to interview him once a year. Sometimes the Board recommends him for discharge after he has served six years. Usually the period is seven, eight, nine years and longer. But when he is eventually discharged from prison this man is placed on a five years' period of probation. He is not allowed to consort with fellow ex-convicts (what other friends has he got, incidentally, in the outside world that has forgotten him during those long years behind bars?). He is not allowed to frequent pubs. And if at any time during the five years of probation he gets convicted on the most minor offence, something for which he could get a five pound fine or a few days' imprisonment, he goes back to prison to serve the indeterminate sentence all over again.

As they say in prison, he goes back to do his second blue-coat. This time he serves a longer stretch than for the first indeterminate sentence. When he comes out the second time, it is the same thing over again. The five years' ticket-of-leave. I believe there are some men in the Swartklei Great Prison today busy with their fourth blue-coat. It is possible, through the indeterminate sentence system, for a man to spend thirty years and more in prison, with intervals of only a few weeks or a few months or a few days at a time, and all through his having committed a number of offences while out on ticket. It is possible, of course, to spend as long as forty or fifty years behind bars in this way - that is, if you live that long.

The ordinary convict wears a brown corduroy jacket, rather ill-fitting and shapeless, and knee-breeches and long woollen stockings, black with red stripes, and a peculiar kind of footwear, halfway between a shoe and a boot. But instead of the brown corduroy jacket the indeterminate sentence convict wears a blue serge jacket, as a distinctive garb. Hence the term "blue-coat". At exercise in the yards, in the workshops, in the cell corridors, everywhere, except in the first offenders' section, the sprinkling of prisoners wearing blue jackets is a characteristic feature of life in the Swartklei Great Prison. I noticed that, with each year that passed, the percentage of convicts wearing blue jackets got higher. The imposition of the indeterminate sentence did not seem to act as a deterrent to recidivism. Oh, yes, I almost forgot - on the breast pocket of the blue-coat the letters "I.S." are sewn on in red. The letters stand, of course, for "Indeterminate Sentence", but in terms of prison irony the letters "I.S." have long ago been interpreted as signifying "I'm Settled".

In prison the blue-coat occupies a position of some degree of importance. He doesn't rank as high as head-warder, maybe. But his social standing is certainly a considerable cut above that of a warder-recruit. A blue-coat is even higher than a murderer. One's prestige inside the prison is in direct proportion to the length of the sentence one is serving and is also based on the number of times one has been convicted. Thus, a first offender who is doing a life sentence, while he rates pretty high as a prison "head", hasn't got quite the same status as a lifer with a number of previous convictions. The more time you do, the better you are supposed to know the ropes. And nothing is more annoying to the genuine long-timer, somebody engaged on a stretch of from ten to twenty years, or life, than to find an inferior person, sentenced to a trivial matter of two or three years only, giving himself the airs of a "head", and speaking out of his turn generally.

And so the blue-coat goes on doing his time, year in and year out. Seven years, eight years, nine years. And then out for a short while on ticket, finding himself in a world that has changed utterly; alone and friendless, certain of one thing only, and that is that before the five years of probation are up doom will have descended on him again in the form of a conviction, for a serious or a trivial offence, it doesn't matter which, and he will have to start on the indeterminate sentence all over again. And how the world changes while you are doing a stretch. When you come out you find that the places you used to know in Johannesburg have vanished. Skyscrapers have gone up where there were tin shanties. And people's habits. They are altogether different. Whether the people have changed their ways, or whether it is you who have altered, having grown so inured to the prison methods of doing things - this is something that you just don't know, and that you don't care about, either.

But when I walk about the streets, and I see the crowds of men and women, with all the multitude of expressions on their faces, and all the different sorts of light in their eyes; and I feel the warm glow of human beings, and my nostrils are filled with the heady stink of human beings, and something inside me comes alive to the joy and pathos of humanity - then I sometimes think, for a few fleeting moments, of the blue-coats in the Swartklei Great Prison. I think of the long prison years in front of them and behind them. I see them hemmed in by brown walls and brown years. I think of these men leading their silent lives. And I hope that God will go with them, through all those years.

3

Now for the murderers. Compared with the blue-coats, they are rather a jolly lot. The majority of them are first offenders. That is not surprising, of course. Murder being the crime it is, it is unlikely that anybody will feel like committing it a number of times. For that matter, you're not allowed to commit murder a number of times ... The result is that by far the majority of murderers doing stretches in the Swartklei Great Prison are first offenders. A murderer never comes back to prison, either. It is almost as though murder, the capital crime, is the only one that appeals to him. The other offences under common law seem too tame, by comparison, to be able to tempt him. The murderer is a strange figure; not pathetic, like the blue-coat; but lonely somehow; almost like the eagle. But also with the lost bewilderment of a child.

In the prison, the murderer, unlike the blue-coat, does not wear a distinctive garb. He is not dressed by the authorities in a way to single him out from the other convicts - bank-robbers, forgers, illicit gold-buyers, rapists and the rest. There is no need for men to put any distinguishing marks on a murderer's clothes. Cain's mark is there for all to read. Murder is a doomed sign to wear on your brow.

4

Disguise it how one will, the fact is that the Swartklei Great Prison is dominated, spiritually as well as architecturally, by the gallows chamber, whose doors rise up, massive and forbidding, at the end of the main wing in the building - the penal corridors.

The hangings are the worst part of life inside the prison. When a man has been condemned to death on the Rand or in any other Transvaal centre he is brought over to the Swartklei Great Prison, where he is lodged in the condemned cell adjacent to the gallows until such time as he is either reprieved or hanged. The period of waiting in that cell next to the gallows varies from about five weeks to two months. Then the case is settled one way or the other. Either the sheriff arrives with a printed document bearing the title "Greetings" in heavy black scroll and he notifies the condemned man that his execution has been set down for the morning after the next, or the Governor of the prison walks in, accompanied by the chief warder, and he informs the prisoner that the Governor-General has decided to commute his sentence to one of imprisonment, the term varying usually from ten years to life.

But during all this time the shadow of his hanging lies like a pall over the inmates of the prison, warders as well as convicts. During most of the months of the year the condemned cells are empty. There is nobody waiting up there at the end of the penal section with the death sentence suspended over him. But when the condemned cells are occupied, things in the prison are rotten all round. There is something inside the most hardened warder or anti-social convict that makes him shudder at the thought of death, of violent death, of the gruesome ceremony of doing a man to death above a dark hole, at a set time, with legal formality that does not extend beyond handcuffs and leg-irons and a sack drawn over the condemned man's head and a piece of coarse rope knotted behind his ear.

On the morning of a hanging the cells are unlocked half an hour later than usual. The prisoners arrive at their workshops half an hour late. The cells are all locked at the hour of the hanging and the morning bell doesn't ring until the execution is over. The man in the condemned cell must not be allowed to know how near his hour has actually come. They say it is all done very efficiently. They say that it takes less than two minutes from the moment the hangman has unlocked the door of the condemned cell until he has got the prisoner trussed and pinioned and with the rope round his neck, waiting for the trapdoor to fall. When the trap drops it is with a reverberation that shakes the whole prison building, and the bell rings, and the cells are unlocked and the convicts march out to work.

I dislike according so much space to the details of the hangings, but these things loom like a shadow over the prison all the time, like an unpleasant odour, and they make life inside the prison a lot gloomier than it would otherwise be. The six hundred convicts and the hundred warders in the prison share to some extent the feelings of the man who is being dropped through the trapdoor, and the fountain-head of life grows discoloured. I don't suppose very much can be done about it. After all, prison isn't supposed to be a place where you can just spend a few happy, carefree years at will.

5

I remember that I had company in the condemned cell. There was another man there, also under sentence of death, when I arrived. We were separated from each other by two rows of bars and wire netting, which formed a little passage in which the warder on duty paced up and down. The warders watched us night and day, working in four-hour shifts, with the lights on all the time. That other man's name was Stoffels. We were provided with cigarettes, which the warder would light for us through the wire netting. I remember the smell of disinfectant in that cell. It is a kind of disinfectant that they use in a number of Government institutions. The smell is strong but not unpleasant. Only the other day I got a whiff of this same disinfectant in a post office corridor. And in one punch that odour brought the past back to me like it was now. I even looked round to see whether the sanitary pail was still there, in the corner.

But I can recall only the external impressions, the surface things, which I have learnt are not realities at all.

I can remember the jokes Stoffels and I made, talking to each other through two sets of steel netting and bars, with the warder in between. And the questions we asked the warders about life inside the prison. We had to ask these questions of the warders, we two, who were in the prison but not of it. And the stories the warders had to relate to us, in the long nights when we couldn't get to sleep, made life as a convict inside a prison seem very alluring – just simply because it was life. And when we heard the convicts march out to work in the mornings, their footsteps heavy on the concrete floor of the hall far removed from us, their passage sounded like the tread of kings. And

when a warder mentioned to us the fact that he had that morning had occasion, in the course of an altercation, to hit a convict over the head with his baton, I know how I felt about that convict, how I envied him, how infinitely privileged I felt he was to be able to be regarded by a warder as a live person, as somebody that could be hit over the head. For no warder would dream of hitting a condemned man with a baton. To a warder a condemned man was something already dead.

Because we had been sentenced to be hanged, Stoffels and I were accorded certain privileges. For one thing, we didn't have to get our hair cropped short, like the other convicts, with a pair of number nought clippers. And when I was taken out on exercise, into the prison yard, twice a day, and I saw other convicts from a distance, and I saw how short their hair was, and I felt my own hair, long and wavy, and I understood what my long hair signified - then I didn't feel too good. I even hoped that, somehow, by mistake, somebody would come in and say that the chief warder had ordered my hair to be cut short. Just so I wouldn't have to flaunt, in the exercise yard, that awful thing that made me different from the hard labour convicts. Long hair and the rope ... A short rope.

Of course, Stoffels and I affected unconcern, there in the condemned cell. We spent much of our waking hours in pulling the warders' legs. We didn't know, then, that we were in actual fact engaged in a time-honoured prison pastime. We didn't know that "kidding" to warders was a sport regularly indulged in by prison lags, and that this form of recreation had venerable traditions. We didn't know all that. We merely followed our natural bent of trying to be funny, and we found, afterwards, that we were all the time conforming to accepted prison custom. It must be that prison was, after all, the right place for Stoffels and me. Because of this aspect of it, at all events, to the part of it connected with pulling a warder's leg, we took like ducks to water.

There was one warder whom Stoffels and I nicknamed the Clown. He had not been in the prison service very long and had only recently been transferred to the Swartklei Great Prison from a native goal in Barberton. We joshed him unmercifully. He was a young fellow in his early twenties, but Stoffels and I addressed him as though he were a man of the world with infinitely wide experience and an oracle of learning. He afforded us many nights of first-class entertainment, during the dreary hours between ten at night and two in the morning, when we could not sleep and were afraid to trust our heads to the hard pallet, in case when we woke up in the morning it would be to find the sheriff standing at the door, with the death warrant.

The Clown had a very simple heart. One night, through a process of not very subtle flattery, we got him to acknowledge that he could dance rather well. We also got him to admit that, in general, men were envious of his ballroom accomplishments, and that, behind his back, they said many nasty things about him, such as that he danced like a sick hippopotamus, or the way a duck waddles. All because they were jealous of him. We even got him so far as to show us a few of the latest dance-steps. For this purpose he took off his heavy warder's boots. At the Clown's demonstration, in his stockinged feet, of the then fashionable black-bottom, Stoffels and I laughed uproariously. We explained to him, of course, that we were laughing at the thought that jealous males could have come to such ludicrously erroneous conclusions about his dancing, merely because they viewed everything he did through the green gaze of envy. Thereupon the Clown joined in the laughter, thus making Stoffels and me roar louder than ever.

"Didn't they perhaps, in their jealousy, even say –" I started off again, when we all suddenly stopped laughing. For a key grated in the outer door and the night head-warder entered.

"What's all this?" he demanded, "The convicts the other end of the hall are complaining they can't sleep, the way you men in the condemned cell keep on laughing all night. And this isn't the first night, neither."

The night head-warder looked at us sternly. There seemed something gravely irregular in a situation in which two condemned men were keeping a whole prison establishment awake with indecorous laughter.

"You condemned men mustn't laugh so loud," he said, "The hard labour convicts got to sleep. They got to work all day. You two don't do nothing but smoke cigarettes all day long and crack jokes. You'll get yourselves in serious trouble if the Governor finds out you keep the whole prison awake night after night, romping about and laughing in the condemned cells."

I wondered, vaguely, what more serious trouble we could get into than we were already in. But at that moment the night head-warder happened to look down at the Clown's feet. So it was his turn to laugh. The Clown certainly cut a ridiculous figure, with shapeless pieces of feet leaking out of his socks.

"Where's your boots?" the night head-warder demanded, his tone midway between a threat and a guffaw, "Don't you know as you can't come on duty improperly dressed? What sort of an example do you think you are to these two condemned men? And look at all them pertaters in your socks. I never seen so many pertaters in a sock. More pertater than sock. With all them pertaters you ought to be working in the kitchen. Come on, now. Quick about it. Put on the other boot, too. What you want to take them off for, anyway? To show these condemned men your pertaters, I suppose. Or maybe you got bunions. Yes, must be bunions. I suppose you got bunions on your feet through walking about the streets looking for trollops."

With that sally, and still guffawing, the night head-warder departed. There certainly seemed to be something in the atmosphere of the cell adjacent to the gallows that was provocative of a spirit of clean fun. The condemned cell air seemed to be infectiously mirth-making.

"Now, isn't that just what we have been saying?" Stoffels asked of the Clown when the three of us were alone together, once more. "How do you like that for jealousy? The moment the head-warder sees you he starts picking you out. What do you think of that? And so ridiculous, too. How can he say you got those bunions on your feet –"

"But I haven't got bunions," the Clown asserted, "You know as well as I do that I took off my boots to show you my –"

"Those terrible bunions," Stoffels persisted, ignoring the Clown's remonstrances, "How can he say you got those corns and bunions *and blisters* walking after whores in the street? Come on, answer me, has he ever seen you?"

"I don't know what he's seen or what he hasn't seen," the Clown answered, "I only know that the only times I've ever walked about looking for a whore it was in the other end of the town from where he stays. It was –"

6

Warders all say that the job in a prison they like least is that of guarding a condemned man. They say it makes them too melancholy. I think I can understand why. If I was a warder I would also get a bellyful of this sort of nonsense. Gallows half-laughs.

There was one warder who gave Stoffels and me a bit of trouble at the start. I don't mean that he bothered us in any way, or that he was offensive. The trouble was simply that we couldn't get him to talk. No matter how cunningly we baited our traps, he would never fall. He was too wise. His name was Van Graan, and he had been in the prison service for a good many years. We tried him with practically everything. He would have none of it. We tried him on that hardy annual, promotion. We also held out the bait of a discussion on long leave.

(We had found that this was also a sore point with the warders. According to what they told us, the granting of long leave was intimately bound up with nepotism. Only the Governor's favourites got granted it.)

One evening we again tried Van Graan out on promotion.

"I suppose you have been in the prison service a very long time?" I essayed, "Funny how one can always tell the difference between an old hand and a new recruit. I can't imagine you ever having been a recruit, meneer. The way you know the ropes. Anybody can see it on you. Nobody would ever try any stunts on you."

"But I also made mistakes at the start," Warder van Graan acknowledged, "I also had to learn. But perhaps it come a bit easier to me than to most -"

"Brains," Stoffels vociferated, "Brains. What I say is if a man has got brains you can't keep him down. Unless it's jealousy. Look at you, now, meneer. Look what brains you got. And look how many years you been in the service. And what's your reward? You're not even a head-warder."

"I'd sooner be just a ordinary warder, like what I am," Warder van Graan answered, turning nasty, "Than be in your boots."

So that attempt had also gone awry. But we got Warder van Graan in the end. We could never have believed that he would have succumbed to so obvious a snare.

"Why I wouldn't like to be a warder," Stoffels announced one evening in a tone the very casual and disarming quality of which should have put Warder van Graan on his guard, "is because of all the backbiting that goes on in a prison. Now, that is where I would be different if I was a warder. I wouldn't go and talk about other warders, behind their backs, to convicts. I would have too much self-respect."

"Some people got no self-respect at all," Warder van Graan nodded his agreement, "And what does one man want to go and scandal behind another man's back? Does he think he'll get more pay for it?"

"And to convicts, too," I interposed, "I mean if a warder has fallen so low that he talks to other convicts about a fellow warder, what won't he go and say about this same warder to the chief, or even to the Governor? A warder that's so low as to gossip with convicts will fall so low, after a while, as to talk to the Governor also -"

"Perhaps he has already fallen so low," Warder van Graan exclaimed, "But who is this warder you are talking about?"

He was a goner then, of course. Poor old Warder van Graan.

"No, no," Stoffels replied, "It's nothing at all, meneer. I was only thinking that I wouldn't like to be a warder, here in the Swartklei Great Prison, if you understand what I mean. I wouldn't like to think that day after day I do my duty honestly, the best I can, and then all the time there is that other warder going behind my back and saying things about me that –"

"Oh, so it's him, is it?" Warder van Graan demanded. "That bastard Snake-Eye. I could have knowed Snake-Eye was up to no good. And him a elder in the church and all. And I know what he says about me, also. He says I lumbers."

"Lumbers?" I repeated. It sounded like halitosis.

"He says I smuggles in tobacco and things," Warder van Graan explained, "Now, I been suspecting that about him a long time, that he goes about saying as I lumbers."

"Whereas, of course, he is the one that lumbers," I replied, very brightly, "It is only when you are yourself guilty of a thing that you accuse others."

"What I knows about him," Warder van Graan said, and he lowered his voice and spoke very slowly and solemnly, "If I was to say what I knows about Snake-Eye, he'd be sitting here where you are."

I affected a start.

"Not as bad as that, surely, meneer?" I exclaimed, "You don't mean to say that what you know about him can get him hanged. Who did he murder? I always felt there was something about that Snake-Eye –"

"No, no, not murder," Warder van Graan exclaimed, "Not as bad as the condemned cell. What I mean to say is he'd be in prison if I was to tell all I know. He made over fifty pounds the month before last, lumbering in tobacco to convicts whose people have got the money. He lumbers it in hidden under his rain-cape. What would he say if I asked the Governor why does Snake-Eye wear a rain-cape when it is a clear, hot night in the middle of the summer, and not a cloud in the sky?"

"But, of course, you would never do a thing like that," I responded, "We all know you got principle."

"And what about that refrigerator that was sent for repairs to the fitters shop from the reserve?" Warder van Graan demanded, "Through whose backyard did eight convicts carry that refrigerator one Tuesday morning. I ask you. Through whose?"

"Surely not -" I began hesitantly, "Surely not through -"

"Yus," Warder van Graan said, "Through none other's backyard. I seen it with my own eyes."

Warder van Graan was caught. He was porridge in our hands, after that. If Stoffels or I would have wanted brandy or dagga smuggled in-

to the condemned cell for us, Warder van Graan would have lumbered it in.

I should like to include just this final story about the Clown.

I have explained that the warder walks up and down that little passage between the two condemned cells. The warder is also locked in. They do that so as to keep a condemned man doubly secure: first, locked inside his own cell, and, secondly, locked in with the warder in a larger cell, comprising the two condemned cells and the warder's passage. But the warder is all right, there. He's got a revolver. Only, he can't get out during the four hours of his shift. The section-warder has to come and unlock him. But he's got a bell-button that he can push whenever there's trouble. Each warder, when he enters the cell, is provided with a tin vessel, cylindrical and about a foot high – like a native's dinner-pail, but taller – containing drinking-water. When the Clown came on duty, at 10 p.m., it was customary because of the lateness of the hour, to put two tins of water into the warder's passage, one for the Clown and one for the warder who came on duty after him. That meant that the cleaner in the section did not have to be awakened at two o'clock in the morning to get the next warder a tin of drinking-water.

But because the Clown had been transferred to Swartklei from Barberton only recently, he was not conversant with all the niceties of condemned cell routine. Consequently, he thought that both tins were for his own use. He would drink water out of one tin, whenever he got thirsty, and regularly, about ten minutes before the next warder (whom we nicknamed Jannie) came in to relieve him, the Clown would wash his hands in the other tin of drinking-water. He used my soap and towel, or Stoffels' soap and towel, whichever was nearer to hand. (Unfortunately, I find that I must again interrupt with a parenthesis. But that is the prison's fault, not mine. I can't help it that prison routine should be so absurdly complicated. Anyway, each time, last thing at night, after Stoffels and I had had our supper, the section-warder would order us to put our empty enamel dixies outside - and also our pieces of soap and our towels. This measure was probably incorporated into the regulations in order to prevent condemned criminals from suffocating themselves with the towels, or from making themselves unnecessarily ill through eating pieces of prison soap.)

Anyway, two pieces of soap and two towels - mine and Stoffels' respectively - would be lying in the corner of his passage when the Clown came in, and there would also be two tins of water. As I have said, the Clown would regularly drink up the water in one tin, and wash his hands in the other.

Most nights, Jannie, the warder who relieved the Clown, would stay on duty right through until six o'clock, without getting thirsty. But those nights when he wanted a drink of water and he picked up the tin that the Clown had washed his hands in, Jannie would curse the whole prison up and down. Prison warders as a class are not distinguished in respect of being particularly clean-mouthed. And Jannie seemed to be much more fastidious about what went into his mouth than he was about what came out. In fact, what came out of his mouth each time he tasted that water in which the Clown had performed his ablutions, were words and expressions that I felt no soap in the world would ever wash clean again.

"— the cleaners," Jannie would splutter, "The — water tastes — soapy again. The lazy bastards of — of — cleaners are too — lazy to wash the — blasted soap off from the inside of the — tin when they put in water for me."

This went on for about a week. Some nights Jannie went off duty without having a drink of water. That was all right. But whenever he drank the Clown's soapy water he would get into a rage that had him cursing for the better part of the night. Stoffels and I never thought of enlightening Jannie about the true state of affairs, preferring to let him blame it on the cleaners. Similarly, we did not think it worthwhile to inform the Clown that every time he washed his hands it was in another man's drinking-water. The situation seemed pregnant with possibilities that we didn't want spoilt.

Then, one night, it happened. It was past one o'clock. The Clown was somewhat circumspect about ringing the bell for the section-warder in a matter of that nature ...

Stoffels and I said no word to each other about what we had witnessed. We went to lie down under our blankets, and lay hoping for the best. The Clown went off duty, Jannie coming in to relieve him. Nothing had been noticed. Could it really be possible that so unique a piece of enjoyment could come the way of two sorry felons such as Stoffels and I? Surely, it was too much to hope for ... Could two men, condemned to death, resting for a brief while at the foot of the gallows, be placed in the way of so rare a thrill? The genius that watches over criminals was with Stoffels and me that night. In the early hours of the morning, when I could hardly stand the tension any longer, Jannie got thirsty. I heard the bottom of the tin grate against the concrete of the floor. I heard Jannie draw in his breath before drinking. Then, oh, rich and ineffable and unforgettable ecstasy, oh, memorable delight, I heard - glug, glug, just like that - I heard Jannie drink. And he went on drinking. Eventually, he sighed, deeply, and I heard him put down the tin.

"Yes, I am thirsty, tonight," Jannie muttered, half to himself. I couldn't stand it any longer.

"Meneer," I said, "The tin. The tin you drink out of. There was no soap in it tonight, was there?"

"No," Jannie answered, "But it tasted funny, all the same."

"Like - like what did it taste, meneer?" I enquired, struggling hard to keep my voice level.

"Well, if I didn't know better," Jannie said, "If I didn't know that it was quite impossible, I would say that it tasted a lot like —."

So Stoffels and I both jumped up from our blankets and informed Jannie that it was.

CHAPTER TWO

1

We kept on indulging in spasmodic frivolities and pulling the warders' legs right until the end. But, of course, it wasn't the same any more when I was left alone in the condemned cell after Stoffels got hanged. Still, I did my best. And there were several nights, when I was there, alone with the warder, on which the night head-warder had to come round and request me to laugh and talk in more subdued tones. I was giving the condemned cell a bad name, he said. But I admit frankly that it wasn't the same, any more, after Stoffels was no longer there.

I am afraid that the reader will have got rather a nebulous sort of impression of this man Stoffels. I am afraid he won't appear to the reader as a creature of flesh and blood. And that is only because I was never able to feel about Stoffels either, that he was a man in a world of men. Perhaps it was because he was going to be hanged, and although he himself naturally entertained hopes of a reprieve, hoping against hope all the time, there was something inside him, his inner life-force, that knew otherwise. At all events, I only realized, after Stoffels had been hanged, how much I missed him, and how little I knew about him, really.

When I entered the condemned cell he was already there. He had got there a few weeks before me. And I was with him for about a month. During all this time I made no real human contact with him. It must have been that the thing inside him knew that he was doomed to die, with the result that he gave out no more human warmths or light or shadow.

As my companion in the death cell for more than four weeks, Stoffels had done a good deal to cheer me up. And yet, on the morning of his execution, there was nothing I could think of saying to him. I could think of no last quip to make. I could think of no final word of comfort. In the shadow of the gallows, I had found, a jest or a solemn speech meant just about the same thing. But even if I could have thought up something to say, I would have had no opportunity of saying it. For early that morning two warders came and fetched me out of my own cell and locked me in a cell two doors away. They didn't lock the door, though, but only the grille gate. And from the sounds I heard later on, when the hangman came to perform his office, it sounded as though everything went off very efficiently. There was the tramping of feet on the iron stairs and the sound of doors being locked and unlocked, and no sound of voices. No orders had to be given. Each man knew what was expected of him, even Stoffels - who played his part tolerably well, considering the fact that he was not rehearsed in it and was getting no pay for it.

The rest of the actors in this early morning drama of the gallows - the Governor, the warders, the doctor, the hangman, the chaplain - were all salaried officials of the administration. Only Stoffels was giving his services free.

I heard what sounded like a quick scuffle, then many footfalls. And then a muffled noise in which I recognized Stoffels' voice, but with difficulty, for only part of that noise seemed to come out of his throat. The rest of it seemed to have come out of his belly. More heavy footfalls and doors creaking on hinges. And still no rapped out words of command. Then a mighty slam that shook the whole building, rattling the pannikin on the floor of the cell in which I was. And it was all over. I looked at the warder guarding me on the other side of the grille. His face was a greenish-white. Then the bell rang. And there were voices, and the sound of much movement, and the noise and commotion of a prison with six hundred convicts beginning the day's routine. I was not as badly shaken by this experience as I thought I would have been. Perhaps it was because, as I have indicated, I had not felt in Stoffels' veins and lungs the blood and breath of life any more during the period of our having known each other.

2

I don't want to waste any more time writing about the condemned cell. I want to get on with the next part of this story. In fact, I want to get out of the condemned cell as quick as possible. As quick as I got out of it that afternoon when the Governor came up and informed me that I had been reprieved. I was asleep on my blankets on the floor, that afternoon. I was dreaming, but I forget what about. And I awoke to find the Governor and the chief warder and the section-officer and the warder on duty in the death cell, all together standing in a ring around me. I woke up and rubbed my eyes. The Governor was talking. And on a sudden the import of his words and his visit dawned on me. It was the Governor who had called on me, and not the sheriff. Not the sheriff. Then I got the gist of it. The Governor was saying that my sentence had been commuted to a term of imprisonment with hard labour for so many years. I got out of that condemned cell in such a hurry that I didn't hear all of the years. And afterwards when I did find out

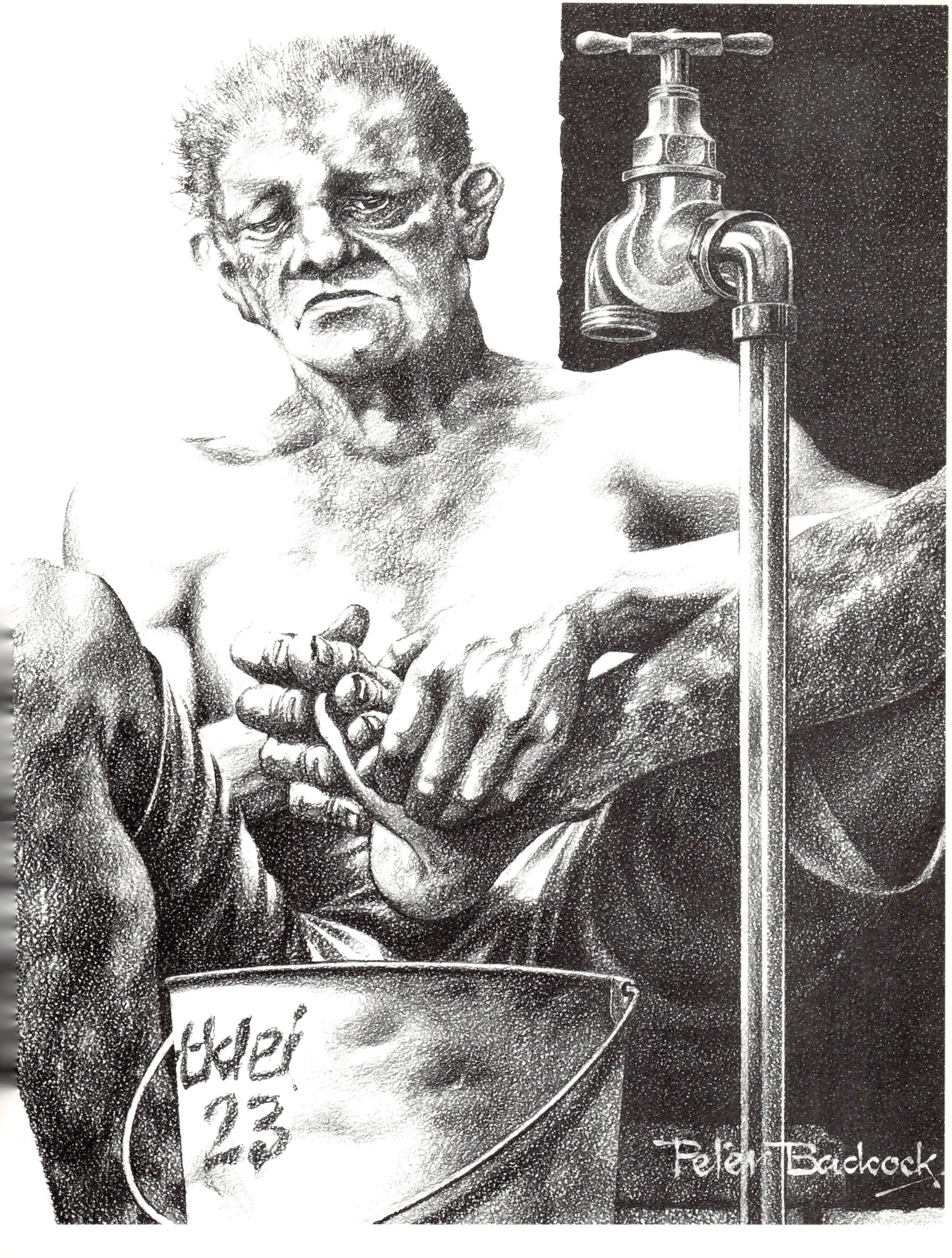
Peter Badcock

(because they took me down into the hall later on and got the number of years written on my ticket) that knowledge did not sober me up.

On the way down to the hall the head-warder addressed me in terms of stern admonition.

"You're a bleeding hard labour — convict now," he said, "See? And we don't want none of your — sanguinary cheek here. You broke your — mother's heart and we'll break your — heart. We tame lions here. First peep out of you, my man, and I'll see you get six days' solitary on spare diet. Pick up your step, there! You're not a blooming condemn' cell favourite no longer. You'll be — sorry it wasn't the hangman by the time we finished with you. You'll find out — double quick there's no blasted favouritism here."

"Yes, sir," I answered the head-warder and followed a discipline-warder across the length of the hall and then in through a grille gate and then up a flight of iron stairs that brought me onto a landing consisting of two sets of cages. They were steel cages, partitioned from each other by bolted steel plates, like you see in a ship. One row had steel plates in front as well; the other row had bars and wire mesh. I hoped they would put me in a cage with bars and wire mesh in front. You could see a little way out into the passage through the wire. And the all-steel cage looked somewhat cold. But my luck was out. The section-warder took me along a passage, unlocked an all-steel cage, waited for me to enter and then, without a word, slammed the steel door shut on me; and left.

I found out, when we were next unlocked, that I was in A2 Section, the first offenders' section, and that long-timers were kept in the all-steel cages and only short-timers were allowed in the cages with wire fronts.

In that cage in A2 Section I spent quite a number of years.

I spent about six months of my time in the stone-yard, sitting down chopping stones. Then they started on the large-scale excavation of the side of the koppie, and the work became more interesting. But with all this new activity of moving part of a mountain with a crane and coco-pans and wheel-barrows, and all this dressing stones and mixing mortar for that long, towering wall – as a result of all this fevered rushing around there began to develop a certain measure of friction as between warder and convict and between convict and convict which was not there in those placid days when we were only making largish stones smaller and had not embarked on this ambitious construction project. The warders wanted more work out of the convicts, and more efficient work. The convicts were sullen in their response, and visited their ill-humour on each other.

"What you want is my boot up your backside again," a warder would shout at a young convict, "But you're used to having other things up your backside. That's why you can't work during the day. Too many blue-coats –"

Or he would shout, "Swing that — pick higher. Put some more blasted guts into it. If I catch you loafing again I'll report you to the Governor, you blasted, motherless, cock-eyed sod." This addressed to some other convict, and so it would go on.

There was a convict in the stone-yard that they called Slangvel. He got his nickname from the bluish appearance of his skin, a sort of slaty mottle. From deeply engrained grime, I suppose. He had a powerful physique, with enormous shoulders and a thick, bull-neck. He washed once a month. I was always interested in Slangvel's ablutions. For some obscure reason he would never wash in the section. But once a month, in the afternoon, a few minutes before the fall-in signal, when we were allowed to relax for a little on smoking days, Slangvel would go to the tap with a bucket and a piece of soap. He would fill the bucket at the tap and walk some distance away and sit on a pile of bricks, with the bucket in front of him, and he would start washing. The first thing he did, always, was to take off his boots and stockings. Incredible quantities of filth were revealed when he peeled off his stockings. Then he put his feet in the bucket. In no time the water would be black with dirt and greasy with floating slime. Then he would take out his feet, dry them on the towel hanging from the back of his breeches, and start washing his hands. When this operation was completed, he would kneel down in front of the bucket and in the filthy, black, greasy, soapy, stinking water ... he would proceed to wash his face.

At various times some of the other convicts spoke to Slangvel about this singular procedure, explaining that if he washed his face first it would be in clean water. They said he should reverse the operational order of his ablutions. But Slangvel could never see the point. "I wash," he said, "And when I'm clean I'm clean."

Slangvel was a man of few words, and those few were uttered in a low sort of growl. He was a heavy dagga-roker. He resented the new activities connected with the extension of the prison wall. He very much preferred the old days, when he could sit down all day long, after a boom-rook, and just allow his hammer to fall up and down, and he didn't have to think and he didn't have to talk.

There was a sawmill on the edge of the stone-yard. About a dozen convicts worked there under the supervision of a warder. They sawed up tree-trunks for the carpenters' shop and they also sawed up the bones from the bone-yard. One day a convict sawed up his hand. Two fingers were severed completely. This caused a bit of excitement. The convict was in a bad way. He collapsed into the sawdust in front of the machine and the warder ordered a couple of the convicts to pick him up and carry him through to the hospital. They had to go through the mortuary-gate. I have explained that the rules lay it down that every convict passing through from the workshops into the section has got to be searched. The warder on duty at the mortuary-gate that day was a middle-aged man who was said to be somewhat unfeeling in his attitude towards the convicts, who nicknamed him Billy the Bastard.

The little procession approached the mortuary-gate: a couple of convicts carrying the injured man between them, and a discipline-warder walking a few paces behind. Billy the Bastard halted them. The discipline-warder explained what had happened. The man was unconscious; half his hand had been sawn away; he was bleeding profusely. They had to hurry, the discipline-warder said.

"You know the regulations," Billy the Bastard replied, imperturbably, "And I got to carry out me orders. I can't let any convict through from the workshops without I search him."

So he made the two convicts lay the unconscious man down on the ground and he proceeded to search them methodically. After that he stooped down and ran his fingers up and down the bloody form of the unconscious convict who had had his hand mangled. Then he said, all right, they could pass through.

Afterwards, when another warder mentioned the matter to Billy the Bastard, and enquired from him, by way of conversation, as to why he had thought it necessary to search the unconscious man as well, he was overheard to answer, "How do I know he didn't have dagga on him? For all I know the whole thing could have been a lurk to lumber dagga into the hospital. Where would I be then?"

The sequel to that little incident was rather funny. The accident at the sawmill occurred in the early part of the day on which Slangvel indulged in his monthly wash. Slangvel took up the bucket and went up to the tap. He was very blue with dagga. He had been smoking it all day, they found out afterwards. And so it was with the most beatific visions swimming before his eyes that he came to the tap. He was in a lovely world of bright-hued unreality. At that moment a convict at the sawmill discovered, in the sawdust, a bloody piece of finger that had come off the injured man's hand earlier in the day. The convict picked up the finger. Then he spotted Slangvel at the tap. He decided to pull his leg. He guessed Slangvel would be blue, but he didn't know how blue. He walked up to Slangvel, who had just started to fill his pail.

The convict held up his hand. Between his own fingers he grasped the bloody stump he had picked up out of the sawdust.

"Look, Slangvel," the convict exclaimed, "I got six fingers. Look, you can count them. Six fingers!"

Out of that gaudy paradise into which the blue smoke of the dagga had taken him, out of that slow, sensuous world of silken movements and voluptuous women, Slangvel was suddenly transported, by the convict's shout, into a sort of in-between region that he didn't know at all well. He looked at the convict's hand. He blinked. Those fingers. Six. And one of them loose. Yes. One finger loose from the others. Slangvel looked again. Yes, he hadn't been mistaken. What he had seen, at the start, was right. It wasn't just a dagga hallucination. That convict there really was holding up – really was holding up –

Slangvel moaned. It was too much for him. His mind, not too bright at the best of times, couldn't cope with this at all. Slangvel moaned again, a long slow moan, and then he dropped the bucket and subsided forward into the concrete gutter in front of the tap. In falling he struck his chin against the edge of the concrete. He was out for the count. The dagga, and the shock about that finger, and his violent contact with the concrete – these were too much for him. Slangvel lay unconscious beside the tap, which was still running: some of the water ran over him without reviving him: there was a deep gash in his chin.

So there was another convict ready for hospital.

This time it was a stone-yard detail that carried an unconscious convict through the mortuary-gate into the hospital. For the second time that day Billy the Bastard was confronted with an unconcious convict, with blood running from him, being carried through the mortuary-gate. It was pretty tough-going: convicts were fainting all over the place like ducks on a hot day on the farm.

The discipline-warder argued, but Billy the Bastard was adamant. The convicts had to be searched. So Slangvel was put down on the ground in front of the mortuary-gate. And this time Billy the

Bastard's luck was dead in. He said he had to search the convicts for dagga ...

He found enough dagga on Slangvel to render a whole city unconscious.